Beyond "Bilingual" Education

Also of interest from the Urban Institute Press:

Clearing the Way: Deconcentrating the Poor in Urban America, by Edward G. Goetz

Federalism and Health Policy, edited by John Holahan, Alan Weil, and Joshua M. Wiener

Choosing a Better Life? Evaluating the Moving to Opportunity Social Experiment, edited by John Goering and Judith D. Feins

Beyond "Bilingual" Education

New Immigrants
and Public School
Policies in California

Alec Ian Gershberg,
Anne Danenberg, and
Patricia Sánchez

THE URBAN INSTITUTE PRESS
Washington, D.C.

THE URBAN INSTITUTE PRESS
2100 M Street, N.W.
Washington, D.C. 20037

Library of Congress Cataloging in Publication Data

Gershberg, Alec Ian.
    Beyond "bilingual" education : new immigrants and public school policies in California / Alec Ian Gershberg, Anne Danenberg, and Patricia Sánchez.
        p. cm.
    Includes bibliographical references and index.
    ISBN 0-87766-723-3 (pbk. : alk. paper)
    1. Immigrants—Education—Government policy—California—Case studies. 2. English language—Study and teaching—Foreign speakers—Government policy—California—Case studies 3. Education, Bilingual—Government Policy—California—Case studies. 4. English-only movement—Government policy—California—Case studies. I. Danenberg, Anne, 1954– II. Sánchez, Patricia, III. Title.
    LC3732.C2G37 2004

                                                                2004012816

Printed in the United States of America
10 09 08 07 06 05 04   1 2 3 4 5

THE URBAN INSTITUTE is a nonprofit policy research and educational organization established in Washington, D.C., in 1968. Its staff investigates the social, economic, and governance problems confronting the nation and evaluates the public and private means to alleviate them. The Institute disseminates its research findings through publications, its web site, the media, seminars, and forums.

Through work that ranges from broad conceptual studies to administrative and technical assistance, Institute researchers contribute to the stock of knowledge available to guide decisionmaking in the public interest.

Conclusions or opinions expressed in Institute publications are those of the authors and do not necessarily reflect the views of officers or trustees of the Institute, advisory groups, or any organizations that provide financial support to the Institute.

To Carmen and Izel, two beautiful bilingual toddlers

Contents

Acknowledgments

T he research and fieldwork upon which this book is based were very
generously funded and institutionally supported by the Public
Policy Institute of California (PPIC) in San Francisco. I spent the first
half of 2001 as a visiting fellow at PPIC, during which time the primary
research was conducted. David Lyons, the president of PPIC, runs a
sharp organization in which policy-relevant, scholarly-based research
can thrive. Mike Teitz, PPIC's research director in 2001, first encouraged
me to apply for the fellowship and then provided much-needed guidance and support while and after I was in residence. Julian Betts helped
me formulate the key ideas and introduced me to Anne Danenberg, who
eventually became my coauthor. Mark Baldassare, the research project
director, pushed, stroked, guided, and challenged the research team—
and ultimately helped greatly in shaping the end results.

PPIC offers an intellectual environment, and I benefited greatly from
my many relationships there, particularly with Chris Jepsen, Kim
Rueben, Debbie Reed, Peter Richardson, Belinda Reyes, Howard Shatz,
Paul Lewis, Margaret O'Brien-Strain, Gary Hart, Jon Sonstelie, and especially Maureen Waller. The other visiting fellows—David Neumark,
Freya Sonenstein, and Steve Rivkin, who in particular offered intellectual
encouragement, insight, and friendship—provided an extraordinarily
stimulating community of scholars and much lunchtime interchange.
Along with my coauthors, I thank Diep Le and Miriam Ebrat for

administrative assistance, and Elizabeth Roach for her field research and analytic input. Appreciation also goes to Kay Lavish, Suzanne Shoemaker, and Karen Newton, who transcribed our qualitative interviews, and without whose help our qualitative analysis would have been impossible. And Tammy Harkey kept the computers and the humor running.

I cannot say enough, in fact, about my coauthors Anne Danenberg and Patricia Sánchez. I learned from and leaned on both of them and am delighted that this book became such a joint effort. Both are devoted researchers, analysts, and writers, and persevered through many challenges, including injury, bureaucracy, and new motherhood.

I also owe thanks to Edward Blakely, dean of the Milano Graduate School of Management and Urban Policy, New School University, who reluctantly granted me a leave (funded by PPIC) during his first year as dean, a time when he could have used his "full team on the court." Also at Milano, Hector Cordero-Guzman reviewed the early empirical work and Darrick Hamilton provided helpful insights on racial and ethnic categories and definitions. And without my friend and colleague David Howell, I never would have been working on immigrant education to begin with. Students in my education policy seminar at Milano provided a sounding board for many ideas. Ben Meade provided excellent, timely, and accurate research assistance, and also performed the interview coding and analysis upon which the qualitative work in chapter 4 is partially based. Jesse Wolovoy, too, provided valuable research assistance early in the project.

Amy Ellen Schwartz at New York University was my coauthor on my first work in immigrant education and together we learned how to think about immigrants as more than just language minorities, as well as how to squeeze insights out of hopelessly imperfect data. Insights I gained with her are seminal in this work. I also benefited from conversations with and/or insights and commentary from Mark Hugo Lopez, Ingrid Ellen, Kathy O'Reagan, Wayne Cornelius, Deborah L. Garvey, Lydia Tugendrajch, and two anonymous reviewers. Martin Carnoy kindly arranged for me to have a visiting professorship at the Stanford University School of Education, which gave me an important university base while I was in California. Susanna Loeb and her Stanford seminar students offered helpful comments. Michael Fix at the Urban Institute provided enormous encouragement and led me to work with the Urban Institute Press, where Rick Custer, Kathleen Courrier, and Suellen Wenz guided the book project from finished research study to fruition. I am particularly happy to be associated now with the important work on immigrants and children produced by the Urban Institute.

My friend and colleague at the National Bureau of Economic Research (NBER), Bob Kaestner, talked with me so much about this project that he is probably the second happiest person to know that it is over. Neeraj Kaushal, Sanders Korenman, and Ted Joyce, also at NBER, provided helpful analytic ideas. Mike Grossman, Marinella Moscheni, and Chris Nagorski, all at the NBER offices in New York, provided me with the most supportive and productive scholarly working environment I could hope for.

At the California State Department of Education, David Dolson provided data, feedback, and key contacts. And in each of the five case study districts—Fresno, Long Beach, Los Angeles, San Diego, and San Francisco—district officials made the time and effort to speak openly about sensitive issues and to help our research team set up the school-level interviews with teachers, principals, and other school staff. No one has taught me more than Don Winkler about how to study and attempt to navigate and usefully organize the messy complexity of schools and school systems, and the government bureaucracies that govern them. Without the support of all these individuals, this project could not have been completed. All errors remain the authors' and the opinions and views expressed in this book do not reflect views of the Public Policy Institute of California, the Urban Institute, or any other institution or individual.

My family, as always, supported me and made timely visits that forced me to "smell the roses" in the Bay Area, as did Doc Schwartz. Carmen Padro gave me my first contact with immigrants and helped raise me to appreciate and respect them. Her spirit continues to live in my work. And finally, Lisa Servon—my colleague, friend, and life partner—informed me that she was going to spend a year in the Bay Area and told me I had to find a way to come along. This was but the most tangible way in which she motivated, loved, and supported me during this project. My dedication of this book is hers to share only with the immigrant children in U.S. public schools, children who hold so much promise and deserve the best education public money and the public sector can provide.

Alec Ian Gershberg
New York City
November 2003

I am grateful to the many people across our case districts who made time in their busy schedules to share their experiences and insights with us. Only through their participation is this book possible.

Anne Danenberg
San Rafael, California
June 2004

Our acknowledgments would be incomplete without a large "thank you" on my part to Carmina Brittain, professor at San Jose State University, who, as a visiting lecturer at the University of California, Berkeley, provided the only course dedicated to immigrants and education. Her review of an early draft of chapter 4 was invaluable. I also thank the other graduate students in the seminar—Maris Thompson, Leticia Leyva, and Kristin Hull Cortes—with whom I shared numerous conversations about the project's ongoing research. In addition, I am especially grateful to my cousin Lucina Gutiérrez, who transcribed in great detail two lengthy interviews in Spanish. Pedro Noguera (now a professor at New York University), Carol Stack, and Harley Shaiken—faculty members in the Social and Cultural Studies program at Berkeley's Graduate School of Education—were supportive and insightful. Finally, a well-deserved "thank you" goes to my coauthors, Anne and Alec; my dear friends Emma Fuentes and Shabnam Koirala; my partner, Fabricio Pineda; and my mother, Antonia Sánchez—all of whom repeatedly heard my frustration and elation about this project for the past three years.

Patricia Sánchez
Berkeley, California
June 2004

Abbreviations

API   **Academic Performance Index**
A school-level index computed using Stanford 9 test scores. The API is used to rank and compare school performance and progress.

CABE   **California Association of Bilingual Education**
A professional organization established in the mid-1970s that promotes equity and achievement for students with diverse cultural, racial, and linguistic backgrounds.

CBO   **Community-Based Organization**

CDE   **California Department of Education**

EIEP   **Emergency Immigrant Education Program**
A federal program authorized under Title VII of the Elementary and Secondary Education Act (ESEA). This program provides funds to states to assist local educational agencies serving areas in which immigrant student enrollment has increased dramatically.

ELL   **English Language Learner**
The term used to identify those students determined to have insufficient English to succeed in English-only classrooms. ELL is equivalent to LEP (limited English proficient). In California, the term "English learner (EL)" is used officially.

ESL   **English as a Second Language**
The term used to describe an educational approach in which English language learners are instructed in the use of the English language. Includes both "bilingual" and "English-only" approaches.

ESOL   **English to Speakers of Other Languages**
The term used to describe English language programs for ESL/EL/ELL/LEP students as well as students in international settings who are learning English through their employer or for the pursuit of higher education in the United States.

FEP   **Fluent English Proficient**
The term used to identify and redesignate former LEP or EL/ELL students who can comprehend, read, write, and speak English well enough to receive instruction in the regular school curriculum. To achieve FEP status, a student in California, for example, must meet several criteria, such as certain levels of standardized test performance, teacher recommendations, and usually a minimum grade point average of 2.0.

HLS   **Home Language Survey**
Survey administered to a parent or guardian to determine if a student should be tested for language proficiency.

L1   The term used to describe a student's native language.

L2   The term used to describe a student's second language.

LEA   **Local Educational Agency**
A district or county office of education.

LEP   **Limited English Proficient**
The term used to identify those students who have insufficient English to succeed in English-only classrooms, as determined by some standardized assessment system and criteria. The term is considered by the federal government to be equivalent to "English language learner (ELL)."

LPS   **Language Placement System**
The series of surveys, tests, and other assessment measures used to place students in language classes such as "bilingual" or "English only."

MEP   **Migrant Education Program**
A federal program funded under the Elementary and Secondary Education Act, Title I, Part C, that supports the education of the children of agricultural and seasonal workers.

MSS   **Mean Scaled Score**
The average test score at a school.

NABE   **National Association for Bilingual Education**
An organization that promotes educational excellence and equity through bilingual education. It is the only national organization exclusively concerned with the education of language-minority students in U.S. schools.

NCELA **National Clearinghouse for English Language Acquisition and Language Instruction Educational Programs**
Formerly the National Clearinghouse for Bilingual Education (NCBE), this online reference offers useful ESL resources primarily for teachers and students, although other groups, such as administrators, business people, researchers, and parents, may find them helpful as well. (NCBE was originally established by Congress in 1974 to help school districts meet their responsibility to provide an equal education opportunity to ELL students. After the No Child Left Behind Act was passed in 2001, NCBE's services were reduced to an online resource.)

NCLB   **No Child Left Behind**
The primary education legislation enacted by Congress and the Bush administration in 2001.

NEP   **Non-English Proficient**
An alternate term used to describe EL, ELL, or LEP students.

OBEMLA   **Office of Bilingual Education and Minority Language Affairs**
A federal office established by Congress in 1974 to help school districts meet their responsibility to provide equal education opportunity to ELL children. From 1974 through 2001, OBEMLA administered federal education grants under the Bilingual Education Act (Title VII of the Elementary and Secondary Education Act), and provided national leadership on promoting effective schooling for linguistically and culturally diverse students.

OLEA   **Office of English Language Acquisition, Language Enhancement, and Academic Achievement for Limited English Proficient Students**
The official redesignation (January 8, 2002) of the Office of Bilingual Education and Minority Language Affairs (OBEMLA) resulting from the enactment of the No Child Left Behind Act of 2001. In the new law, federal grants for improving the instruction of English language learners are addressed under Title III, Language Instruction for Limited English Proficient and Immigrant Students.

PAC   **Parent Advisory Committee**
A parent organization at the school level. One form of the PAC is the English Language Advisory Committee (ELAC). These committees are required by law to exist in schools where there are 21 or more ELLs. The district-level version of this committee is known as the District English Language Advisory Committee (DELAC).

SEI   **Structured English Immersion**
A method of ESL instruction often referred to as "English only" to distinguish it from "bilingual" instruction.

STAR   **Standardized Testing and Reporting**
The main standardized tests used in California. Also called Stanford 9, or SAT9.

1

Immigrant Education— The Program and Policy Landscape

America's experience of immigration should give it a lead in the developed world for several decades to come. . . . But it is not numbers alone that will give America an advantage. Even more important, the country is culturally attuned to immigration, and long ago learned to integrate immigrants into its society and economy. . . . The one big obstacle to the full integration of recent immigrants in America is the poor performance of American public schools.
—Peter Drucker

In 1999–2000, California was home to more than 1.4 million students who were classified as English language learners (ELLs).[*][1] This number represented nearly 40 percent of all public school ELL students in the United States and nearly 25 percent of the total student population in California (Kindler 2002). Currently, about 1 in 10 students in pre-kindergarten through grade 12 across the nation are English language learners, and their numbers have grown dramatically over the past decade, doubling since 1990. Furthermore, in 1999–2000, nearly 200,000 California students were classified as recent immigrants (foreign-born students attending U.S. schools for fewer than three years), corresponding to nearly 25 percent of all recent immigrant students in the United

*Students for whom English is a second language and who are not completely proficient in English (as determined by an assessment system) are often referred to as LEP (limited English proficient), ELLs (English language learners), and ELs (English learners). We generally use "ELL" throughout this book to reflect the most current usage in other related research studies.

1

States (National Clearinghouse for English Language Acquisition 2002). And by 2002, there were more than 252,000 recent immigrant students and nearly 1.5 million ELL students in California's public schools. Without a doubt, recent immigrant and ELL students greatly impact California schools.

Not Just California's Problem

California is not the only state facing huge immigrant challenges, however. Nationally, more than three-quarters of recent immigrant students are concentrated in a few states: California, New York, Texas, Florida, Illinois, and New Jersey. Together, these states contain nearly 40 percent of the current total U.S. population. In addition, states like Arizona, Massachusetts, and Colorado have significant immigrant populations relative to their total populations. Thus, educating immigrant students is an issue of national importance with potentially local impact on nearly half of our nation's taxpayers as well as our country's economic competitiveness. Immigrant education, primarily as it relates to debates over language curricula, has become a hot topic—not only in education policy circles, but also in state politics. Following California's lead, for example, Arizona and Massachusetts have passed ballot initiatives restricting the use of "bilingual" education in favor of some version of an "English-only" curriculum.[2] Colorado voters, on the other hand, have defeated a similar measure that received much public attention when two opposing millionaires financed rival ad campaigns. In addition, the debate has recently entered federal policymaking through President Bush's education legislation, the No Child Left Behind Act. Therefore, examining California's experience in educating immigrant students is timely because the state has by far the most immigrant students and has for many years been a trendsetter in the most prominent debates about educating these children. As more states face increasing immigrant student populations, and as these states implement many of the school policies first tested in California, the California experience holds significant lessons that we bring to bear on potential strategies in other states and at the federal level.

Like the citizens of other immigrant-rich states, Californians and their state and local governments can do little on their own to affect immigrant flows because relevant policies are set federally.[3] Thus, Californians and residents of other states can expect their school systems to be educating significant immigrant and English language learner populations for the foreseeable future. As Peter Drucker comments, immigrants are likely to continue to play an increasingly integral role in the economic success of the United States. And, as Drucker argues, our public schools' poor performance in educating immigrant and ELL students has impeded the kind of positive economic outcomes we might expect as a result of this country's comparative advantage in integrating immigrants into its economic and social life. In other words, the stakes are high.[4] States have a strong interest in improving the educational outcomes of their immigrant and ELL students, outcomes for which they are directly responsible. The federal government, too, has a similar interest given the implications for the country as a whole and the fact that immigration policy is by definition federal.

The Focus of Our Study

We recognize the politicized and often value-laden nature of the policy arenas we are entering and seek to frame our study to motivate as many participants as possible—regardless of politics, ethics, or values—around a shared policy goal. Ultimately, the core of the *policy* issue is not whether immigrant students *deserve* better from their school system.[5] In order to bring advocates of different values together for constructive debate, we begin by raising the specter of the economic costs associated with failing to effectively educate immigrants—although our discussion itself does not focus on the economic impact of immigrant students.[6] With the above points in mind, this book explores the following key research questions about education in California:

1. How are recent immigrant students distributed across districts and schools, and how does this distribution compare with that of English language learners and California's schoolchildren?
2. What are the characteristics of the schools attended by the typical recent immigrant, and how do these schools differ from those attended by the typical student and the typical ELL student?
3. How well do schools with high proportions of immigrants perform on standardized tests?
4. On average, do these schools have higher or lower levels of resources?

5. What challenges do recent immigrant students face, aside from language barriers and learning English at school?
6. Which newcomer programs are schools and districts pursuing? Which broader policies affect recent immigrant students and in what ways do these policies affect these students?
7. What educational choices are available to schools and parents, and how are these choices made?
8. What are the implications of the California experience for other states, as well as for federal education policy?

This book paints a statistical portrait of English language learners and recent immigrant students in five large urban districts in California—Fresno, Long Beach, Los Angeles, San Diego, and San Francisco. We also highlight the key issues immigrant students face as they pursue success in California's schools, as well as the concerns confronting educators and school and district staff charged with educating these students. In addition, we draw lessons learned for other states with significant immigrant populations. In doing so, we attempt to disentangle the reality of being an immigrant student (especially a recent immigrant) from that of being a student in need of language assistance. Naturally, the two concepts go hand in hand, and we do address both. However, we argue that the discussion about educating immigrants has been dominated by the debate over educating ELL students.

The Bigger Picture

The policy debate that has most dominated this arena is, of course, that spawned by the implementation of Proposition 227, a ballot initiative overwhelmingly passed in 1998 that requires ELL students to be placed in structured English immersion (SEI) classrooms unless parents choose to waiver out of SEI and into some form of "bilingual" education. We seek to broaden this debate. Simply put, even if a lot of recent immigrant students are ELLs, there is something to be gained by thinking more broadly about the students' immigrant experience beyond their efforts to learn English (and the schools' efforts to teach them English). It is important to state that we do not attempt to evaluate or by any means settle the debate concerning "English only" versus "bilingual" instruction. In fact, we attempt to remain neutral about it. Rather, we seek to shed light on key aspects of the discussion while also highlighting other issues that have been largely ignored because of the debate.

Most states, including California, have no coherent education policy strategy for immigrants, particularly new immigrants, and the same can be said for the federal government. Current policies impacting immigrants, such as English as a Second Language (ESL), are aimed at ELL students and are directed almost exclusively toward teaching them English. While this strategy addresses one critical issue relevant to immigrants and education, it may be too narrowly focused to optimize the myriad strategies for organizing and supporting schools and teaching new immigrants, other ELL students, and mainstream students. In California, the differences even between the raw numbers of recent immigrant students and ELL students are striking. More than 300 school districts educated enough recent immigrants in 1999–2000 to qualify for federal funds through the Emergency Immigration Education Program (EIEP), the only federal program that targets monies based on the number of immigrant students rather than the number of English language learners. In these EIEP districts, 32.2 percent of the students were classified as English language learners, while 4.8 percent were recent immigrants (table 1.1).

English language learner students who are not recent immigrants fall into two basic categories: (1) immigrant students who have been in the school system more than three years and are still classified as ELL, and (2) ELL students who are not immigrants (e.g., children of immigrants

Table 1.1. *EIEP and California Public Schools Profile, 1999–2000*

	Districts receiving EIEP funds	All California districts
Districts	334	1,046
Schools	5,120	8,563
Students	4,036,510	5,951,612
English language learner	1,300,833 (32.2%)	1,480,527 (24.9%)
Recent immigrant	192,991 (4.8%)	NAª

Source: California Department of Education.

Notes: EIEP = Emergency Immigration Education Program. "Recent immigrant" students are foreign-born students with fewer than three years in U.S. public schools. Figures in parentheses are the percentage the adjacent number represents in relationship to total enrollment in that type of district.

a. NA = not applicable; recent immigrant students are counted only in EIEP districts.

or Puerto Ricans). Both categories imply worrisome outcomes because they indicate that such students may not be served well by their schools.[7] This study also sheds light on the challenges of educating ELL students who are not recent immigrants.

Disentangling the different issues for recent immigrants and ELL students is important because each group's challenges are different.[8] Recent experiences with newcomer programs (primarily in New York City, San Francisco, Los Angeles, and Illinois), which focus on serving recent immigrants exclusively, highlight these distinct challenges.[9] In addition, Rivera-Batiz (1995) and Schwartz and Gershberg (2000, 2001) found that the impact of a high proportion of recent immigrants on a school could be the *opposite* of the impact of a high proportion of ELL students.[10] For instance, all else equal, students in New York City schools with high concentrations of recent immigrants scored *higher* on standardized tests, while students in New York City schools with high concentrations of ELLs scored lower. These findings are consistent with theories that immigrants are more driven to succeed than many of their native-born counterparts (Ogbu 1991). Once we account for the difference in language ability, recent immigrants are in higher-than-average-scoring schools.

A Unique Look

Most academic studies of immigrants and education have been ethnographic.[11] Although such studies reveal a wealth of information essential for understanding how immigrant children learn and interact with native-born children, the lessons are difficult to generalize. Furthermore, quantitative analytic work to date has often used data aggregated at the district or state level, a limitation that renders such analyses indicative of certain trends but also difficult to generalize. School-level quantitative studies have focused almost exclusively on English language learners and issues of bilingual education. This study fills a critical gap through its marrying of quantitative and qualitative work, presenting a picture of the key policy issues in California for educating new immigrants, ELL students, and the mainstream students who, increasingly, learn beside them. We concentrate on elementary and, to some extent, middle schools because these are likely the school levels at which the stakes are highest in terms of lifetime outcomes and at which the school system is most likely to be able to impact students' futures.[12] Elementary school is also where, for better or for worse, the majority of the resources for language assistance and other immigrant education programs are concentrated (Ruiz-de-Velasco and Fix 2000). We concentrate on recent immigrants because the first years after arrival are critical for this group. As the immigrant scholar Carola Suárez-Orozco notes: "There are energies we could harness as a society, but we're not. Kids come in with energy and quickly lose hope."[13]

The Outline of Our Study

The remainder of this chapter surveys briefly the major policy debates relevant to recent immigrant and ELL students in California.[14] Chapter 2 provides a statistical portrait of these immigrant and ELL students. We examine and categorize the kinds of schools that typical ELL students attend and compare these with typical schools attended by recent immigrant and native-born students. We also measure segregation of recent immigrant and ELL students compared with other segregated student populations. In chapter 3, we perform statistical analyses to examine further the patterns and distribution of school resources and outcomes for schools attended by recent immigrant, ELL, and other students. Chapters 4, 5, and 6 rely on a qualitative study involving more than a hundred open-ended interviews with district- and school-level staff in California's five largest school districts. We offer insights relating to the impressions of key stakeholders in the education system—often through their own words. Chapter 4 examines the major challenges (in addition to learning English) faced by recent immigrant students. We describe what teachers, schools, and districts are doing both formally and informally to serve recent immigrants—so-called newcomer programs, policies, and practices. We discuss how these approaches both relate to and differ from programs that serve ELL and native-born disadvantaged students. The particular challenges to parental involvement and other important school governance issues related to recent immigrants are also highlighted. Chapter 5 concentrates on the challenge of teaching English to recent immigrant and ELL students. It focuses primarily on the controversial choice between "bilingual" and "English only" education, and the views educators and other stakeholders have regarding how the choice is made for each student. Chapter 6 examines and analyzes California's assessment and accountability systems, concentrating on the implications for recent immigrants and the schools that teach them. Finally, chapter 7 concludes the book with policy recommendations and directions for future research.

Policy Debates around Recent Immigrant and ELL Students in California

An enormous amount has been written about the debate over "bilingual" versus "English only" education, much of it specifically in response to Proposition 227.[15] The California Department of Education (CDE) is in fact performing its own evaluation of the proposition's effects (Parrish 2001). The debate over the passage of Proposition 227 has evolved now into various debates over its implementation. For instance, Ron Unz—the author of Proposition 227—has claimed the initiative led to huge successes for ELL students and recently clashed publicly with the State Board of Education (SBE) over changes in rules governing the waiver process and the requirement that children annually receive 30 days of "English-only" instruction.[16] (We discuss both these issues in chapter 5.) In addition, Unz has spread the debate nationally through ballot initiatives in at least three more states, eyeing as well such bastions of "bilingual" education as New York and Texas. On the other side of the debate, García and Curry-Rodríguez (2000) assert that Proposition 227 did not produce a "'sea of change' in programmatic efforts . . . [or] achievement gains."[17] The issue was also prominent in both the debate over and the final version of President Bush's education bill of 2002, the No Child Left Behind (NCLB) Act. For example, according to bill sponsor Congressman John Boehner, bilingual education is "one of the components [of the Elementary and Secondary Education Act] that is most badly in need of reform."[18]

Unfortunately, far less has been written about other issues related to the schooling success and failure of immigrant students. To deal effectively with the issue of immigrant education, these policy debates must be broadened beyond the question of bilingual education. In fact, NCLB consolidates the Bilingual Education Act and the EIEP and changes the criteria for funding districts. Though it is too soon to determine the full consequences this change will have at the state and district levels, the initial signs are worrisome for the one federal program that targets immigrant but not ELL students.[19] NCLB requires states to comply with the legislation by channeling monies to districts with high levels of *growth* in recent immigrants. The implication is that districts with large but steady numbers of recent immigrant students (like San Diego, Long Beach, and San Francisco) have fewer relevant needs than those with small but growing numbers, and remarkably many districts with larger immigrant populations now do not qualify for federal funding for immigrant education. California has experienced perhaps the starkest change resulting from NCLB. In the year following NCLB's enactment, the count of recent immigrants qualifying for funding dropped from 205,540 to just below 133,000, and the funding per pupil plunged from $153 to $67. This policy change, buried deep in the NCLB legislation, certainly raises some questions.[20] In particular, districts that have implemented EIEP-funded programs to address issues arising largely from federal immigration policy must now find ways to fund the programs with state or local monies, or cut them.

More Research Needed

Nearly a decade has passed since a RAND study helped put the so-called newcomer issue on the research landscape. That study found:

> The most notable characteristic of immigrant education policy at the state level is its total absence, aside from programs for [ELL] students. Across the six states we studied, there are no policies specifically targeted to students on the basis of their immigrant status. Rather, state policy focuses on students with limited English-language skills, whether they be immigrants or native born (McDonnell and Hill 1993, 24).

Little additional scholarly research exists that informs either the debate or the policy changes at the state or federal level. A few reports and organizations provide some heartening exceptions, but policymakers and the media have failed to pick up on their findings. California Tomorrow, an advocacy organization, has written extensively about the newcomer experience and issues (especially in high schools); however, despite the organization's efforts, the concept is nearly invisible in the policy landscape of California or most other states, and may indeed be disappearing.[21] California Tomorrow has argued that educators must consider the broad experience that newcomer students face in becoming a part of the U.S. educational system:

> The law focuses on language as the barrier to immigrant student achievement, but in the lives of students, language is just one part of the gap they must leap in trying to bridge cultures and nations. And learning the language is just a small part of what goes on for immigrant students in negotiating their place in school (Olsen and Jaramillo 1999, 204).

Challenges beyond Language

The Urban Institute has issued several reports dealing with immigrant students in a much broader context than their language ability, in particular Ruiz-de-Velasco and Fix's (2000) "Overlooked and Underserved: Immigrant Students in U.S. Secondary Schools."[22] And in "Immigrant Children and Their Families: Issues for Research and Policy," the Board on Children and Families (of the National Research Council) declared that "immigrant children have been rendered largely invisible in policy spheres" (BCF 1995, 72). The Board stressed both the "value of looking at immigrant children in the context of their families" and the "need for policymakers to address such policy issues as education and health care." The report asked several questions that provide an important backdrop for our study:

> The pressing practical issue, then, is not whether policies and programs for immigrant students exist, but to what extent appropriate policies for immigrant children and existing policies (such as those for [ELLs]) overlap, and whether special policies and programs are needed for immigrant children. *Among the crucial questions: Are there social services that schools might provide or coordinate which would benefit recent arrivals? Do immigrant students need educational services different from those provided to [ELL] students? What might those services be and how should they be integrated into the educational system?* (BCF 1995, 80; emphasis added).

The Board noted the "paucity of research on immigrant children" and appealed for research on immigrant children to "throw light on the issues affecting these populations, removing them from obscurity and validating their experiences" (83). We seek to answer this call using the Board's "crucial questions" as a springboard.[23]

Thus, in chapter 4, we determine what educators perceive to be the biggest challenges recent immigrant students face, aside from learning the language. Some of these challenges relate to the socioeconomic condition of these families—poverty, minimal prior schooling, inadequate and costly housing, and family separation. Many of these difficulties, however, relate to issues at the school and school-district level—stigmatization of immigrant and ELL students, difficulties fostering parental participation, legal and immigration-related issues, and immigrants' difficulties in navigating the school system and accessing adequate health care and other social services. We focus on these issues because schools and school districts can do and are doing something about them. For instance, we document in chapter 4 the extent to which schools serve as "connections brokers," linking immigrants to a wide range of social services (e.g., health care). We examine a few government programs organized to facilitate this role and mitigate the challenges; for the most part, however, schools do this without explicit support.

The "Long-Term ELL Problem"

Ruiz-de-Velasco and Fix (2000) focus on high school students and highlight the challenges associated with two subpopulations: adolescent youth with significant gaps in their schooling upon arrival in the United States, and long-term ELLs.[24] Our study echoes these themes and, in fact, some of our empirical results support their idea that our schools (and, thus, our society) have more of a "long-term ELL problem" than an "immigrant problem" (as is so often stated in the popular media). Part of the solution to that "problem" may lie in more nuanced approaches beyond, or in addition to, simply providing language assistance for recent immigrants who arrive in elementary and (to some extent) middle school. Ruiz-de-Velasco and Fix provide ample insight into the practices (realized and unrealized) that support long-term English language learners once they are in secondary school. However, these authors offer little evidence as to the factors that produce long-term ELLs, particularly those factors that relate to the education and other services these students receive upon entering the school system, often as recent immigrants, and often in elementary school.[25] School officials and Californians in general who want to reduce the number of long-term ELL students should be concerned with understanding the nature of the three "sources" of these students: (1) recent immigrants, (2) nonrecent immigrants, and (3) non-immigrant ELL students.[26] While our quantitative work does not provide any immediate answers to this obviously important and difficult problem, it does, along with our qualitative work, provide insight—especially into the first group—that should prove beneficial to current policymakers and in future research.

Newcomer Programs

As mentioned earlier, there are few explicit newcomer policies and programs in elementary and middle schools. Los Angeles and, to a much lesser extent, San Francisco have small programs. Like newcomer schools in New York City—which focus on serving recent immigrants—these California schools and programs appear to have arisen as local, isolated, almost organic responses to dire need (especially overcrowding), not from any sort of organized district, state, or federal policy or funding initiative to better educate recent immigrants.[27] To a large extent, public fears over segregation and isolation of newcomer students have quashed any potential experimentation with newcomer schools and programs, and such programs appear to be waning in California. Many educators in our study, especially those in San Francisco, had high praise for newcomer schools in their districts. Others, however, expressed grave concern. Thus far, neither the policy analytic nor the policymaking communities have shed any light that would help build or support consensus one way or the other. Throughout this study, we also seek to highlight state and district programs that appear to positively affect the educational experience of immigrant students, even if many of these programs do not explicitly target these students. Examples include home-school liaisons, the Healthy Start Initiative,[28] and other health-related programs.

Whether or not districts or states choose to encourage even limited experimentation with newcomer policies and programs, newcomer policy *is* happening every day in every school and classroom with significant populations of recent immigrants. As we explore in chapters 4 and 5, teachers and other staff in such schools and classrooms are making daily decisions that amount to de facto newcomer policies and practices. Examples range from placing all recent immigrants in the same class (creating an unofficial "newcomer" class) to partnering recent immigrants with experienced students who tutor, translate, and even comment upon their work. We argue in this book that state departments of education, along with the most immigrant-rich districts, should examine seriously and likely support experimentation with the range of potential strategies and classroom practices we only touch upon here.

Facing the Challenge

Immigrants face many challenges to achieving educational success. And, as participants in this study reveal, immigrant students present many challenges to California's schools. These challenges (particularly the challenge of teaching English) have been the primary focus of the policy-making and political rhetoric relating to immigrant students. Such rhetoric is unlikely to cool down without considerable effort. For instance, Putnam (2002) shows that in the months since the terrorist attacks of September 11, U.S. citizens have become more tolerant and more accepting of diversity, and show signs of increasing social capital in all of the wide range of measures he examines except one: the country has become markedly more hostile toward immigrants. At the same time, recent immigrant students present also enormous and important *opportunities*—opportunities the United States and California can ill afford to squander. At stake are not only their own citizens' economic well-being (both native and foreign born), but also the progressive social fabric upon which Peter Drucker (2001) argues the new "knowledge society" will be built in the near future. In order to reap the benefits of the opportunities provided by immigrant students, states and the federal government need to foster educational environments that help overcome the challenges facing recent immigrants. Drucker argues that, in general, the United States is "culturally attuned to immigration" compared with other developed nations, and that this fact is a key aspect of the nation's comparative advantage in the world economy. We argue, following Drucker, that the education of immigrants in California is not as effective as it must be and that this obstacle is in part created by a school system that does not appear adequately attuned to recent immigrants, culturally or otherwise. The same could be said for other states across the country. Teaching language is only one important aspect of educating immigrants effectively.

NOTES

The epigraph to this chapter is drawn from "Survey: The Near Future," *The Economist,* November 2, 2001.

1. Note that these data exclude Puerto Rico and other outlying jurisdictions from English language learner counts. Including Puerto Rico, California had 25 percent of all the ELL students in the nation.

2. We employ the term *"bilingual" education* to refer to any course of instruction in which the teacher is permitted to use a language other than English to a significant degree in the classroom, and in which non-English instructional materials will often be used. We often put quotation marks around "bilingual" because we believe that true bilingual education has fluency and full proficiency in both languages as its ultimate goal. While some programs still state this to be the case, most do not appear in fact to do so; however, the term *"bilingual" education* is still widely used. (For additional discussion, see Rossell [2000a, b].) A similar argument could be made about the term *English only.* In fact, we believe our study makes clear that the dichotomous nature of the political and policy debates does not reflect actual teaching practices and students' needs in real and diverse classroom learning environments.

3. Some may argue that states that deny or lower the quality of social services to immigrants will decrease immigrant flows. See Borjas (2001), chapter 6, for a review. However, recent studies by Kaestner and Kaushal (2001) and Kaushal (2002) show that new immigrants' location decisions are unaffected by the accessibility of means-tested programs such as Temporary Assistance for Needy Families (TANF), food stamps, and Medicaid. Immigrants locate primarily based on historical patterns of family and social networks. These studies also indicate that immigrants do not need a bigger incentive than do the native born to become economically self-sufficient. The belief that immigrants need a bigger incentive to become economically self-sufficient led to welfare reform, in part to exclude immigrants from benefits.

4. Economic analysts such as George Borjas (2001) and Jasso, Rosenzweig, and Smith (1998) have argued that immigrants' education and skill levels have declined steadily over the past three decades, as has their potential economic productivity. Cornelius and Marcelli (2000) argue that recent immigrants to California from Mexico have, by some measures, higher educational attainment than earlier cohorts. They show that the average number of years of schooling has risen for certain key groups of Mexican immigrants. If, however, the quality of their education is low, or their educational attainment *relative* to U.S. native-born students has fallen, then Borjas's implications still hold. Previous work at the Public Policy Institute of California (PPIC) (Cheng 2001) hints at some of the disparities in school readiness among ethnic and immigrant groups. In a sense, however, it does not matter who is "right" here; if schools are performing poorly in educating immigrant children, then policy alternatives focusing on these children can potentially improve this performance.

5. Our personal values would lead us in that direction, however.

6. In this sense, we can agree with Borjas (2001, 188) when he argues that although "moral issues may influence the direction and tone of the immigration debate, as well as determine the likelihood that some policies are adopted or rejected, it is still valuable to describe the . . . policy that the United States would pursue if it wanted to maximize the economic well-being of its native population." There is relevance here for immigrant education policy in California.

7. However, Hakuta, Butler, and Witt (2000) summarize well the prevailing consensus in the education literature that even successful English learners likely take four to seven years to achieve proficiency. This conclusion indicates that the federal definition for recent immigrant students (foreign-born students attending U.S. schools for fewer than three years) is not adequate if the goal is to support students until they achieve proficiency. Nevertheless, even if all recent immigrants were English learners (an assumption we do not make), more than 27 percent of ELL students either immigrated more than three years ago or were never immigrants. This number seems large enough despite the inapplicability of the three-year definition to raise concern over the effectiveness of the state's system for educating recent immigrant and ELL students.

8. We discern, a priori, four main reasons why immigrants have an effect on schools: (1) immigrants' limited English proficiency; (2) immigrants' varying levels of academic preparation; (3) the stressors of expected acculturation immigrants face; and (4) overcrowding of individual schools with already scarce resources. This project's qualitative work, in particular, will shed light on the non-ELL issues mentioned here and the potential policy responses.

9. See Gershberg (2000) and Avila (2002).

10. That is, they found that regression coefficients for "recent immigrants" and "ELL students" had opposite signs in models of either test scores or school-level resources. See Rivera-Batiz (1995) and Schwartz and Gershberg (2000, 2001).

11. See, for instance, Valenzuela (1999). Rivera-Batiz (1995) also summarizes nicely the extensive ethnographic and anthropological research to date that is relevant in explaining these potential outcomes. In short, Ogbu (1982, 1991), Ogbu and Simons (1998), and Suárez-Orozco (1991) have all argued that immigrants appear to be more motivated to succeed than native-born students of similar background. In addition, these experts argue that immigrants, particularly members of racial minority groups in the United States, perceive and overcome social obstacles in ways that are more beneficial to their schooling success. Kao and Tienda (1995) and Vernez and Abrahamse (1996) provide some quantitative support for these qualitative arguments.

12. In addition, Ruiz-de-Velasco and Fix (2000) look at similar issues, concentrating exclusively on secondary school students, and derive considerable insight from schools and districts in California.

13. Cited in Zehr (2001). Also, recent work by the New York City Board of Education (2000) found that the academic success of ELL students—measured primarily by their exit from ESL/bilingual programs—depends critically upon the grade at which they enter the New York City public schools. Those entering in elementary school, especially kindergarten and first grade, do the best, followed by those entering in high school. But more than a third of elementary school ELL students did not exit by the target date. The implication is that the immigrant experience and the needs of immigrants differ significantly between elementary, middle, and high school.

14. In addition, appendix A summarizes the state-level programs and policies in place to support these students.

15. The volume of literature on this topic is large, and even summarizing it is beyond the scope of this study. Readers interested in work supporting the abolishment of "bilingual" education could start with Rossell (2000a, b), Rossell and Baker (1996), and Santosuosso (1999). Readers interested in work supporting "bilingual" education could begin with August and Hakuta (1997), de Cos (1999), Johnson and Martinez (2000), and Crawford (1997). Two works that appear to be impartial and relatively neutral evaluations are Greene (1998) and Lopez (2000). Parrish (2001) also provides a nice summary of the research findings to date on instructional programs for ELLs. The underlying pedagogical theory upon which much of the push for bilingual education is based can be found in Cummins (1981, 1986, and 1994), Krashen (1994), and Leyba (1994).

16. Mendel (2002). See also California Department of Education (2002b).

17. See the special issue edited by Eugene E. García (2000) for a series of articles from this camp.

18. See Boehner (2001); this document contains a summary of NCLB's changes to bilingual education.

19. "At the current appropriation level, the Emergency Immigrant Education program is not authorized. That program and the bilingual education program previously authorized by Title VII of the Elementary and Secondary Education Act were replaced by a new state formula program. Eighty percent of state allocations [are] based on the number of limited English proficient students in the state and 20 percent [are] based on the number of immi-

grant students. States use these funds for services to limited English proficient students, whether or not they are immigrants. However, states may reserve up to 15 percent of their allocation for special grants to school districts that 'have experienced a significant increase, as compared to the average of the two preceding fiscal years, in the age or number of immigrant children and youth.' The No Child Left Behind Act holds states and school districts accountable for teaching limited English proficient students English and holding them to the same high academic standards as all other students." E-mail message from Ki Lee, U.S. Department of Education, to Alec Gershberg, February 13, 2002.

20. Other aspects of NCLB, not addressed in this study, also impact recent immigrant students (e.g., the testing NCLB requires). Note also that much of the fieldwork and research for this study took place before NCLB was implemented, so we continue to refer to the EIEP and do not analyze the impact of the dramatic changes resulting from NCLB. These data are taken from California Department of Education ("Immigrant Student Demographics").

21. See Olsen (1997); Olsen and Chen (1988); Olsen and Dowell (1989); Olsen and Jaramillo (1999); and Olsen et al. (1994, 1999) for the most relevant work by California Tomorrow. Much of California Tomorrow's work over the past 15 years has focused on immigrant students and their right to a quality public education. The organization has promoted active school-level counseling and support focused on the transitional phase of immigration and the special concerns and problems facing immigrant children. California Tomorrow advocates that this support be designed to foster the development of a positive self-concept incorporating the binational, bicultural, and bilingual experiences of the foreign-born child.

22. See also Fix, Zimmermann, and Passel (2001) for a broader context than immigrant children and their schools.

23. Of course, some education scholars have highlighted "an overemphasis on language of instruction," which in turn overshadows "other issues critical to the education of language minority students" (Schirling, Contreras, and Ayala 2000). However, their arguments have focused largely on pedagogical issues in the classroom rather than on broader policy issues for districts and school, and they also emphasize the ELL aspect of students over the recent immigrant aspect of students.

24. Ruiz-de-Velasco and Fix (2000) cite a northern California district where "over 42 percent of the districts' secondary [ELL] students are still classified [ELL] after six or more years in U.S. schools," even though most of these students are "orally proficient" (47). They use the term "long-term LEP."

25. They say language development in secondary schools is not happening in content areas and that school staff members do not know how to work with ELLs. These insights, while potentially important, concentrate on language issues.

26. This last group comprises mostly children of immigrants and Puerto Ricans.

27. Illinois has recently experienced a more organized push for newcomer schools and centers, supported by the nonprofit Center for Applied Linguistics (Avila 2002). See also Schnur (1999).

28. The Healthy Start Initiative was created to improve the lives of children, youth, and families by placing comprehensive school-linked services at or near schools.

2

Recent Immigrant and ELL Students and Their Schools

ompared with other states, California's public school system is experiencing the greatest impact from recent immigrant and ELL students. Furthermore, the experiences of each of these two groups may differ considerably. In this chapter we explore these propositions by offering statistical portraits of ELLs and recent immigrant students in California. Specifically, we introduce several quantitative methods and provide data analysis on recently arrived immigrant students, including descriptions of schools providing recent immigrant data. We examine and categorize the kinds of schools that typical English language learners attend and compare them with the typical schools attended by recent immigrant and other students. To do this we analyze test score data, school-level resources, and other school characteristics. We also explore segregation of recent immigrant and ELL students from other students.[1]

We perform these analyses at the school level for the five districts that have historically been the largest districts in the state—Fresno, Long Beach, Los Angeles, San Diego, and San Francisco.[2] Of the 329 districts submitting recent immigrant counts in 1999–2000, these 5 districts accounted for 22 percent of schools, almost 27 percent of students, more than 24 percent of recent immigrant students, and more than 33 percent of English language learners. Although we received data from 12 districts, our school-level quantitative analysis focuses on the 5 largest districts for three reasons. First, our overall qualitative analysis is conducted in and yields additional insights about these districts. Second, the other seven districts providing school-level data represent a very small proportion of schools in recent immigrant districts and are not representative of the rest of California's recent immigrant districts. Third, an analysis of these large, urban districts is most closely comparable with research conducted in the New York City school system by Schwartz and Gershberg (2000, 2001) and should provide insights for similar urban districts in other states.[3] Thus, this school-level analysis provides a richer picture of students' actual experiences because it allows us to uncover the characteristics of schools where different kinds of students are actually educated.

Table 2.1 shows statewide, recent immigrant,[4] and ELL enrollment in each of five academic years—1997–1998 through 2001–2002.[5] While overall and ELL enrollment increased over those periods, recent immigrant enrollment—still a significant student population of over 200,000 and representing about 3.3 percent of all students—declined somewhat.[6] Clearly, most of the state's 1.6 million English language learners are not recent immigrants.[7]

Table 2.1. *Recent Immigrant and English Language Learner (ELL) Students in California, 1997–98 to 2001–02*

Academic year	Total state enrollment	Recent immigrant students	ELL students
1997–98	5,727,303	234,935 (4.1%)	1,406,166 (24.6%)
1998–99	5,844,111	212,697 (3.6%)	1,442,692 (24.7%)
1999–2000	5,951,612	192,991 (3.2%)	1,480,527 (24.9%)
2000–01	6,050,895	192,540 (3.2%)	1,511,299 (25.0%)
2001–02	6,147,375	205,540 (3.3%)	1,559,248 (25.4%)
Percent change, 1997–98 to 2001–02	6.9%	−14.3%	10.9%

Source: California Department of Education (CDE) ("English-Learner Students," "Immigrant Student Demographics," and "Limited-English-Proficient Students") and authors' calculations from CDE, California Basic Education Data System (CBEDS), and Emergency Immigrant Education Program (EIEP) datasets.

Notes: "Recent immigrant" students are foreign-born students with fewer than three years in U.S. public schools. Figures in parentheses are the percentage the adjacent number represents in relationship to total enrollment for that period.

Students' Cultural Roots

In 1999–2000, immigrants from more than 175 countries and students speaking at least 56 languages were enrolled in California's public schools.[8] Although most of these students came from Mexico and spoke Spanish, such an array of cultural diversity suggests certain challenges for students and schools. Chapters 4, 5, and 6 discuss some of the challenges. This section examines student nationality and native language distribution in the five cases.

National Origins of Recent Immigrant Students

Table 2.2 shows 16 categories of national origin for recent immigrant students statewide and in each of the five largest districts for 1999–2000. It is particularly noteworthy that during that school year close to 20 percent of the state's recent immigrant students lived in Los Angeles. Still, recently arrived immigrant students represented a relatively low percentage of all students in Los Angeles—less than 5 percent were recent immigrants. On the other hand, recent immigrants in San Francisco represented nearly 9 percent of the district's total enrollment, while accounting for less than 1.5 percent of the state total. So although Los Angeles is home to a greater share of the state's recent immigrant students, San Francisco may have a higher proportion of students who need special services designed to help recently arrived immigrants make a transition to the United States. This higher proportion may also translate into higher per-pupil costs if fulfilling recent immigrant students' specialized needs is costly. Thus, it is particularly ironic that San Francisco did not qualify for federal funds for recent immigrants under the new rules dictated by NCLB.

Looking at the national origin of California's recently arrived students, it is no surprise that most (almost 70 percent in 1999–2000) came from Mexico. Recently arrived Southeast Asian and Filipino students ranked second and third, respectively. However, national origin varied more among the five case districts. For example, San Francisco reported that only about 13 percent of its recently arrived students were Mexican, whereas Long Beach had over 67 percent. Given San Diego's distinction as the district closest to the Mexican border, it is somewhat surprising that its district did not demonstrate the highest percentage of recently arrived Mexican students—in fact, fewer than half of its recent immigrants were from Mexico.[9]

Table 2.2. *National Origins of Recent Immigrant Students in California's Five Largest School Districts and Statewide, 1999–2000*

		District (total enrollment rank)				
	State-wide	Los Angeles (1)	San Diego (2)	Long Beach (3)	Fresno (4)	San Francisco (5)
Percentage of California's total recent immigrant students	—	18.8	2.0	1.1	1.1	1.4
Percentage of students who are recent immigrants	3.2	4.7	2.1	2.4	2.5	8.7
Percentage of recent immigrant students from						
Mexico	69.1	58.4	40.3	67.1	59.6	13.4
Central America	2.8	15.5	1.3	7.1	1.2	9.7
Other Latin America	1.6	2.6	1.3	2.5	1.0	2.0
Caribbean[a]	0.1	0.1	0.8	0.1	0.0	0.0
Philippines	3.7	4.0	17.8	10.1	1.4	10.5
Southeast Asia	3.7	1.5	6.8	6.3	19.8	5.0
Northeast Asia (except Korea)	3.0	0.5	3.6	0.4	0.2	11.2
Korea	2.2	4.5	1.2	0.1	0.3	1.7
Mainland China	2.0	1.4	1.4	0.5	0.6	29.0
South Asia	3.1	2.1	1.6	1.0	3.4	1.2
Western Europe and developed economies	2.9	1.7	6.2	0.8	2.3	4.5
Eastern Europe	3.4	5.0	2.6	1.1	7.3	8.5
Africa	0.5	0.6	13.2	0.8	1.5	0.8
Middle East	1.4	1.9	1.8	1.7	1.1	1.6
Pacific Islands	0.5	0.1	0.2	0.5	0.2	0.8
Other[b]	0.0	0.0	0.0	0.0	0.0	0.0
Total	100	100	100	100	100	100

Source: Author's calculations from CDE, CBEDS, and EIEP datasets.

Notes: "Recent immigrant" students are foreign-born students with fewer than three years in U.S. public schools. Figures may not total 100 percent due to rounding.

a. Non-Spanish-speaking Caribbean countries.

b. Although the "other" category is empty in 1999–2000, in some years it contains counts in the EIEP data.

Ranking and comparing the recent immigrant composition among the districts yields some interesting results. Relative to the other four districts, Long Beach was home to the highest percentage of Mexicans in 1999–2000. Los Angeles showed the highest percentage of Central Americans (15.5 percent), Koreans (4.5 percent), and Middle Easterners (almost 2 percent). San Diego had the highest percentage of Filipinos (almost 18 percent), Africans (more than 13 percent), and recent immigrants from Western European/developed economies[10] (more than 6 percent). Fresno exhibited the highest percentage of Southeast Asians (almost 20 percent) and South Asians (3.4 percent). Finally, San Francisco was home to the highest percentage of Northeast Asians excluding Koreans (more than 11 percent), Mainland Chinese (29 percent), and Eastern Europeans (8.5 percent). Overall, it is clear that our five large urban case districts display significant variation in the national origin of their recent immigrant students, much like other large urban districts across the country.

Native Languages of English Language Learners

We also group languages into categories that match the national origin categories as closely as possible; however, we have no data on students' national origins for widely spoken languages such as Spanish, Chinese languages, and Arabic.[11] Recall that close to 1.5 million students in 1999–2000 demonstrated limited English language fluency (table 2.1). More than 80 percent of ELL students statewide spoke Spanish, around 5 percent spoke a Southeast Asian language, approximately 3 percent spoke one of the Chinese languages, and the rest spoke some other language.

Table 2.3 shows 13 language categories statewide and in the five largest districts. Again, of the five case districts, Los Angeles was home to the highest percentage of ELLs in 1999–2000—more than 21 percent. In contrast, the other case districts together accounted for just 8 percent of the state's total ELL students. The percentage of English language learners within districts ranged from a low of 22.4 percent in San Francisco to a high of 44 percent in Los Angeles. Moreover, the percentage of ELL students in each of the five districts was higher than each district's share of total ELL students in the state. Therefore, these districts may be disproportionately in need of resources to serve English language learners.

Recall that an average of almost 81 percent of ELL students in 1999–2000 spoke Spanish across all districts with English language learners. However, a look at the languages spoken within the case districts reveals more variation. According to table 2.3, more than 93 percent of

Table 2.3. *Languages Spoken by English Language Learner (ELL) Students in California's Five Largest School Districts and Statewide, 1999–2000*

		District (total enrollment rank)				
	State-wide	Los Angeles (1)	San Diego (2)	Long Beach (3)	Fresno (4)	San Francisco (5)
Percentage of California's total ELL students	—	21.1	2.7	2.3	1.7	1.3
Percentage of students who are ELL	24.9	44.0	28.1	36.9	30.9	22.4
Percentage of ELL students who speak						
Spanish	80.9	93.2	76.9	80.9	55.0	38.7
Filipino language	1.4	0.7	3.7	1.9	0.1	5.2
Southeast Asian language	4.6	0.8	10.7	15.3	41.4	6.0
Japanese	1.0	0.1	0.3	0.1	0.0	1.4
Korean	1.2	1.3	0.4	0.1	0.1	1.4
Chinese language	2.8	0.7	0.8	0.3	0.3	35.8
South Asian language	1.4	0.2	0.0	0.0	0.7	0.7
Western European language[a]	1.2	0.2	0.4	0.1	0.1	0.6
Eastern European language	1.7	1.8	0.4	0.1	1.3	3.7
African language	0.0	0.0	0.0	0.0	0.1	0.2
Middle Eastern language	1.4	0.5	0.8	0.2	0.5	1.9
Pacific Island language	1.2	0.2	0.4	0.1	0.1	0.6
Other language	1.0	0.3	5.2	0.9	0.6	3.9
Total	100	100	100	100	100	100

Source: Authors' calculations from CDE and CBEDS datasets.
Notes: Figures may not total 100 percent due to rounding.
a. Except Spanish.

ELL students in Los Angeles spoke Spanish, while in San Francisco, less than 39 percent of these students spoke Spanish. Although Spanish is the most prevalent native language among English language learners in each of the five districts, other language categories demonstrate a substantial presence. For example, more than 41 percent of Fresno's and more than 15 percent of Long Beach's ELL students in 1999–2000 spoke a Southeast Asian language, and almost 36 percent of San Francisco's ELL students spoke a Chinese language. Taken together with our previous discussion of recent immigrant student national origins, we have reason to believe that the results we report here and in chapter 3 are not solely driven by Mexican and/or Spanish-speaking students. Rather, the results reflect a wide range of immigrant experiences.

According to table 2.3, the language group with the fewest speakers is the African language group—only two of the five districts reported African language speakers. However, many speakers of African languages may be labeled as "other" or understated in the language census (LC) for three reasons: (1) the LC only has one African language (Tigrinya), which is spoken primarily in Ethiopia and in parts of Eritrea in East Africa, (2) Student National Origin Report (SNOR), on the other hand, shows that more than 13 percent of San Diego's recent immigrants are from Africa, and (3) interviews with district and school personnel there lead us to conclude that many of the recently arrived African origin students demonstrate limited English proficiency.[12] In addition, Africans are likely being counted as African Americans (or blacks) in much state data, a practice that raises interesting methodological as well as philosophical issues.[13] Clearly, there is room for improvement in the collection of racial and ethnic data by the state and districts.

Although the numbers in this example are quite small, the challenges— such as language translation and cultural differences—presented by a single student whose native language is not among the more commonly spoken languages in California cannot be underestimated. These difficulties place significant strain on the resources of the teacher, school, and, in some cases, even the district.[14]

Student Demographics

Following Schwartz and Gershberg (2000, 2001), we use descriptive statistics and exposure indices to compare schools typically attended by different kinds of students. An exposure index reveals the school characteristics the typical recent immigrant is exposed to. We also use dissimilarity indices to analyze segregation differences among schools across a district. We compare the level of student segregation with such characteristics as gender, ethnicity or race, free- or reduced-price-lunch eligibility (as a proxy for poverty), recent immigrant status, and ELL status.[15]

In several respects, the student population in the five largest districts is quite different from the student population in the state as a whole. Each district population has a distinctive ethnic or racial composition when compared with other districts and the state (figure 2.1). All of the districts in 1999–2000 included higher proportions of black or African-American students (ranging from 11 to 20 percent) than the state (8.6 percent). All had fewer white students and more Asians (except Los Angeles). In addition, all were relatively similar to the state overall for Hispanic students except Los Angeles, which was 70 percent Hispanic.

Table 2.4 presents school-level statistics for the five case districts combined. Whereas figure 2.1 illustrates the student composition in each district compared with the state, this table describes the average school, the average student, the average recent immigrant student, and the average English language learner. For example, the average school across the five largest districts was characterized in 1999–2000 by a student population that was 16 percent black or African American, slightly more than 53 percent Hispanic, 10 percent Asian, nearly 17 percent white, almost 67 percent free- or reduced-price-lunch eligible, 4 percent recent immigrant, and

Figure 2.1. *Ethnic or Racial Categories in California's Five Largest School Districts and Statewide, 1999–2000*

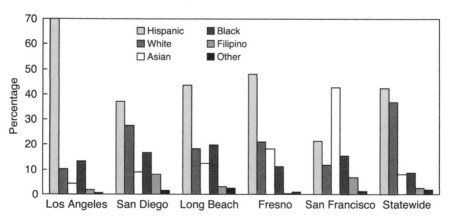

Source: Authors' calculations from CDE and CBEDS datasets.

Table 2.4. *Exposure Indices for Student Demographic Variables in California's Five Largest School Districts, 1999–2000*[a]

	(1)	(2)	(3)	(4)	(5)
	Number of schools	Percentage of students at the average school who are	Percentage of the average student's schoolmates who are	Percentage of the average recent immigrant's schoolmates who are	Percentage of the average ELL student's schoolmates who are
All schools[b]					
Black	1,131	16.0	14.2	10.6	10.7
Hispanic	1,131	53.2	59.1	66.6	72.2
Asian	1,131	10.0	8.7	8.7	6.9
White	1,131	16.6	14.1	10.5	7.6
Eligible for free/ reduced- price lunch	1,100	66.8	69.1	74.6	81.1
Recent immigrants	1,131	4.0	4.4	7.9	5.4
ELLs	1,131	37.1	39.1	47.7	54.1
Elementary schools (K–6)[c]					
Black	752	15.0	13.5	8.8	9.9
Hispanic	752	54.6	62.3	72.7	75.4
Asian	752	9.7	7.6	6.8	6.0
White	752	16.6	12.9	8.8	6.3
Eligible for free/ reduced- price lunch	746	71.4	77.1	83.2	86.7
Recent immigrants	724	4.4	4.5	6.9	5.4
ELLs	752	43.1	50.1	60.9	63.1

(*continued*)

Table 2.4. *Continued*

	(1)	(2)	(3)	(4)	(5)
		Percentage of students at the average school who are	*Percentage of the average student's schoolmates who are*	*Percentage of the average recent immigrant's schoolmates who are*	*Percentage of the average ELL student's schoolmates who are*
	Number of schools				
Middle schools (6–8)[c]					
Black	139	16.0	14.6	13.1	11.8
Hispanic	139	51.5	58.8	62.8	68.6
Asian	139	12.2	9.0	9.5	7.7
White	139	15.8	13.9	11.2	9.1
Eligible for for free/ reduced- price lunch	139	66.9	68.9	72.0	75.7
Recent immigrants	138	4.0	4.1	5.7	4.7
ELLs	139	30.1	31.8	36.5	39.3
High schools (9–12)					
Black	155	18.1	14.3	12.3	11.9
Hispanic	155	49.9	54.0	57.7	63.1
Asian	155	10.9	11.3	11.9	10.2
White	155	16.7	15.8	13.5	11.4
Eligible for reduced- price lunch	154	46.6	54.2	59.6	61.8
Recent immigrants	155	3.8	5.2	9.0	6.4
ELLs	155	17.9	23.7	29.2	29.9

Source: Authors' calculations from CDE, CBEDS, and EIEP datasets.

Notes: ELL = English language learner. "Recent immigrant" students are foreign-born students with fewer than three years in U.S. public schools.

a. California's five largest school districts are Los Angeles, San Diego, Long Beach, Fresno, and San Francisco.

b. The "all schools" category includes all the elementary, middle, and high schools plus those schools that do not fit neatly into the three grade spans.

c. Some districts include grade 6 in elementary school, while others include it in middle school.

slightly more than 37 percent English language learner. Columns 3, 4, and 5 present what we will call throughout this study "exposure indices." These indices measure the degree of contact between immigrants and other types of students, and are one of several measures of interaction with, or exposure to particular "social experiences by group members" (White 1986).[16] Another way to think of an exposure index—in this case for recent immigrant students—is that it describes the percentage of schoolmates of a particular type who attend school with the *average* recent immigrant student.[17]

There are few differences of great interest between the experiences of average students and average recent immigrant students, but the results do indicate that the average recent immigrant student attends a school with schoolmates who are somewhat different from the schoolmates of the average student. In 1999–2000, there were fewer black and white students and more free- or reduced-price-lunch eligible, Hispanic, ELL, and

Figure 2.2. *Schoolmate Characteristics in K–6 Schools in California's Five Largest School Districts, by Student Type, 1999–2000*

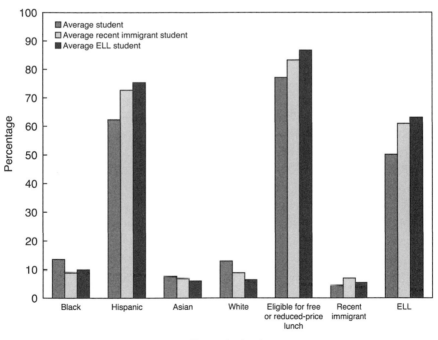

Source: Authors' calculations from CDE, CBEDS, and EIEP datasets.
Notes: ELL = English language learner. "Recent immigrant" students are foreign-born students with fewer than three years in U.S. public schools.

recent immigrant students in a school the average recent immigrant attended (figure 2.2).

The patterns are similar for the average ELL student, who was in a school where the percentage of black schoolmates was about the same as it was for the average recent immigrant student. However, the percentages of Asian, white, and recent immigrant schoolmates were lower, and the percentages of Hispanic, free- or reduced-price-lunch eligible, and ELL schoolmates were higher for the average English language learner than they were for the average recent immigrant student. Hispanic, free- or reduced-price-lunch eligible, recent immigrant, and ELL students also attended larger schools than the average student (not shown). At first glance, therefore, it appears that while similar, there are differences between the characteristics of schools attended by the average recent immigrant and the average English language learner.

Note that public schools in these districts have higher concentrations of Hispanic, black, ELL, and recent immigrant students than are found in the general population (not shown). Evidently, there *is* some segregation of all these groups in public (as opposed to private) schools. In other words, a higher proportion of white, non-Hispanic, native-born English speakers in these districts go to private schools. Thus, public schools are segregated in a way the data in figure 2.2 cannot capture. While this is not the focus of our study, any segregation between public schools must be viewed in light of the concentration of certain ethnic, racial,[18] language minority (non-native English speaking), and immigrant groups in the public school system to begin with. That is, segregation of all these groups is likely worse than our data in figure 2.2 show. Even so, figure 2.2 paints a striking picture. It compares average, average recent immigrant, and average ELL student exposure to students with various characteristics in K–6 schools across the five case cities.

Both the average recent immigrant student and the average English language learner in 1999–2000 attended a K–6 school with slightly lower percentages of Asian, black, and white schoolmates and higher percentages of Hispanic, free- or reduced-price-lunch eligible, recent immigrant, and ELL schoolmates than the average student (see also table 2.4). The statistics for Hispanic, free-lunch-eligible, and ELL students' schoolmates in figure 2.2 are in some sense stunning. The average elementary student attended a school that was more than 50 percent ELL, 70 percent poor, and 60 percent Hispanic. The figures are higher still for average recent immigrant and ELL students. In fact, the typical ELL elementary student was in a school that was more than 85 percent poor! It is hard to escape the concentration of race, poverty, and language minorities in the public schools in these five large urban school districts. Given the characteristics of the state as a whole and the likely characteristics of each of these five districts, there is clearly some segregation of poor, minority students in public schools, caused in part by the choices made by nonpoor, nonminority families either to send their children to private schools or not to live in large urban area school districts. But do these patterns indicate segregation *between and within* public schools, too, and, if so, how severe is this segregation?

Segregation of English Language Learners and Recent Immigrant Students

While an exposure index measures the degree of contact between schoolmates of different types, a "dissimilarity index" gauges the degree of segregation that might be occurring. This index runs from zero to one, with segregation increasing as the index increases. It presents the proportion of a particular group of concern (such as recent immigrants or blacks) that would need to change schools in order for that group to be evenly distributed across schools. We often, however, express this index in terms of the percentage rather than the proportion of students who would have to move. (See appendix B for a full definition.) The index is calculated for a pair of categories—immigrant and nonimmigrant, for example. We perform this analysis for several student categories across schools in *each* of the five districts to compare segregation within the districts, which we emphasize as the most appropriate unit of analysis.[19] Although students may change districts during the course of their schooling, we do not construct these indices across all recent immigrant districts in the state, in part because policies that may affect the distribution of students in one district may not pertain to another district. On the other hand, policy in a given district has the potential to greatly affect which school a particular student attends in that district.

Across K–6 schools in each of the districts, recent immigrant and ELL students are generally (though not always) less segregated than other groups of concern, and English language learners are generally more segregated than recent immigrants (table 2.5). For instance, in Los Angeles, 56 percent of black and 43 percent of ELL students in 1999–2000 would have had to change schools for each school in the district to achieve the

Table 2.5. *Dissimilarity Indices for California's Five Largest School Districts, by Grade Span, 1999–2000*

Grade span and student type	Los Angeles	San Diego	Long Beach	Fresno	San Francisco
All schools[a]	N = 655	N = 177	N = 86	N = 97	N = 116
Recent immigrant	0.25	0.45	0.27	0.23	0.36
Black	0.56	0.33	0.22	0.25	0.38
Hispanic	0.52	0.39	0.27	0.26	0.40
Asian	0.54	0.38	0.31	0.28	0.38
White	0.64	0.46	0.47	0.43	0.38
ELL	0.43	0.46	0.38	0.35	0.30
Eligible for free/ reduced-price lunch	0.49	0.49	0.46	0.38	0.37
Elementary schools (K–6)[b]	N = 446	N = 122	N = 56	N = 56	N = 72
Recent immigrant	0.23	0.55	0.25	0.20	0.30
Black	0.59	0.36	0.21	0.27	0.46
Hispanic	0.55	0.45	0.31	0.27	0.42
Asian	0.60	0.42	0.31	0.28	0.39
White	0.70	0.51	0.56	0.46	0.45
ELL	0.40	0.49	0.39	0.33	0.31
Eligible for free/ reduced-price lunch	0.56	0.55	0.51	0.44	0.30
Middle schools (6–8)[b]	N = 72	N = 20	N = 16	N = 14	N = 17
Recent immigrant	0.20	0.31	0.37	0.20	0.27
Black	0.54	0.30	0.20	0.15	0.31
Hispanic	0.48	0.29	0.26	0.21	0.40
Asian	0.49	0.26	0.20	0.19	0.35
White	0.60	0.38	0.44	0.43	0.33
ELL	0.29	0.36	0.30	0.26	0.23
Eligible for free/ reduced-price lunch	0.32	0.44	0.40	0.43	0.30
High schools (9–12)	N = 96	N = 16	N = 8	N = 14	N = 21
Recent immigrant	0.26	0.23	0.24	0.22	0.41
Black	0.52	0.32	0.23	0.22	0.31
Hispanic	0.48	0.30	0.21	0.28	0.35
Asian	0.44	0.32	0.31	0.23	0.37
White	0.56	0.39	0.32	0.42	0.31
ELL	0.24	0.36	0.14	0.28	0.33
Eligible for free/ reduced-price lunch	0.40	0.39	0.19	0.30	0.25

Source: Authors' calculations from CDE, CBEDS, and EIEP datasets.

Notes: ELL = English language learner. "Recent immigrant" students are foreign-born students with fewer than three years in U.S. public schools.

a. The "all schools" category includes all the elementary, middle, and high schools plus those schools that do not fit neatly into the three grade spans.

b. Some districts include grade 6 in elementary school, while others include it in middle school.

average percentage of black and ELL students, respectively. In contrast, only 25 percent of recent immigrant students would have had to change schools. In San Diego, however, the recent immigrant and English language learner groups were the most segregated groups for elementary schools (0.55 and 0.49, respectively). These statistics suggest not only that recent immigrants attend neighborhood schools close to where they live in particular areas of San Diego, but also that such neighborhoods contain higher concentrations of recent immigrants than are found in other cities. Unlike San Francisco and Los Angeles, San Diego is without newcomer schools, a possible source of the segregation. So while opponents of explicit newcomer schools and programs voice fears of segregation, it happens that a district with no explicit newcomer programs is the most segregated with respect to recent immigrants.

A look across all schools in table 2.5 reveals some variation among the districts. For example, recent immigrants in San Diego in 1999–2000 appeared to be the most segregated across all schools (0.45); San Francisco ranked second (0.36), while Fresno featured the least segregated recent immigrant population (0.23). Although San Francisco's recent immigrant high school students were relatively segregated (0.41), this situation may be at least partially the result of the district's exclusively newcomer high school. In terms of ELL students, San Diego (0.46) and Los Angeles (0.43) demonstrated the highest degrees of segregation, while San Francisco had the lowest (0.30) across all schools.

More importantly, in terms of overall trends, two main patterns emerge. First, there is some segregation of immigrant and ELL students, which is variable across school levels and districts. That segregation, however, is not categorically worse than for other groups of concern. Second, in general, segregation falls as students move from elementary to high school. These results support research by Betts, Rueben, and Danenberg (2000) and most of the student characteristics analyzed by Schwartz and Gershberg (2000, 2001). Higher segregation in grade K–6 schools is not surprising because these schools reflect residential segregation across neighborhoods (Massey and Denton 1993) more strongly than do middle schools and high schools, which typically enroll students from "feeder schools" over a wider area. To the extent that the state and school districts have policies to reduce segregation, ELL and recent immigrant students could be legitimate target groups of concern. Of course, the goal of less segregation may not always be either desirable or compatible with supporting successful newcomer schools and programs.

Resource Distribution across Schools

Examining the distribution of students across and within the case districts leads us to an analysis of resource distribution. Betts, Rueben, and Danenberg (2000) demonstrated considerable inequality in measures that capture student-teacher interaction within districts as well as across districts in California. These measures include school characteristics, such as pupil-teacher ratio and average class size, as well as teacher characteristics, such as experience, education, and certification. One of the most common measures of school resources is spending per pupil. Although this measure does exist at district level in California, it is remarkably unavailable for school-level analysis. And while there is debate over whether teacher-characteristic measures accurately capture the quality of a teacher, these measures represent a relatively objective set of criteria. Therefore, in the absence of better information, we focus on these types of measures throughout our analysis for consistency and comparability of resources.

We analyze a number of school and teacher characteristics across schools in our five case districts.[20] Except for some teacher characteristics, very little variation occurs in most of the school resource measures. That is, by most measures available, recent immigrant and ELL students overall attend schools similar to those of average students. This is in some sense good news: the state has the most direct control in regulating these measures (such as class size), and its policies appear to be achieving some measure of equity in some key areas. Figure 2.3 shows, however, that compared with the average elementary school student, average English language learner and recent immigrant students in 1999–2000 attended a K–6 school with fewer highly experienced and highly educated teachers, more teachers with low levels of experience and education, and more teachers who lacked full credentials. Again, in most cases, recent immigrants were slightly better off than ELL students, although in elementary schools these differences were very small.[21] Table 2.6 contains these measures for all schools and for all three grade spans.

The general trend observed across all schools in the five case districts holds true within individual districts, yet there is some variation among the five districts (table 2.7). For the average student, the average recent immigrant student, and the average ELL student within districts, there are only a few, small differences in pupil-teacher ratios and average teacher experience either across or within districts. However, the average recent immigrant student attends a larger school with generally larger

Figure 2.3. *Teacher Characteristics in K–6 Schools in California's Five Largest School Districts, by Student Type, 1999–2000*

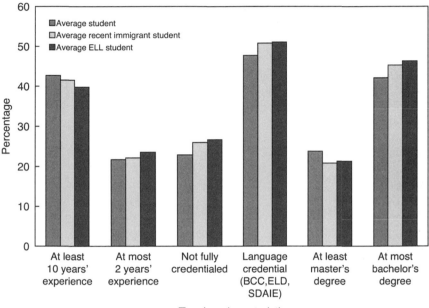

Source: Authors' calculations from CDE, CBEDS, and EIEP datasets.

Note: BCC = Bilingual cross-cultural; ELD = English language development; SDAIE = Specially designed academic instruction in English.

class sizes than the average student or the average ELL student. On average, Los Angeles had the largest schools in 1999–2000, while San Francisco featured the smallest schools. Fresno had the highest percentage of highly experienced teachers, whereas San Diego had the highest percentage of novice teachers (up to two years of experience).

Another measure that has received much attention—particularly in light of federal No Child Left Behind (NCLB) legislation mandating a fully qualified teacher in every classroom—is the percentage of teachers with a full teaching credential. On average in 1999–2000, San Diego and Fresno boasted low percentages of teachers who lacked full credentials— approximately 5 to 8 percent for the average, recent immigrant, and ELL student, while Los Angeles and Long Beach averaged between 25 and 30 percent in this category, depending on the type of student. Still, recent immigrant students appear to be slightly better off than English language learners in terms of being exposed to (and presumably taught by) teachers with full certification.

Table 2.6. *Exposure Indices for School and Teacher Characteristics in California's Five Largest School Districts, 1999–2000*[a]

School type and characteristic	Number of schools	The average school	A school attended by the average student	A school attended by the average recent immigrant student	A school attended by the average ELL student
All schools[b]					
Total enrollment	1,131	959.2	1,636.8	1,770.3	1,537.0
Student-teacher ratio	1,130	20.1	21.7	21.8	21.0
Average class size	1,130	25.8	26.9	27.3	26.8
Average teacher experience (y)	1,130	11.6	11.6	11.4	10.7
≥ 10 y (%)	1,128	46.4	46.2	45.2	42.2
≤ 2 y (%)	1,128	20.0	20.4	20.6	22.4
Teachers not fully credentialed (%)	1,130	19.7	21.1	23.0	25.0
Teachers with language credential (BCC, ELD, SDAIE, bilingual) (%)[c]	1,130	39.7	39.8	42.9	45.3
Teachers with at least a master's degree (%)	1,130	28.5	27.9	26.7	24.2
Teachers with at most a bachelor's degree (%)	1,130	36.0	38.5	40.8	43.2
Elementary schools (K–6)[d]					
Total enrollment	752	750.3	947.6	1,052.2	1,082.2
Student-teacher ratio	752	19.2	19.6	19.6	19.6
Average class size	752	26.1	26.2	26.7	26.6
Average class size, grades K–3	748	18.3	18.5	18.5	18.6
Average class size, grades 4–6	733	28.3	28.8	28.4	28.7
Average teacher experience (y)	752	11.2	10.9	10.7	10.2
≥ 10 y (%)	750	44.0	42.7	41.6	39.8
≤ 2 y (%)	750	21.0	21.7	22.2	23.6
Teachers not fully credentialed (%)	752	20.7	22.9	26.0	26.6

(continued)

Table 2.6. *Continued*

School type and characteristic	Number of schools	The average school	A school attended by the average student	A school attended by the average recent immigrant student	A school attended by the average ELL student
Teachers with language credential (BCC, ELD, SDAIE, bilingual) (%)[c]	752	45.0	47.7	50.8	51.0
Teachers with at least a master's degree (%)	752	25.5	23.7	20.8	21.2
Teachers with at most a bachelor's degree (%)	752	38.9	42.1	45.2	46.3
Middle schools (6–8)[d]					
Total enrollment	139	1,478.0	1,806.0	1,850.9	1,918.7
Student-teacher ratio	139	23.1	23.8	23.8	23.8
Average class size	139	28.8	28.0	28.6	27.4
Average math class size	139	28.0	28.2	27.5	28.0
Average English class size	139	24.9	24.6	24.3	24.5
Average teacher experience (y)	139	11.5	11.4	11.2	10.9
≥ 10 y (%)	139	46.0	45.4	44.5	43.3
≤ 2 y (%)	139	22.2	22.4	22.6	23.2
Teachers not fully credentialed (%)	139	20.7	22.8	24.0	24.9
Teachers with language credential (BCC, ELD, SDAIE, bilingual) (%)[c]	139	31.4	32.4	33.5	34.2
Teachers with at least a master's degree (%)	139	30.1	29.1	28.8	27.4
Teachers with at most a bachelor's degree (%)	139	32.2	37.9	38.3	39.5
High schools (9–12)					
Total enrollment	155	1,652.8	3,060.3	3,111.3	3,285.3
Student-teacher ratio	154	22.6	24.5	24.8	24.6
Average class size	154	24.2	27.9	27.9	27.7
Average math class size	149	24.7	27.9	28.1	27.7

(*continued*)

Table 2.6. *Continued*

School type and characteristic	Number of schools	The average school	A school attended by the average student	A school attended by the average recent immigrant student	A school attended by the average ELL student
Average English class size	150	22.2	23.7	23.6	23.6
College prep ("a–f") classes (%)	154	62.5	63.5	60.6	63.1
Number of advanced placement (AP) classes offered	154	10.9	20.0	18.8	19.7
Average teacher experience (y)	154	13.5	13.3	12.9	12.8
≥ 10 y (%)	154	56.6	53.8	52.8	52.3
≤ 2 y (%)	154	14.3	16.2	16.3	16.4
Teachers not fully credentialed (%)	154	15.4	17.0	17.1	18.2
Teachers with language credential (BCC, ELD, SDAIE, bilingual) (%)[c]	154	27.2	30.7	34.0	32.8
Teachers with at least a master's degree (%)	154	37.5	34.9	35.4	32.8
Teachers with at most a bachelor's degree (%)	154	28.1	32.2	34.3	33.7

Source: Authors' calculations from CDE, CBEDS, and EIEP datasets.

Notes: ELL = English language learner. "Recent immigrant" students are foreign-born students with fewer than three years in U.S. public schools.

a. California's five largest school districts are (historically) Los Angeles, San Diego, Long Beach, Fresno, and San Francisco.

b. The "all schools" category includes all the elementary, middle, and high schools plus those schools that do not fit neatly into the three grade spans.

c. BCC = Bilingual cross-cultural; ELD = English language development; SDAIE = Specially designed academic instruction in English.

d. Some districts include grade 6 in elementary school, while others include it in middle school.

Table 2.7. *Exposure Indices for School and Teacher Characteristics in All Schools in California's Five Largest School Districts, 1999–2000*

Characteristic	The average school	A school attended by the average student	A school attended by the average recent immigrant student	A school attended by the average ELL student
Los Angeles (N = 654[a])				
Total enrollment	1,084.0	1,845.9	1,905.6	1,672.3
Student-teacher ratio	20.1	22.0	21.8	21.1
Average class size	22.9	25.9	26.4	26.6
Average teacher experience (y)	11.6	11.4	11.2	10.8
≥ 10 y (%)	45.7	45.0	44.2	42.2
≤ 2 y (%)	20.5	21.1	21.2	22.4
Teachers not fully credentialed (%)	24.7	25.8	26.1	28.5
Teachers with language credential (BCC, ELD, SDAIE, bilingual) (%)[b]	43.5	42.0	45.0	46.8
Teachers with at least a master's degree (%)	24.5	24.6	24.2	22.3
Teachers with at most a bachelor's degree (%)	46.3	46.8	46.8	49.0
San Diego (N = 177)				
Total enrollment	795.2	1,092.6	1,438.6	1,049.2
Student-teacher ratio	19.6	20.4	21.2	19.7
Average class size	22.0	23.7	24.9	22.3
Average teacher experience (y)	11.0	11.2	11.8	9.3
≥ 10 y (%)	43.6	43.8	46.3	35.5
≤ 2 y (%)	25.5	25.5	23.6	32.4
Teachers not fully credentialed (%)	6.0	5.4	4.5	8.0
Teachers with language credential (BCC, ELD, SDAIE, bilingual) (%)[b]	40.1	38.1	34.3	50.0
Teachers with at least a master's degree (%)	51.9	52.3	54.4	45.7
Teachers with at most a bachelor's degree (%)	44.2	43.9	41.8	49.9

(*continued*)

Table 2.7. *Continued*

Characteristic	The average school	A school attended by the average student	A school attended by the average recent immigrant student	A school attended by the average ELL student
Long Beach (N = 86)				
Total enrollment	1,063.6	1,714.6	1,715.9	1,421.8
Student-teacher ratio	21.9	23.1	22.9	22.0
Average class size	25.2	26.9	27.0	25.9
Average teacher experience (y)	11.3	11.6	10.7	10.2
≥ 10 y (%)	44.4	45.5	42.0	39.1
≤ 2 y (%)	18.7	18.4	20.3	21.3
Teachers not fully credentialed (%)	26.1	26.2	28.7	30.2
Teachers with language credential (BCC, ELD, SDAIE, bilingual) (%)[b]	39.4	35.6	35.0	38.0
Teachers with at least a master's degree (%)	28.0	30.2	28.8	25.8
Teachers with at most a bachelor's degree (%)	25.9	25.3	28.0	30.2
Fresno (N = 97)				
Total enrollment	842.6	1,239.9	1,223.5	1,218.9
Student-teacher ratio	20.4	21.7	20.7	20.9
Average class size	21.8	23.0	22.7	22.8
Average teacher experience (y)	13.9	14.1	13.1	12.8
≥ 10 y (%)	58.8	59.2	54.6	53.5
≤ 2 y (%)	9.5	9.5	10.5	10.8
Teachers not fully credentialed (%)	8.3	6.2	6.7	6.9
Teachers with language credential (BCC, ELD, SDAIE, bilingual) (%)[b]	39.2	38.1	40.3	40.3
Teachers with at least a master's degree (%)	11.6	10.9	9.9	10.1
Teachers with at most a bachelor's degree (%)	2.4	0.2	0.0	0.1

(continued)

Table 2.7. *Continued*

Characteristic	The average school	A school attended by the average student	A school attended by the average recent immigrant student	A school attended by the average ELL student
San Francisco (*N* = 116)				
Total enrollment	525.0	872.3	920.9	728.7
Student-teacher ratio	19.0	20.1	21.9	19.9
Average class size	51.7	51.7	46.2	53.5
Average teacher experience (y)	11.4	12.3	12.7	11.8
≥ 10 y (%)	45.6	49.4	52.7	48.1
≤ 2 y (%)	18.9	17.3	15.6	18.1
Teachers not fully credentialed (%)	17.3	15.8	15.8	16.8
Teachers with language credential (BCC, ELD, SDAIE, bilingual) (%)[b]	18.0	26.4	35.3	23.5
Teachers with at least a master's degree (%)	29.4	29.7	31.7	28.7
Teachers with at most a bachelor's degree (%)	1.1	1.2	1.3	1.2

Source: Authors' calculations from CDE, CBEDS, and EIEP datasets.

Notes: ELL = English language learner. "Recent immigrant" students are foreign-born students with fewer than three years in U.S. public schools.

a. Except "total enrollment" = 655, and "teacher experience ≥ 10 years and ≤ 2 years" = 652.

b. BCC = Bilingual cross-cultural; ELD = English language development; SDAIE = Specially designed academic instruction in English.

Perhaps the most interesting resource measure is the proportion of teachers who have *at most* a bachelor's degree: The percentage of such teachers ranged from a low of close to 0 percent in Fresno during the same time period to a substantial 50 percent in a school attended by the average ELL student in San Diego.[22] Los Angeles is not far behind San Diego (46 to 49 percent). Again, the average recent immigrant student appears to fare slightly better than the average ELL student in terms of teacher characteristics. Chapter 3 explores the relationships between student and teacher characteristics across schools in these districts in more detail.

Given the generally small differences in exposure to teachers' characteristics that serve as measures of quality, a natural question arises: how does the average achievement in a school attended by the average recent immigrant student compare with the achievement in a school attended by the average student and the average ELL student?

Academic Performance in Schools Attended by Recent Immigrant and ELL Students

Test scores serve as our final set of measures across schools in California's five largest school districts.[23] We focus on reading and mathematics mean scaled scores (MSS, the average test score at the school for the given type of student) and the percentage of students scoring at or above a nationally normed median (p50) in grades 2 and 5. Grade 2 represents an "entrance point" to elementary school, while grade 5 represents an "exit point" for many students as they move from elementary school to middle school.[24] We present scores for three groups of students: all students, ELL students, and non-ELL students.

As shown in table 2.8, the average English language learner and recent immigrant student in K–6 schools attends a school in which—for either subject and by either test measure we use—the scores of all second grade students are lower than those in a school attended by the average student overall. ELL students are in schools with slightly lower scores than recent immigrants. This pattern repeats for both ELL and non-ELL second grade test scores, and for fifth grade scores as well. Because these data present only descriptive relationships, they do not control for other characteristics, such as gender, ethnicity, and socioeconomic status. That is, we can say, for example, that recent immigrants are in schools with lower test scores, but it could simply be that recent immigrants tend to be ELLs, and ELL students attend lower-scoring schools. Further statistical analysis used in the next chapter will help to untangle these factors.

Birds of a Feather Singing Different Tunes?

This chapter has focused on recent immigrant and ELL students in California, along with several other student characteristics such as gender, race/ethnicity, and socioeconomic status. It has also examined various school characteristics, including pupil-teacher ratio, class size, and such teacher characteristics as experience, education, and certification. We find that the two student populations perform differently and receive different

Table 2.8. *Exposure Indices for Performance in Second and Fifth Grades in California's Five Largest School Districts, 1999–2000*[a]

	Average score	Average score at a school attended by the		
		Average student	Average recent immigrant student	Average ELL student
Second grade				
All students				
MSS reading	574.0	568.8	563.0	560.5
P-50th reading	42.3	37.0	30.7	28.4
MSS math	572.8	568.8	564.7	562.5
P-50th math	50.4	46.4	41.6	40.0
ELL students				
MSS reading	558.9	556.4	554.7	553.4
P-50th reading	26.8	24.2	22.1	21.0
MSS math	564.3	562.0	560.5	559.6
P-50th math	42.2	39.7	37.3	37.0
Non-ELL students				
MSS reading	582.0	578.1	574.9	572.2
P-50th reading	50.9	47.0	43.5	41.0
MSS math	575.5	571.7	568.9	565.9
P-50th math	53.4	49.7	46.5	44.2
Fifth grade				
All students				
MSS reading	638.3	633.5	628.9	626.1
P-50th reading	33.4	28.6	23.6	20.8
MSS math	639.2	635.1	631.7	629.0
P-50th math	40.5	36.0	31.9	29.2
ELL students				
MSS reading	614.9	612.8	611.8	611.1
P-50th reading	8.3	7.2	6.6	6.2
MSS math	622.8	620.4	619.4	618.4
P-50th math	21.5	19.0	17.6	16.9
Non-ELL students				
MSS reading	648.2	645.0	642.9	640.5
P-50th reading	43.4	39.6	36.6	34.1
MSS math	645.9	643.0	641.8	639.3
P-50th math	48.5	45.4	43.7	41.2

Source: Authors' calculations from CDE, CBEDS, and EIEP datasets.

Notes: MSS is mean scaled score for the given grade's scores at the school; P-50th is the percentage of students in the given grade scoring at or above the national 50th percentile of scores. MSS scores can be compared across grades but not between academic subjects. "Recent immigrant" students are foreign-born students with fewer than three years in U.S. public schools. ELL = English language learner.

a. From elementary (K–6) schools, pooled. California's five largest school districts are Los Angeles, San Diego, Long Beach, Fresno, and San Francisco.

schooling experiences, yet in many respects they share similar characteristics and experiences.

In conclusion, recent immigrant enrollment is declining mildly, while
English language learner enrollment is increasing mildly. Also, the average
student attends school in a district with fewer than 6 percent recent immigrant students but approximately 25 percent ELL students. In addition,
although segregation among recent immigrant students is milder than
among other groups, there is, in fact, some segregation of English language
learners and recent immigrant students. This segregation is strongest at
the elementary school level and is acute in some districts. Nevertheless,
blacks and free-lunch-eligible students are more segregated than ELLs and
recent immigrant students in most districts, but not all. Furthermore,
recent immigrant and ELL students are exposed to teachers who are less
experienced, less educated, and less likely to be fully certified teachers.
Finally, although the average recent immigrant student attends a school
with higher overall test scores than the average English language learner,
both groups attend schools with lower-than-average test scores.[25]

NOTES

1. All data for this study, except school-level counts of recent immigrant student
populations, come from databases made available by the California Department of Education (CDE). The school-level analysis is for the 1999–2000 academic year. Appendix B
describes all relevant data and collection issues. The school-level data on recent immigrants were gathered from individual districts for this study. They derive from the census
taken in schools each March to comply with the federal Emergency Immigrant Education
Program (EIEP), which provides funds to states and school districts with significant recent
immigrant student populations. Unfortunately, we do not have school-level data on the
national origin of recent immigrants. For more description and discussion of the EIEP, see
appendix A, Gershberg (2002), NCBE (1999), and Schwartz and Gershberg (2001).

2. Following Betts, Rueben, and Danenberg (2000), we categorize schools as elementary schools (grades K–6), middle schools (grades 6–8), and high schools (grades
9–12). Schools serving a grade span that does not fit into one of these three categories are
included in the analyses across all schools and are omitted from the analysis by grade span.
Most of the observations lost in this process concern schools that are different in structure
and nature (e.g., special education, alternative) and thus not comparable with schools that
clearly fit in one of the three categories. Sixth grades in elementary and middle schools tend
to have distinctly different structures: sixth grades in the former tend to be self-contained
classrooms, whereas sixth grades in the latter tend to be departmentalized.

3. The EIEP district data are collected each year under the federal guidelines; however,
there are no requirements for data collection at the school level. Therefore, we requested
school-level EIEP student counts directly from the participating districts. We received data

that could be matched to our other 1999–2000 datasets from 12 districts, including our 5 case districts. Appendix B describes the nature of the data we received in more detail.

4. Note that since the EIEP dictates our definition of recent immigrant, we use the terms *recent immigrant student* and *EIEP student* interchangeably throughout the study. Both refer essentially to foreign-born students with fewer than three years in U.S. public schools.

5. For table 2.1, we supplement the data in our database with data for two additional school years from the California Department of Education (2003, "Immigrant Student Demographics").

6. It must be stressed, however, that recent immigrant enrollment may be understated due to enrollment thresholds in the federal EIEP requirements and the voluntary nature of the program. Appendix B describes the datasets and data collections more fully.

7. Note that the year after the NCLB replaced the EIEP with the Title III Immigrant Education Program, the count of recent immigrants plummeted to 132,000.

8. The Student National Origin Report (SNOR) is among the reports submitted to the federal recent immigrant program, and the language census (LC) is an annual count of nonnative English students by native language in California. We collapsed the SNOR and LC into 16 and 13 categories, respectively, using a combination of geographic, economic, political, and cultural factors (see appendix B).

9. It is also possible that San Diego School District officials are more conservative than other district officials in the manner in which they define *recent immigrants* in their census, though it is not clear how that would systematically underreport Mexicans.

10. See appendix B for the list of countries that comprise this category.

11. Spanish is the most difficult yet important language to match to national origins because it is the primary language of the overwhelming proportion—approximately 73 percent—of recent immigrants in each of the three academic years. An analysis of the Spanish-speaking countries in the SNOR (not shown) reveals that almost 90 percent of the Spanish speakers are from Mexico, slightly more than 5 percent are from Central America, and the rest are from other parts of Latin America and Spain. Although we designed the language categories to match the national origin categories as much as possible, it must be stressed that many English language learners may not be recent immigrants, or indeed, immigrants at all. This section discusses only the ELL population; as such, any references to particular language speakers refer to the limited English speakers only as compared, for example, with fluent English speakers whose native language is not English, or with foreign language speakers whose native language is English.

12. Administrators in San Diego later confirmed that African language ELLs in their district are counted as "other" on the LC.

13. We use "black" rather than "African American" because we have confirmed that recent immigrant students from Africa are counted as African American in many districts. Asians do not include Filipino or Pacific Island students. The combined categories of American Indian or Alaska Native, Filipino, and Pacific Islander account for approximately 5 percent and are excluded from much of this chapter.

14. See chapter 4 for a discussion regarding translation issues.

15. Appendix B provides a complete description of exposure and dissimilarity indices.

16. For a complete discussion of this and other measures of diversity and segregation, see White (1986). See appendix B for a full definition of exposure indices.

17. Care must be taken in the interpretation of the meaning of "average" recent immigrant student. We do not mean average in any sense related to performance, but average with respect to the other characteristics of the student population included in table 2.4.

18. The term *ethnicity* is generally based on geographical, language, or religious ancestry, while *race* has traditionally been based on phenotypical or traditional groupings. In terms of racial grouping, there are mainly three historical racial groups—Negroid (i.e., black), Caucasoid (i.e., white), and Asiatic. Most common usages do not adhere to these categorizations, and we tend to believe that race itself often amounts to an ethnic grouping. The original thought was that racial groupings were based on scientific groupings. However, modern science has largely shown that these so-called scientific differences are not valid. Much of the controversy as to whether to use *race* or *ethnicity* surrounds Hispanics, whose members are a conglomerate of blacks, whites, and Asians. Thus in this study, we use both terms largely to make this distinction. The authors thank Darrick Hamilton for helpful insights on this issue.

19. Pooling would have the advantage of garnering information from a larger sample of schools, but is theoretically difficult to interpret. For instance, if the dissimilarity index indicates the proportion of black students that would have to change schools for each school to achieve the average number of blacks, how would we interpret students moving from a school in, say, Fresno to one in San Diego?

20. In K–6 schools, which typically have self-contained classes, we examined average class sizes across grades K–3 and grades 4–6; in middle schools and high schools, which typically have departmentalized classes, we examined average math and English class sizes. We also examined the proportion of college prep and advanced placement (AP) classes in high schools.

21. Not surprisingly, however, the average ELL student attends a school in which there are a higher percentage of teachers with a credential that authorizes them to teach English learners.

22. Note that San Diego has a lot of internship programs with the goal of attracting recent college graduates to the teaching force. These interns most likely have at most a bachelor's degree. Thus, this situation may be the result of an explicit policy that district officials would argue could improve teacher quality.

23 Test scores are measured using results from California's Standardized Testing and Reporting (STAR) program, which tests students statewide in grades 2 through 11 in key areas each spring. The Stanford Achievement Test Series, Ninth Edition, Form T (Stanford 9), is a multiple-choice test that allows comparisons with a national sample of students. Students in grades 2 through 8 are required to take tests in reading, mathematics, language arts (written expression), and spelling. Students in grades 9 through 11 are required to take tests in reading, writing, mathematics, science, and history/social science.

24. All scores are school-level average scores for each group of students. Test scores for grades 8 and 11 appear in appendix table B.6.

25. Isolating the scores of ELL and non-ELL students reveals similar patterns.

3

School Achievement and Resources

The Differing Experiences of Recent Immigrant and ELL Students

I n this chapter, we continue to explore the relationships between schooling resources and outcomes, on the one hand, and the representation and characteristics of recent immigrant and ELL students on the other. More specifically, we use statistical analyses to compare the proportion of English language learners and recent immigrant students in California public schools with test score outcomes at those schools. We then examine the differences in some of the resources available at those schools.[1] We also concentrate on disentangling the experience of recent immigrant students from that of ELLs and introduce other student characteristics, such as race and poverty. In short, we find that the ELL and recent immigrant experiences are different enough to warrant policymakers' attention to program and policy development that at times treats them differently. This chapter focuses on issues of equity and distribution, not efficiency and efficacy, though we believe our work has implications for the design and implementation of effective education programs.

A Brief Review of Current Research

Relatively little economic research has investigated the experience of immigrant students and their treatment in or impact on schools. Most academic studies of immigrants and education have been ethnographic. There have been, however, several important quantitative studies of immigrants and educational attainment, including Betts and Lofstrom (1998) and Vernez and Abrahamse (1996).[2] Two important findings emerge from this literature. First, immigrant children are at least as likely as native-born children to enroll in school. Second, the educational attainment of immigrants is, in many respects, comparable with that of the native born.[3] Unlike much of the popular press, social scientists tend to view immigrants as unusually motivated and future oriented, willing to make sacrifices for their children. In addition, Betts (1998) and Betts and Lofstrom (1998) find some evidence that immigrants' success comes at the direct or indirect expense of the educational attainment of the native born. Put simply, immigrants can potentially "crowd out" the native born in competition for educational resources or opportunities.

The research on educational resources and immigrants has focused on the costs associated with limited English proficiency. Duncombe and Yinger (1997), Downes and Pogue (1994), and Wyckoff and Naples (2000), for example, find that increasing the share of ELL students in the overall student population increases district costs. And although additional resources may be available for schools and districts serving English language learners, these resources may be insufficient to cover the additional costs, thereby decreasing resources available for other educational programs.[4]

Rivera-Batiz (1996) examines the impact of immigrants on schools per se by using New York City school-level data to examine the determinants of passing rates on standardized reading and math exams.[5] He finds that higher proportions of recent immigrants in a school positively affect outcomes while shares of English language learners have a negative impact. Schwartz and Gershberg (2000, 2001) build upon this research. Using school-level data for New York City schools, they investigate the relationship between the concentration of recent immigrant and ELL students in a school and that school's resources and performance. They find that ELL and recent immigrant student experiences in New York are significantly different from each other: school resources generally decline with the representation of recent immigrants but increase with the representation of English language learners; furthermore, more recent immigrant students indicates better performance, while more ELL students indicates lower performance.[6]

Our analysis builds upon this body of research, particularly that of Schwartz and Gershberg. While our data are not as rich in the level of detail with which we can examine different kinds of recent immigrants, we do have district-level data for the entire state of California and school-level data for the five largest districts in the state. Following Schwartz and Gershberg (2000, 2001), we model the distribution of several different resource and performance measures and frame the interpretation in equity terms. The resource "equity" models describe equality in the distribution of resources across schools, capturing the relationship between resources and the representation of recent immigrants, controlling for other student characteristics. The performance "equity" models describe equality in the distribution of "outputs" across schools, capturing the relationship between output and the representation of recent immigrants, again controlling for other student characteristics. This process is important because we previously found that differences in school performance, for example, were not very pronounced for the average recent immigrant and ELL students.[7]

Analysis of School-Level Student Outcomes and Performance

We model the distribution of student outcomes across schools in relation to a selection of student characteristics. It is very important to stress that we do not assert that the models are causal.[8] Thus, we are examining the kinds of schools recent immigrants attend. It is worth explaining these statistical concepts in laymen's terms as much as possible. For example, in some cases we will report findings that, all else equal, recent immigrants attend a higher-scoring school. This result does not mean, however, that the recent immigrants necessarily cause higher scores, though the possibility exists. The *all else equal* statement is important. It means that in controlling for other student characteristics, we are attempting to isolate the independent association of recent immigrants with school-level test scores. For example, we control for the proportions of both recent immigrants and English language learners at the schools in our sample. Therefore, in some cases we find that, all else equal, recent immigrant students can be found in higher-scoring schools while ELL students attend lower-scoring schools. Since many recent immigrants are also English language learners, this conclusion does not necessarily mean that recent immigrants are, on average, in

higher-scoring schools. It means instead that, once we account for the negative association of language ability (for which ELL status is a proxy), the
independent association of recent immigrants with test scores is positive.[9]
Therefore, one can think of this process as isolating the effect of being a
recent immigrant, controlling for language ability and other characteristics
such as ethnicity and poverty. In other words, if two schools are equal in
every way (including proportion of ELL students) except that one serves a
higher proportion of recent immigrant students, then the school with the
higher share of recent immigrants will have higher test scores. The fact that
we cannot assert causality means that while the previous statement is true,
we cannot say that the scores in the second school are higher *because* of the
recent immigrants or some other unmeasurable factor.

We thus seek to examine and describe the outcomes at schools
attended by different kinds of students. Tables 3.1 and 3.2 present results
from these statistical models for second and fifth grade test scores in math
and reading for all schools in the five case districts—Los Angeles, San
Diego, Long Beach, Fresno, and San Francisco. We examine these two
grades because they represent early and late elementary school grades,
and depending upon the model run, the sample contains between 538
and 707 schools.[10] This section refers to these test score measures as "outcome measures" and as "dependent variables," and we attempt to make
our discussion as accessible as possible to those without a background in
statistics. All data collection issues are addressed in appendix B and, to
some extent, in the relevant sections of chapter 2.

For both math and reading scores, we run three models for each grade
level: columns (1) and (4) use the scores for all students in a school as
the outcome measures, columns (2) and (5) use the scores for English
language learner students only, and columns (3) and (6) use the scores
for non-ELL students only (i.e., the average test score for all students at
a school, excluding the scores of ELLs).[11]

Second Grade Math and Reading Models

The second grade results using all test scores (table 3.1, columns [1] and
[4]) show that, all else equal, poor (free- or reduced-price-lunch eligible)
and ELL students attend schools with lower test scores. This is hardly surprising. In addition, we discern no impact at this grade level with respect
to the proportion of recent immigrant students, a clear difference from
the result for English language learners. That is, as we explained above,

Table 3.1. *School-Level Outcome Equity OLS Regressions with District Fixed Effects, Second Grade, 1999–2000*

| | Dependent variable (mean scaled score on SAT9 test) | | | | | |
| | Math scores | | | Reading scores | | |
Independent variable = student characteristic	(1) All scores	(2) ELL scores	(3) Non-ELL scores	(4) All scores	(5) ELL scores	(6) Non-ELL scores
Intercept	633.011**	600.973**	627.657**	633.815**	602.557**	627.216**
	(10.86)	(15.106)	(11.656)	(9.167)	(11.848)	(10.309)
Eligible for reduced-price lunch (%)	−0.072*	−0.019	−0.114**	−0.063*	0.00603	−0.119**
	(0.040)	(0.057)	(0.042)	(0.034)	(0.044)	(0.037)
English language learner (%)	−0.425**	−0.112	−0.646**	−0.533**	−0.168*	−0.575**
	(0.080)	(0.123)	(0.091)	(0.068)	(0.096)	(0.080)
Recent immigrant (EIEP %)	0.062	0.046	0.461*	−0.081	−0.084	0.242
	(0.199)	(0.231)	(0.245)	(0.168)	(0.180)	(0.217)
Asian (%)	0.189**	0.348**	0.226**	0.125**	0.237**	0.162**
	(0.074)	(0.106)	(0.081)	(0.063)	(0.083)	(0.072)
Hispanic (%)	−0.424**	−0.222**	−0.338**	−0.457**	−0.245**	−0.412**
	(0.066)	(0.104)	(0.072)	(0.056)	(0.081)	(0.063)
Black (%)	−0.485**	−0.186**	−0.507**	−0.498**	−0.289**	−0.481**
	(0.048)	(0.081)	(0.048)	(0.041)	(0.063)	(0.0422)
Filipino (%)	−0.192**	0.070	−0.191**	−0.155**	0.199*	−0.210**
	(0.081)	(0.152)	(0.076)	(0.068)	(0.119)	(0.067)
Other race (%)	−0.819**	−0.062	−1.096**	−0.656**	−0.316	−0.715**
	(0.369)	(0.598)	(0.362)	(0.312)	(0.467)	(0.320)

(continued)

Table 3.1. Continued

Independent variable = student characteristic	Dependent variable (mean scaled score on SAT9 test)					
	Math scores			Reading scores		
	(1) All scores	(2) ELL scores	(3) Non-ELL scores	(4) All scores	(5) ELL scores	(6) Non-ELL scores
ELL* Hispanic	0.00226**	0.000267	0.00386**	0.00192**	−0.000306	0.00388**
	(0.00084)	(0.0014)	(0.000968)	(0.000707)	(0.00110)	(0.000856)
Female (%)	0.250	−0.340	−0.054	−0.063	−0.316	0.147
	(0.221)	(0.289)	(0.238)	(0.186)	(0.227)	(0.211)
San Diego dummy	0.769	−0.728	2.437	−1.022	−5.866**	2.432
	(1.733)	(2.324)	(1.798)	(1.463)	(1.817)	(1.590)
Long Beach dummy	8.036**	5.571**	10.693**	4.133**	4.611**	4.414**
	(1.898)	(2.512)	(2.003)	(1.601)	(1.961)	(1.771)
Fresno dummy	−19.920**	−21.478**	−18.742**	−22.176**	−23.300**	−21.100**
	(1.852)	(2.798)	(1.818)	(1.563)	(2.189)	(1.608)
San Francisco dummy	−8.001**	13.418**	−17.280**	−9.303**	6.953	−17.556**
	(2.877)	(5.437)	(3.304)	(2.428)	(4.362)	(2.929)
Adjusted R-square	0.67	0.35	0.67	0.80	0.50	0.72
Number of observations	707	574	689	706	567	686

Source: Authors' calculations from CDE, CBEDS, and EIEP datasets.

Notes: OLS = ordinary least square; ELL = English language learner. "Recent immigrant" students are foreign-born students with fewer than three years in U.S. public schools. Figures in parentheses are standard errors.

* = significant at 10% level, ** = significant at 5% level.

Columns (1) and (4) are weighted by total enrollment; (2) and (5) by ELL enrollment; (3) and (6) by non-ELL enrollment.

Table 3.2. School-Level Outcome Equity OLS Regressions with District Fixed Effects, Fifth Grade, 1999–2000

| | Dependent variable (mean scaled score on SAT9 test) | | | | | |
| | Math scores | | | Reading scores | | |
Independent variable = student characteristic	(1) All scores	(2) ELL scores	(3) Non-ELL scores	(4) All scores	(5) ELL scores	(6) Non-ELL scores
Intercept	679.608**	639.405**	683.229**	688.794**	636.681**	689.340**
	(8.469)	(10.143)	(9.351)	(7.236)	(8.600)	(8.128)
Eligible for reduced-price lunch (%)	−0.081**	0.023	−0.098**	−0.088**	0.024	−0.108**
	(0.032)	(0.039)	(0.344)	(0.027)	(0.033)	(0.030)
English language learner (%)	−0.518**	−0.019	−0.526**	−0.600**	0.068	−0.482**
	(0.063)	(0.083)	(0.075)	(0.054)	(0.071)	(0.065)
Recent immigrant (EIEP %)	0.349**	0.568**	0.285	0.168	0.174	0.222
	(0.160)	(0.159)	(0.204)	(0.137)	(0.135)	(0.177)
Asian (%)	0.274**	0.128*	0.274**	0.082*	−0.109*	0.079
	(0.058)	(0.071)	(0.067)	(0.050)	(0.060)	(0.058)
Hispanic (%)	−0.306**	−0.089	−0.384**	−0.338**	−0.145**	−0.367**
	(0.052)	(0.072)	(0.059)	(0.044)	(0.061)	(0.051)
Black (%)	−0.480**	−0.289**	−0.524**	−0.480**	−0.319**	−0.511**
	(0.052)	(0.055)	(0.040)	(0.033)	(0.047)	(0.034)
Filipino (%)	−0.165**	0.056	−0.182**	−0.147**	0.178**	−0.196**
	(0.064)	(0.099)	(0.062)	(0.055)	(0.084)	(0.054)
Other race (%)	−0.168	0.717*	−0.397	−0.553**	0.0772	−0.728**
	(0.292)	(0.405)	(0.300)	(0.250)	(0.342)	(0.260)

(continued)

Table 3.2. *Continued*

Independent variable = student characteristic	Math scores			Reading scores		
	(1) All scores	(2) ELL scores	(3) Non-ELL scores	(4) All scores	(5) ELL scores	(6) Non-ELL scores
ELL*Hispanic	0.0023**	-0.00171*	0.00487**	0.00215**	-0.00198**	0.00347**
	(0.000661)	(0.000962)	(0.000797)	(0.000564)	(0.000820)	(0.000693)
Female (%)	0.060	-0.162	0.108	0.051	-0.173	0.121
	(0.172)	(0.193)	(0.191)	(0.147)	(0.164)	(0.166)
San Diego dummy	0.696	4.870**	1.141	0.210	2.748**	2.437*
	(1.385)	(1.630)	(1.478)	(1.184)	(1.382)	(1.285)
Long Beach dummy	1.819	5.949**	2.074	-1.011	4.554*	-0.533
	(1.525)	(1.749)	(1.660)	(1.303)	(1.482)	(1.443)
Fresno dummy	-19.685**	-8.605**	-19.134**	-20.847**	-7.996**	-19.284**
	(1.466)	(1.935)	(1.509)	(1.252)	(1.642)	(1.311)
San Francisco dummy	-9.295**	10.301**	-10.106**	-10.088**	11.28**	-9.141
	(2.268)	(3.240)	(2.709)	(1.937)	(2.766)	(2.354)
Adjusted R-square	0.75	0.44	0.69	0.84	0.42	0.75
Number of observations	695	541	693	695	538	692

Source: Authors' calculations from CDE, CBEDS, and EIEP datasets.

Notes: OLS = ordinary least square; ELL = English language learner. "Recent immigrant" students are foreign-born students with fewer than three years in U.S. public schools. Figures in parentheses are standard errors.

* = significant at 10% level, ** = significant at 5% level.

Columns (1) and (4) are weighted by total enrollment; (2) and (5) by ELL enrollment; (3) and (6) by non-ELL enrollment.

students with poor English ability are in lower-scoring schools while, all else equal, recent immigrants are not. With the possible exception of non-ELL scores, recent immigrants do not appear to be in schools with discernibly higher or lower test scores once we control for other student characteristics, such as language ability. In fact, even the simple correlation between ELL and recent immigrant percentages (0.36, not shown) is not as high as one might expect, implying that the two measures are substantively different.[12]

Asians are in higher-scoring schools while blacks and Hispanics attend lower-scoring schools in all six models. Filipinos attend schools with lower overall and non-ELL test scores but higher ELL scores. Poorer student populations, represented by the proportion of students qualifying for the federal free- and reduced-price lunch program, are also generally found in schools with lower test scores, though not with lower scores among their English language learners.

Tables 3.1 and 3.2 also include an interaction term between ELL and Hispanic (ELL*Hispanic) in an attempt to differentiate Hispanic and non-Hispanic ELL students.[13] In virtually all specifications for both grades, the coefficient is positive and significant. This implies that, having controlled for the other student characteristics (which include ELL and Hispanic independently) schools with higher proportions of Hispanics among their ELL population have higher test scores than schools with lower proportions of Hispanics among their English language learners. One way to frame the results is that the impact of high proportions of Hispanic ELL students is still negative, but it is less negative than high proportions of non-Hispanic ELL students.[14] That is, non-Hispanic English language learners are in lower-scoring schools than Hispanic ELL students.[15]

Fifth Grade Math and Reading Models

The results for the fifth grade scores are different in at least one important way (table 3.2). While English language learners are still generally in lower-scoring schools, recent immigrant students are in *higher*-scoring schools relevant to math tests. These results are similar to those reported for fifth and eighth grade scores by Schwartz and Gershberg (2000) as well as several of the studies previously mentioned. All else equal, fifth grade recent immigrant students appear to be in higher-scoring schools (in math) once language ability is controlled for (through the inclusion of the ELL variable). This is an important point because previously we saw little difference in the average scores of schools attended by the average fifth grade recent immigrant and ELL students, and both sets were lower than those for the schools attended by the average student. In table 2.8, for example, the mean scaled test score (MSS) in math was 631.7 for the school attended by the average recent immigrant and 629.0 for the school attended by the average English language learner, but 635.1 for the average student's school. However, controlling for other characteristics of a school's student body, immigrants can be found in higher-scoring schools (for fifth grade math) than either ELL or average students.

What can we say about the magnitude of this association? At first blush, one might say that despite being statistically significant, the effects appear small. For example, in column (1) of table 3.2, the coefficients on ELL and recent immigrant percentages are –0.518 and 0.349, respectively. This can be interpreted to mean that a 1 percentage point increase in the proportion of English language learners at a particular school is associated with a 0.52 point decrease in that school's average math score. Since the mean MSS fifth grade math score for all schools in our sample was 635, these coefficients do seem small. Note first, however, that these coefficients are among the largest in the model; their association with test scores is as strong as or stronger than any of the other measurable student characteristics. Second, the average elementary school student in our sample attends a school in which about 50 percent of his classmates are ELL students and 4.5 percent are recent immigrant students (see table 2.4), and while the mean test score may be 635, a gap of only 106 points separates the highest- and lowest-scoring schools (not shown). This proportion of English language learners, then, is associated with nearly 25 percent of the difference between the highest and the lowest scores.[16] A 1 percentage point rise in the proportion of recent immigrants yields a 0.349 point gain in the MSS, and all the recent immigrants combined are associated with a 1.5 point higher score.[17] In the case of the proportion of recent immigrants, we would place more emphasis on the positive nature of the effect, its difference from the effect of ELL students, and the change in significance from second to fifth grade than on its overall magnitude.[18]

Why and How Being an English Language Learner Is Not the Same as Being a Recent Immigrant

We are not implying that certain forces bring about change in recent immigrant students during the period between second and fifth grade. To the contrary, nearly all the recent immigrant student population in fifth grade was by definition *not* attending school in the United States in second grade. The differences then could stem from the demographic and other characteristics of students (and their families) who come to the United States and first enroll in grades 3 through 5 as compared with those students who first enroll in U.S. schools in kindergarten through second grade. These differences could also spring from immigrants' capacity and natural ability or from their families' residential patterns. These discrepancies could also stem from the schools' ability to educate these students. Finally, these differences could be the result of the schooling the students received in their home country, which we explore below as well as in chapters 4 and 5—particularly for students educated in Mexico.

With respect to fifth grade reading scores, the coefficients on recent immigrant percentages are all positive but not significant, while the coefficients on ELL percentages are negative for the overall and non-ELL scores (table 3.2).[19] The key message is, however, clear: being a recent immigrant student does not appear to be the same as being an English language learner.

Interestingly, the coefficients on ELL percentages for the models of ELL-only scores are insignificant (table 3.2). Thus, higher concentrations of English language learners are not associated with lower scores among this population. In fact, in models without the district fixed effects (not shown), these coefficients are significant and positive, suggesting that analysts and policymakers should further explore whether schools with higher concentrations of ELLs have higher-performing ELL students perhaps due to economies of scale. Exploring this possibility would necessitate employing more sophisticated modeling (with better data).[20]

Higher concentrations of English language learners are associated with lower scores among non-ELL students (table 3.2).[21] Furthermore, higher concentrations of blacks and Hispanics are negatively associated with all test scores; in other words, these populations are evident in the lowest-scoring schools. Finally, once again, the ELL*Hispanic interaction term is generally positive and significant (and of approximately the same magnitude as for second grade), a result that again calls into question the idea that the "ELL problem" is largely a "Hispanic problem."[22]

Understanding how immigrant students arrive and relate to English language learners is essential in order to interpret our results.[23] Once students arrive they begin the process of assimilation into the U.S. education system. In a nutshell, English-speaking immigrants are never classified as English language learners, while those whose parents speak a foreign language are classified as ELLs until they are able to pass an examination. Students who progress rapidly in school likely develop English proficiency fairly rapidly, while others remain English language learners for a number of years. In certain cases, some students never learn English well, and even their children can be classified as ELL upon entry into the school system. Therefore, ELLs are likely to be disproportionately drawn from those students whose academic progress is slow, though this approach is predicated on a good and accurate language assessment system—something we question in the following chapters.

Given that ELL status may be an indicator of poor academic progress for those who have attended U.S. schools for a number of years, English language learners could have systematically lower test scores even if language difficulties did not impede their progress. Because it is not possible to separate long-term English language learners from recent arrivals in the data, we must be cautious in interpreting the findings on ELL students in our test score models. Moreover, the finding that recent immigrants do better conditional on the proportion of English language learners must also be cautiously interpreted because a higher share of immigrants, given the proportion of ELL students, provides some indicator of immigrants' academic progress (greater success will lead to more declassification as ELL). Thus, our results may simply capture the higher skills and greater motivation of immigrants in a particular school. However, given that our primary aim is to show that being an immigrant student is not the same as being an English language learner, we feel our data limitations and our analysis do not preclude us from saying just that, almost conclusively.

Equity in the Distribution of School-Level Resources

We now turn our attention more briefly to the distribution of resources to schools, and examine the variation in school-level resources for schools attended by recent immigrant, ELL, and other students. Betts, Rueben, and Danenberg (2000) detail the pitfalls of such studies for California, particularly the lack of accurate and consistent measures of spending and/or cost per pupil across schools. Analysts are left with poor measures of resources. We concentrate here on the proportion of teachers who are not fully credentialed, the share of inexperienced teachers in elementary schools, and the average class size.[24] Similar to the outcome modeling above, we specify models intended to explore the equity of resource distribution and we do not assert the models are causal.[25]

Table 3.3 shows the resource equity models for the proportion of teachers at a school who are not fully credentialed, the proportion of teachers at a school with fewer than two years of experience ("rookie" teachers), and the average class size at the school level.[26] Again, the ELL and recent immigrant variables have differing and often opposite impacts. All else equal, English language learners (and black students) attend schools with fewer fully credentialed teachers, while recent immigrants (and Asian students) attend schools with more fully credentialed teachers. The sizes of the associations (i.e., the coefficients) are about equal. The magnitude of the coefficients indicates that there are significant resource differences associated with these student characteristics.[27] No other variables are significant (including poverty), indicating that students with these characteristics are in schools with similar proportions of fully credentialed teachers. The story is essentially the same for rookie teachers; ELL students attend schools with a higher proportion of rookies, while recent immigrant students are found in schools with lower proportions of these teachers (controlling for the recent immigrants being ELLs).[28]

On the subject of average class size, English language learners are actually found in schools with larger classes. While this detail is consistent with the pattern of fewer resources being available to ELL students, it is somewhat surprising given that language classes for English language learners tend to be smaller. However, it is possible that this fact could hold true, and that it, in turn, causes other classes to be larger. Overall, recent immigrants are not in schools with larger class sizes (the coefficient on Recent Immigrant in column [5] is insignificant).

We also specified models with the addition of the Recent Immigrant*Hispanic interaction term (columns 2, 4, and 6). These results indicate that the patterns that hold true for schools with high proportions of recent immigrants also hold true for schools with high proportions of recent immigrant and Hispanic students;[29] thus we find no evidence that recent Hispanic immigrants are systematically located in schools with fewer of these resources than are non-Hispanic immigrants. It is not unreasonable to presume that there are rookies teaching non-Hispanic immigrants, all else equal, since the need for Spanish-speaking teachers has been established longer than for other groups. In models not shown, we also found that schools with high concentrations

Table 3.3. *Elementary School–Level Resource Equity OLS Regressions, 1999–2000*

Independent variable = student characteristic	Not fully credentialed		Zero to two years' experience		Average class size	
	(1)	(2)	(3)	(4)	(5)	(6)
Intercept	9.18902	8.40956	14.33002*	12.90168	19.72698**	22.52704**
	(8.54344)	(8.5463)	(8.69295)	(8.6570)	(9.63629)	(9.69014)
Eligible for reduced-price lunch (%)	0.0181	0.01472	0.0059	0.00004475	-0.00146	0.00681
	(0.03092)	(0.0310)	(0.03171)	(0.0316)	(0.03428)	(0.03438)
English language learner (%)	0.30959**	0.31264**	0.23907**	0.24464**	0.18149**	0.17636**
	(0.04155)	(0.0415)	(0.04227)	(0.0421)	(0.0464)	(0.04632)
Recent immigrant (%)	-0.26616**	0.03427	-0.23161*	0.32315	-0.17369	-0.94522**
	(0.13096)	(0.2247)	(0.1332)	(0.2275)	(0.17717)	(0.39138)
Asian (%)	-0.24**	-0.25491**	-0.10419*	-0.13194**	-0.10502	-0.07134
	(0.05639)	(0.0571)	(0.05739)	(0.0578)	(0.06644)	(0.06797)
Hispanic (%)	-0.04712	-0.02832	-0.03619	-0.00179	-0.08814*	-0.13067**
	(0.04711)	(0.0484)	(0.04801)	(0.0491)	(0.05175)	(0.05506)
Black (%)	0.22856**	0.22885**	0.16099**	0.16088**	-0.07504*	-0.07984*
	(0.03825)	(0.0382)	(0.03943)	(0.0392)	(0.04203)	(0.04196)
Filipino (%)	-0.00792	-0.01694	-0.2494**	-0.2662**	0.09928	0.10901
	(0.06404)	(0.0642)	(0.06514)	(0.0650)	(0.07328)	(0.07319)

(continued)

Other race (%)	0.23182	0.23136	0.73155**	0.73116**	-0.00407	0.01977
	(0.29323)	(0.2929)	(0.29826)	(0.2966)	(0.34791)	(0.34702)
Recent Immigrant *Hispanic interaction term	—	-0.00506	—	-0.00935**	—	0.01159**
		(0.0031)		(0.0031)		(0.00525)
Female (%)	0.05138	0.05356	-0.07249	-0.06866	0.07877	0.05953
	(0.17393)	(0.1737)	(0.17697)	(0.1760)	(0.19635)	(0.19595)
San Diego dummy	-17.0084**	-16.98142**	8.69354**	8.7421**	-4.42633**	-4.66624**
	(1.33337)	(1.3319)	(1.35613)	(1.3486)	(1.48328)	(1.48273)
Long Beach dummy	1.12114	1.13848	-3.0092**	-2.977**	-1.41882	-1.67925
	(1.47932)	(1.4776)	(1.50448)	(1.4960)	(1.64466)	(1.64388)
Fresno dummy	-14.92102**	-14.90814**	-10.10145**	-10.0748**	-0.44519	-0.63498
	(1.46298)	(1.4612)	(1.48812)	(1.4798)	(1.61112)	(1.6085)
San Francisco dummy	5.24334**	5.49684**	6.10511**	6.58174**	—a	—a
	(2.25492)	(2.2575)	(2.29471)	(2.2873)		
Adjusted R-square	0.5888	0.5898	0.3368	0.3443	0.0966	0.1021
Number of observations	718	718	716	716	646	646

Notes: OLS = ordinary least square. "Recent immigrant" students are foreign-born students with fewer than three years in U.S. public schools. Figures in parentheses are standard errors.

a. School-level models for average class size exclude all observations from San Francisco due to bad class-size data in that district.

* = significant at 10% level, ** = significant at 5% level.

of ELL students (over 80 percent) have higher proportions of teachers lacking full credentials and lower proportions of teachers with more than 10 years' experience, while schools with fewer than 20 percent English language learners had fewer rookies.[30] Regarding average class size, the interaction term indicates that recent Hispanic immigrants may be in larger classes, which is consistent with the results for average class size for ELL students. However, all else equal, Hispanics and blacks attend schools with smaller, not larger, classes.

These results pool schools from all five districts; thus, they provide a kind of aggregate or average affect. However, in results not shown we found significant differences among districts in the effects of various characteristics. For instance, we discussed above that, all else equal, recent immigrants are in schools with more fully credentialed teachers and fewer rookies. In Long Beach, however, the opposite is true. It is therefore necessary to consider such variations across districts.[31]

Unexplored Opportunities

Overall, at the school level, it appears that English language learners, not recent immigrants, are attending schools with fewer resources or worse achievement.[32] The previous chapter explored the characteristics of recent immigrant and ELL students, their schools, and their distribution across schools and districts. We now see that schools with significant ELL and recent immigrant student populations are significantly different in their characteristics and performance, yet the policy arena makes virtually no attempt to differentiate between them. In fact, we echo Ruiz-de-Velasco and Fix (2000) in the belief that California has much more of a "long-term ELL problem" than it does a "recent immigrant problem."[33] The same may well be true for other states. The policy responses to the two groups could be quite different and have quite different implications for school policy everywhere. In addition, non-Hispanic ELL students may, all else equal, be in the lowest-scoring schools, challenging the notion that the "immigrant problem" is only Hispanic and Mexican. However, schools with higher proportions of recent immigrant and Hispanic students have lower scores among their English language learners, which may suggest the need to differentiate schooling approaches taken to educate different kinds of newcomer students.

One potential response to the results presented in this chapter is that immigrants are not in such bad schools; that is, they are doing fine, so why worry about them? We do not believe such a response is warranted, especially given the near complete lack of consideration for recent immigrant students per se in policymaking circles. We could also ask why school systems have gifted and talented programs, for example. The point is that different kinds of students require different kinds of programs and policy responses, and we believe that our results imply the need to consider programs and policies aimed at supporting recent immigrants. Such an approach emphasizes that recent immigrant students present not only a challenge to but also an opportunity for schools.

On the resource side, schools with recent immigrant students do not appear to get less per se, at least according to the measures we have available. It does appear, however, that schools with ELL students do get less. However, these results do not appear from our interview knowledge to be the result of any explicit policies to channel and allocate resources in such a manner. In addition, we cannot say that the resources available at schools with high recent immigrant student populations are used well, especially with respect to educating those recent immigrants or helping them adjust to life in California. While we find that recent immigrant students are not systematically located in worse schools or schools with fewer resources, we should emphasize that this is true only once we control for other characteristics of the student body. For instance, we control for the proportion of ELL students and Hispanic students (both of whom are in worse schools with fewer resources in many instances). Thus, students in schools with high proportions of recent immigrants who are also English language learners and Hispanic are likely to be in worse schools because of these other characteristics.[34]

Finally, even if we believe the conditions and resources are in place for effectively educating recent immigrant students (an assumption we do not make), the resources currently available are not necessarily being put to good use. Having good ingredients does not make a good chef; rather, having a good recipe and the necessary support to implement it does. Thus, we must ask if California has the right recipe for educating recent immigrants. Our statistical work cannot provide an answer for this question. Therefore we turn to the explanatory, if suggestive, power of our qualitative research and interviews with educators. We explore the nature of these issues more in the qualitative analyses in the remainder of this book.

Our results in this chapter are similar to previous quantitative studies, yet more quantitative studies are needed—studies that could begin to unravel the causal connections between student characteristics, such as national origin and English proficiency, and student and school performance as well as the associated costs and resources devoted to teaching these students. Nevertheless, it is clear that ELL and recent immigrant students are not the same, though even in this one policy area that *has* received attention they are virtually treated as such. There is little public debate over whether, in fact, "bilingual" education and structured English immersion (SEI) have different impacts on or value for recent immigrant and ELL students who have been in the United States for more than three years (or who were born in the United States). While recognizing the need to thicken both quantitative and qualitative analyses in this area in the future, we believe policymakers could expand their perception of recent immigrant students and move beyond debates purely about language (and the pedagogy of language instruction). The changes wrought by President Bush's No Child Left Behind legislation on the Emergency Immigrant Education Program (EIEP)—the only program that provides funds for immigrants not linked to language instruction—do not bode well in this regard. We explore these issues in the following chapters.

NOTES

1. As with most statistical analyses relying on state-level data, we are restricted by the unavailability of accurate measures of spending and cost per pupil across schools. We must make use of the other resource measures available, which are often not resources over which policymakers have direct control.

2. See McDonnell and Hill (1993), Vernez and Abrahamse (1996), or Rivera-Batiz (1995) for a deeper discussion of this literature.

3. This is true for both groups in aggregate, usually controlling for other characteristics. Obviously, not all immigrant and native groups and subgroups are the same.

4. It is also possible that the additional resources may be diverted to benefit non-ELL students or programs. Parrish (1994) suggests most of these resources are not, in fact, spent on supplementary direct instruction.

5. Rivera-Batiz (1995) uses a school-level database to examine the determinants of passing rates on standardized reading and math exams. Controlling for language ability, he finds that the proportion of recent immigrants in a school has a positive impact upon outcomes. That is, the proportion of English language learners and the proportion of recent immigrants have opposite impacts on outcomes. His regression models look at elementary and middle schools for one test for one year and use only the proportion passing exams as an outcome, rather than the actual scores on the exams. In addition, he has a (perhaps too) small number of independent variables for the production function approach he attempts to use and the endogeneity problems likely inherent in that production.

6. Schwartz and Gershberg (2000, 2001) also found that, despite the popular perception of immigrant students as Hispanic or Asian and ELL, a significant portion is black, white, or non-ELL. They did not find strong segregation among recent immigrants or English language learners, but they did find that not all groups of recent immigrants were treated equally. In New York City, for instance, recent black immigrants—who are less likely to be English language learners—seem to receive fewer resources and perform relatively poorly.

7. See Berne and Stiefel (1984) for more on the measurement of interdistrict equity. See Iatarola and Stiefel (2000) for a discussion and application of intradistrict equity and Schwartz (1999) for a discussion and application of the multivariate approach to investigating intradistrict equity.

8. The only independent variables in these models are student characteristics, thus the models should not be construed to be production functions. There are, for instance, no input variables such as spending per pupil, school size, teacher characteristics, or school curriculum. See Hanushek (1986, 1996). In addition, we do not specify "value-added" models as one would for a production function; that is, we do not model *changes* in test scores or use the previous year's test scores as an independent variable. Schwartz and Gershberg (2000, 2001) *do* report a value-added specification. Their inclusion of prior test scores implies that the estimated parameters capture the differences in performance associated with the representation of different groups in the student body, controlling for previous performance, and thus their results might be interpreted as capturing differences in gains in performance between the two years. There are many ways to specify such a model. We omit the lagged test scores because we believe the interpretation of the coefficients is more straightforward. We also believe this specification best captures the distribution of the school outcomes upon which most policymakers focus. We thank Robert Kaestner for spirited and informative comments regarding the specification of the model we chose.

9. We thank Sanders Korenman for insightful comments about the wisdom of looking at the effect of being a recent immigrant conditional upon ELL status. In the end, we agree that care must be taken in the way we interpret such results, but we believe it to be a valuable approach.

10. Some observations are missing due to missing variables in either the dependent or independent variables. In the "all student" models, the omitted observations are generally for schools with fewer than 10 students total in the grade, charter schools, and special education enrollment. Omitted observations due to missing independent variables are the result of missing free-lunch-eligible percentages and missing EIEP data. (The latter missing data are in San Diego, where we were unable to confirm whether "missing" was equivalent to zero EIEP students, so "missing" was left as "missing." In the other districts, either the data we received from the districts had zeros, or we were able to confirm with district officials that "missing" meant zero EIEP students.) In the ELL and non-ELL test score models, the observations omitted due to missing dependent variables are generally schools with fewer than 10 English language learners at the school or in the grade.

11. In each case, the variables are weighted by the appropriate student enrollment. We run a district fixed-effects model to discern the impacts of the student characteristics independent of the district in which the students are found. Most of the variable names are self-explanatory. In most cases, the results from non-fixed-effects specifications were not

substantively different, though in general the sizes of the important coefficients of interest were smaller. The excluded race category is "white," and the excluded district dummy is the "Los Angeles dummy." Descriptive statistics for all models presented in this chapter are available on the project web site at http://www.urban.org/pubs/bilingual.

12. Note that the correlation coefficient is significant at the 99 percent confidence interval. In addition, the correlation is not particularly worrisome from a statistical point of view and thus we believe supports looking at the effect of being a recent immigrant conditional upon language ability. This is, in fact, the case for all regressions we present here with respect to this correlation, unless otherwise mentioned. However, we did perform runs of the models excluding ELL and Hispanic percentages to see if the results for recent immigrant percentages changed in worrisome ways, and they did not. We cannot, of course, rule out problems of multicollinearity in the model specification, but these concerns are similar to those at the core of a long history of educational production functions attempting, for instance, to disentangle the impact of race from that of poverty. See, for instance, Hanushek (1986).

13. The coefficient on the interaction term is in fact a weighted average of the impact on Hispanics and non-Hispanics with the proportion of population in each group as the weight. Naturally, if better data were available, such as the proportion of ELL students who are Hispanic, we would not need to use this interaction term. Care must always be used in interpreting such interaction terms, and all findings that stem from the interpretation must be considered suggestive.

14. For example, the coefficients on ELL and ELL*Hispanic in table 3.1 column (1) are −0.425 and 0.00226, respectively. This means the coefficient on ELL for Hispanics would be −0.425 + (0.00226 × 100) = −0.199. Of course, this is holding constant the separate impacts of Hispanic and ELL, which are both negative. Still, it may be that non-Hispanic ELL students (while there are fewer of them) are in worse schools and *perhaps* more difficult to teach (though, of course, our specification cannot tell us this).

15. However, the correlations between ELL and Hispanic are very high (around 0.85 in most of our samples); thus our results must be interpreted with caution. Still, in specifications without the interaction term, the results do not change substantively, except that the size of the coefficients on ELL and Hispanic are smaller. In addition, even specifications without ELL did not change substantively. However, the correlations between the interaction term and both ELL and Hispanic percentages are very high indeed, about 0.94. This is indeed worrisome, and we explore different, less problematic interaction terms in appendix B.

16. The standard deviation of the MSS math scores is about 16, so a little more than a 30 percent increase in the percentage of English language learners is associated with a one standard deviation decrease in math scores.

17. We also performed all these analyses logging the dependent variable. Those results are available on the project web site (http://www.urban.org/pubs/bilingual) because we did not find them to be any more intuitive than the non-logged version.

18. In addition, we ran models adding the variables ELL^2 and $(Recent\ Immigrant)^2$. The intention here is to capture any nonlinearities in the relationships between these variables and test scores. For instance, while the relationship between the recent immigrant percentage and fifth grade math scores is positive and significant overall, these models show that the relationship may actually be negative up to the mean of about

4.5 percent and positive thereafter. The ELL percentage, on the other hand, appears linearly negative, though we do present results suggesting there may be some economies of scale with larger ELL populations. The results for these models are available at http://www.urban.org/pubs/bilingual.

19. We note that the coefficient on the recent immigrant percentage in the same specification without fixed effects (not shown) was positive and significant.

20. A production function approach, for instance, could examine economies of scale in ELL education.

21. Remember, however, that we are not asserting this is causal (e.g., some kind of crowding out). Rather, it seems likely that those non-ELL students in schools with high ELL concentrations are not the highest-scoring non-ELL students.

22. In tables B.7 and B.8 (appendix B), we specify and discuss similar models except that they employ an interaction term for the proportion of recent immigrant students with the proportion of Hispanic students (EIEP*Hispanic). We find support for these conclusions. Indeed, Hispanic recent immigrants may overall fare well compared with non-Hispanic recent immigrants, all else equal, but our relatively crude measures cannot prove this.

23. We thank Steve Rivkin for his help (and language) in thinking through this framework.

24. Jepsen and Rivkin (2002) explore the use of these measures as proxies for teacher quality.

25. These models are not to be construed with cost functions. Again, there are no independent variables other than the characteristics of the student body. The resource equations cannot be interpreted as cost functions or factor demand equations—(there are, after all, no prices among the independent variables) and no argument is made that these resource allocations have emerged from cost-minimization efforts by schools or school districts. Once again, we run a district fixed-effect model on school-level data from the five case districts.

26. Note that in the California Department of Education data, average class size is a somewhat superior measure to pupil-teacher ratio, since the latter simply divides the number of full-time-equivalent teachers at a school site (whether or not they are teaching in the classroom) by the number of students at the school. Average class size, on the other hand, estimates the actual mean number of students in each classroom. There are, however, some data problems with average class size. Specifically, the school-level data for San Francisco are questionable (since the mean is 59). Therefore, in our models of average class size we have omitted all observations from San Francisco. We modeled teacher-pupil ratio using the full set of schools including San Francisco and did not get results that contradict the findings we present.

27. As with the models of outcomes, the sizes of the coefficients on the variables of concern are as big or bigger than any of the other variables. In these models, however, they may be even larger in an absolute sense. For instance, all else equal, a 1 percentage point increase in the ELL and recent immigrant populations leads to a 0.31 percentage point increase and a 0.27 percentage point decrease, respectively, in the proportion of noncredentialed teachers at a school.

28. The results (not shown) for a school's proportion of highly experienced teachers and teachers with a maximum of a bachelor's degree are similar. At the high end of

teacher education, English language learners are in schools with relatively fewer teachers with a master's or doctoral degree, and recent immigrants are in schools with neither higher nor lower proportions of such highly educated teachers.

29. The coefficient on the interaction term is generally the opposite sign from that on the ELL percentage and usually significant. The coefficient on the recent immigrant percentage in these models is generally not statistically significant.

30. In these specifications, the recent immigrant percentage is not statistically significant.

31. All these results are available upon request from the authors. We thank Steve Rivkin for pushing us in this direction.

32. Care must be taken in overstating this conclusion. If many recent immigrants are also ELLs, then it is more accurate to say that immigrants fare no worse than (other) ELL students in terms of resources at their schools. Given that the correlation between recent immigrant and ELL is only 0.36, however, we chose to make the statement as it appears in the text. Thanks to Julian Betts for pointing this out, and for his help in framing the language. Thanks, too, to Sanders Korenman for relevant insights.

33. The words in quotation are ours, and not taken from the Ruiz-de-Velasco and Fix (2000) report. We use the quotation marks to indicate that these are popular phrases.

34. In fact, in models (not shown) that did not include the ELL variable, the coefficient on Recent Immigrant was either insignificant or negative. We explored many permutations of all models in this chapter, with and without the ELL variable and the interaction terms. These results are available from the authors upon request, but did not require substantive changes in the interpretations of the models we chose to represent.

4

Recent Immigrant Challenges and Public School Responses

T he findings from our quantitative analyses differentiate the recent immigrant student from the English language learner by establishing that the two are indeed different enough to produce different and even opposite results in statistical models. However, the quantitative analyses are limited severely by the nature of the data available, preventing us from addressing many of the most interesting questions. For example, how is the recent immigrant experience different from the experiences of other ELL and native students? What particular challenges do recent immigrants face? What do school- and district-level staff members perceive the needs of these students to be, and how, in fact, do schools and teachers end up trying to address these needs? How do state and district programs and policies help school and district staff in this endeavor?

The Qualitative Research Study on Recent Immigrant Students

To adequately explore such questions, therefore, we conducted and analyzed a series of purposive interviews with district officials in the five case districts as well as with principals at 26 elementary and middle schools in these districts. We visited 11 of these schools and interviewed teachers and other relevant school-level staff. We also interviewed representatives from various community-based organizations (CBOs) that serve immigrant populations. In all, we performed more than 120 interviews, each of which lasted approximately one hour.[1] The interview questions were largely open-ended, and we employed a set of guidelines for "interviews as guided conversations."[2] Chapters 4, 5, and 6 report the findings, and while each chapter employs a somewhat different methodological and analytical approach, each is also built upon a core of principles and practices presented fully in appendix C.

Given the small sample of individuals interviewed and the actual selection process, we make no claims that their answers are representative of any given set of individuals working in the school system. In other words, the results offered here are not generalizable to all cases, districts, and schools. However, the depth of the interviews provides a richness of detail that is much more difficult to capture in quantitative studies. In addition, while not a large sample with respect to the number of individuals working in the school system, the number of interviews is relatively large for qualitative studies of this nature. We present, categorize, and organize the information we received and attempt to discern typical responses or a range of typical responses, as appropriate. This method raises more questions than it answers, which in many ways is the goal of this kind of study.

This chapter presents the challenges faced by recent immigrants and the ways school systems have or have not responded to their needs. We discuss the specific newcomer programs and practices in various districts and schools, as well as a range of programs and practices—both formal (*de jure*) and informal (*de facto* or ad hoc)—that teachers, principals, and other school-level staff referred to when asked about strategies for recent immigrant students. We then selectively discuss those challenges less directly related to language curriculum and instruction for English language learners, which is the focus of chapter 5. The next chapter will, in fact, specifically explore what our interview respondents said about "bilingual" education and English immersion for recent immigrant students.[3] Both chapters 4 and 5 discuss in detail how immigrant parents are involved in the schools their children attend and in the education their children receive.[4] Looking ahead, chapter 6 analyzes the section of our interviews that focused on assessment and accountability measures and practices that relate to recent immigrant and ELL students. Throughout, we attempt to let the voices of the respondents emerge, while interpreting those voices only modestly, remaining aware that others might interpret them differently.

Challenges Recent Immigrants Face

Recent immigrants face numerous challenges as they enroll in American schools. Appendix C presents the full list of and necessary definitions for the challenges that emerged in our interviews. Many of these challenges were mentioned in response to two specific questions:

1. What kinds of challenges—in addition to the language barrier—do you feel immigrant students face when they come to this country?
2. Are these challenges the same ones faced by nonimmigrant students who are disadvantaged? Do you see any differences in the way that immigrant and nonimmigrant disadvantaged students handle these challenges?

Following are those challenges mentioned by at least 20 percent of our respondents:[5]

- Communication/language (89 percent)
- Assimilation/culture (67 percent)
- Poverty (54 percent)
- Navigating the school system (understanding school and school system policies) (46 percent)
- Low prior schooling of students (46 percent)
- Low educational level (years of schooling) of parents (31 percent)
- General health issues (29 percent)
- Housing (28 percent)
- Parental participation/involvement with children in their school work (28 percent)
- Parental participation/involvement at school (26 percent)
- Children not living with their parents (25 percent)
- Child care to assist parents (25 percent)
- Gangs (25 percent)
- Legal issues, immigration/INS issues/related fear (24 percent)
- Stigmatization by the school system, school staff, or others (21 percent)
- Transportation to and from school and/or school events (21 percent)

In this chapter, we concentrate on the major challenges that can be distinguished in our respondents' discussions as clear issues related to recent immigrants. We also concentrate on issues related to or that directly affect the work respondents do at the school level and the services these respondents seek to provide. In other words, we concentrate on areas that can and do impact students more or less directly, primarily parental participation and involvement; navigating the school system; legal issues and fear; communication/language (including translation); and general health and social service issues.[6]

Two-thirds of our respondents were concerned about how recent immigrant students are able to acculturate to American school life, noting that these new students really want to fit in with their schoolmates. Assimilation and acculturation are such vast issues that we do not attempt a single, integrative discussion here. Rather, we address different aspects of integration across the entire study. Broadly speaking, school personnel find themselves as central players in the process they associate with assimilation for both recent immigrant students and their families.

Programs and Practices Affecting Recent Immigrants

How do elementary and middle schools help (or hinder) immigrant students in meeting these myriad and significant challenges? Policies and practices regarding recent immigrant students vary among the five school districts we visited, with the Los Angeles and San Francisco school districts generally demonstrating the most extensive implementation of formal newcomer practices. At the time of our interviews, these two districts each had more than one educational facility for newcomers, as well as an assessment center to determine students' academic needs.[7] Fresno currently has a facility for conducting initial student assessments of recent immigrants. In San Diego, individual schools are responsible for initial assessments of immigrant students, and any newcomer-oriented courses are offered at the secondary level, depending on the school. Long Beach has no newcomer program per se.

Indeed, our interviews show a possible trend toward decentralization of newcomer-oriented coursework and other facilities down to the school level and even to individual teachers and classes. These latter relatively ad hoc practices are examples of de facto newcomer policies, which differ from the more formal de jure policies and practices most often set at the district level. A discussion of these formal programs and informal practices in each of our five case districts follows. Given the broad variation in the socioeconomic and educational characteristics of these districts, we believe this discussion holds relevance for other districts across the country with significant populations of recent immigrant students.

De Jure Newcomer Practices and Programs in Districts

SAN FRANCISCO

The first school district in the United States to establish a high school for newcomers, San Francisco also offers three education centers for elementary-age children—the Chinese, Mission, and Filipino education centers—where new immigrant children can spend their first year in U.S. schools.[8] In addition, a district education placement center identifies the students' needs. Several respondents described the teachers and citizens in general as more supportive of immigrants than those in other parts of the state. Despite such support, San Francisco seems to reflect a larger trend to move away from separating recent immigrant students from other students, and this inclination may be affecting usage of the district's three language centers. At least three respondents reported an increasing movement to send new immigrant students directly to non-newcomer schools. One principal noted that the district is in the process of closing down these three centers, adding that it is very difficult for schools to take on the services that these centers offer. Several respondents indicated there is no system to support new immigrant students who go immediately to regular schools, yet more and more, such students are going directly to the classroom. One elementary principal indicated that immigrant students come directly to his school because the newcomer centers are full. Another elementary principal, who reported that the district wanted to save money on salaries by closing the centers, called for a return to the policy of sending newcomers to these centers first.

LOS ANGELES

The two schools for newcomers in Los Angeles got their start because other school districts had such schools. One district administrator recalls having traveled to San Francisco and Long Beach to observe what these districts were doing for newcomers. One of these schools is housed on the campus of Belmont High School—a large, overcrowded school near downtown Los Angeles—in a part of the city that is densely populated and highly influenced by immigrants. The other, Bellagio Road Newcomer School (grades 4 through 8), is situated within a school in an affluent section of West Los Angeles. Many of its students are bused across town to this site. However, one respondent indicated that the Bellagio Road Newcomer School might close in order for its campus to better serve children living in that part of the city. In reality, though, each of these newcomer schools serves only about 400 students, and combined, the two schools serve just a fraction of the district's recent immigrant students. Several respondents indicated that the schools should be expanded or increased in number, or that newcomer classes should be offered in individual schools. However, more than one respondent said students attending Bellagio Road Newcomer School are too isolated. Thus, there is clearly a tension over the benefits of official newcomer schools.

Neither of these newcomer programs concentrates on elementary students, which make up the majority of recent immigrant students and remain the focus of our study. However, another district program—the immigrant assessment center—is located at an elementary school in an area near downtown. When we began our research, it was serving thousands of newly arrived, immigrant elementary school students in a given part of Los Angeles, offering physical exams, vaccinations, counseling, academic assessment, and school assignments.

Among all the districts we visited, the Los Angeles district is making the most extensive use of federal Emergency Immigrant Education Program (EIEP) funds for programs, such as the newcomer programs, specifically designed to impact and support recent immigrants. It is also the only district where respondents outside the district office refer to the EIEP by name, in part because of the sheer numbers of recent immigrant students in the district. As of spring 2001, the district had 37,000 students who were eligible to take part in the program.[9] In terms of age, most were children in kindergarten through third grade. Material presented in these classes—much of which is created by the EIEP office—is meant not only to help new immigrant children learn English, but also to help them learn about the culture of their new country—with emphasis on the Los Angeles area in particular. Field trips to local points of interest are also part of the program. While in the past EIEP-supported programs put more emphasis on oral English than on reading and writing, the Los Angeles program has become more demanding and academically oriented. Even so, it is still shaking off the reputation of being "the fun program." As part of the program, students also have access to specialized counseling services and a school nurse. Depending on the school, an EIEP curriculum may be offered on Saturdays during the school year, as a summer program, or during intersession breaks if a school is on a year-round calendar. Teachers of EIEP classes, who often teach at the public school their students attend, attend a training workshop before joining the program. Although school participation in EIEP is not mandatory, most eligible schools are participants.

We note that the recent federal No Child Left Behind legislation, and California's resulting proposal to adapt its funding rules for the EIEP, would potentially mean a large reduction of funds to districts like Los Angeles—districts where the recent immigrant student count is likely to always be large but not necessarily growing. The same could be said of nearly any immigrant-rich district across the country.

Fresno

The Fresno school district features a language assessment center for new students where students undergo initial evaluations prior to being assigned to schools (generally according to where they live). The center is partially funded by EIEP monies. The extent of resources available for new immigrant students depends on the resources and philosophy of the individual schools. The Fresno district also uses its EIEP funds centrally to pay its district-level translators. In addition, the district pays teacher salaries for programs such as the nationally recognized Khmer Emerging Education Program (KEEP), an after-school cultural program started by the community in which more than 300 Cambodian students study their family's language and culture. In addition, the district, which has one of the highest populations of migrant workers in the country, sends a bus—equipped with a nurse and school personnel—to the local fields to help migrant workers whose children are students.

San Diego

Compared with other school districts, San Diego has relatively little in place to address the needs of its recent immigrant students per se; that is, newcomer policy is largely inseparable from the strategy governing ELL education and other school and district policies. The district has no central assessment center to evaluate new students upon their arrival; this service is provided at individual schools. However, district officials are considering locating centers in certain parts of the district. Newcomer courses are offered at the middle school and high school levels, but availability varies. Generally, other policies or practices pertaining to immigrant students also vary, depending on the school. In fact, there are fewer newcomer programs now than in the past, according to a district administrator:

> A few years back, we had strong newcomer programs at certain sites. . . . Some sites have maintained newcomer-kind of situations, and others have folded more into their overall program. . . . Some schools felt that the newcomer programs kind of kept the kids apart too much.

Another factor in the decline of newcomer programs has been the disparity in immigrant languages. In addition, the district is in the process of redefining what it means to be a newcomer, as the same administrator explains:

> I don't know if anyone really understands yet, but we are starting to identify newcomers as students who are in older grades—grades four and up, we're saying—who are new to school. . . . They've had no schooling, no prior education . . . or big gaps and breaks in their schooling. They need an orientation to the language and the culture, and [to] being a student. So we're defining that kind of a student as a newcomer as opposed to a late-entry student. A student who might have come from Mexico City or from any other place—that they're educated—already knows about being a student, they just need English.

In this case, San Diego is redefining "newcomers" as older immigrant students who have had limited or no schooling in their home countries as opposed to simply being new to U.S. schools. Meanwhile, the school district makes use of EIEP funds in a variety of ways—funding school-level health care and academic programs, for example. The district also uses some of the EIEP funds centrally, providing some resources and materials to schools that serve new immigrants, supporting the biliteracy program, and funding professional development.

Long Beach

Although Long Beach Unified School District has no newcomer programs for elementary and middle school students, it does offer a number of other programs and services geared toward immigrant students. The International Student Registration Office assesses incoming students, supports vaccination, and helps families prepare the paperwork required for enrollment. According to several respondents, families feel comfortable enough there that they often return for advice with subsequent problems. There is also a separate office to coordinate the district's EIEP program, translation services, and field projects.

According to one district administrator, the district officially encourages teachers to determine students' level of knowledge and to be aware of methods that will help students be able to follow instructions. One elementary school principal reported that the district makes the school aware of new immigrant students and the kinds of services available to them from the district, and encourages the principal to advise parents of those services.

De Facto and Ad Hoc Newcomer Practices in Schools and Classrooms

We discerned two kinds of de facto policies for recent immigrants operating in schools and classes across the districts. First, respondents clearly associate language curricula with programs designed to serve recent immigrants (e.g., "bilingual" education, English immersion, etc.). We define these as *de facto* newcomer policies because, as we have argued throughout this study, we do not believe they have been designed specifically to assist recent immigrants holistically, but rather as a means of serving language minority and ELL students. (These policies will be discussed primarily in chapter 5.) Second, beyond the issues of language curricula, school staff and teachers are making decisions and practices daily that are conceived with recent immigrants in mind. We often call these *ad hoc* newcomer policies, not because we want to give them any negative connotation, but rather because (1) almost by definition they are individual and idiosyncratic in nature at the school and often the classroom level, (2) they are not usually governed directly by any district or state policies or plans, and (3) they arise in a highly decentralized and often organic manner.

AD HOC NEWCOMER POLICIES AND PRACTICES IN SCHOOLS AND CLASSROOMS

Several interviews in San Diego exemplified nicely both the nature of some of the most common ad hoc newcomer practices as well as the thick tension surrounding the issue of special attention focused on recent immigrant students. Although respondents from elementary schools confirmed the lack of specific newcomer programs, they did report that more informal measures are helping recent immigrants. For example, one elementary principal commented that new immigrants are sent to selected classes at each grade level, and the school regularly sends primary language support personnel to those classes:

As far as acclimating them [immigrant students] to the country and all of that—
and depending upon the level of the child when they come—it is the teacher who
needs to either make changes in the curriculum or [teach certain] social skills or
[show them] where the bathroom is. It all falls on the teacher.

But this same principal added,

I do not agree with newcomer classes or newcomer schools. I don't agree. I think
they [immigrant students] need to be integrated. However, just as we send the primary language support to those classes, I think schools who have immigrants
should have certain support services sent to us to assist us with those kids and
their families. But, yeah, it's really the teacher [who] does it all.

Similarly, a teacher whose school previously offered a newcomer program described the placing of newcomers in sheltered or structured
English immersion (SEI) classes, which serve as de facto newcomer
classes even though some students in those classes are not newcomers.
While there was disagreement among respondents about the benefits of
separate (de jure) newcomer programs, there was near-uniform recognition that teachers are acting to help newcomers and that they need
support in doing so.

The principal of a San Diego elementary school without newcomer
programs reported:

One of the things that we have in place is daily small group instruction. You need
to do certain ELD [English language development] with newcomers that you
don't necessarily do with the rest of your class. You need to do that if you have
newcomers in your class. If you have kids who need that, that's your responsibility. Where you find that time is up to you. You have to do it.

This school has four instructional assistants who are on site 3.5 hours
per day to give primary language support to the English language learners in the school's 46 classrooms. The principal pays for them out of the
school's general budget. In addition, a credentialed upper-grade literacy
support teacher offers services to each fourth and fifth grade teacher.

Furthermore, the principal continued, the school commonly practices "partnering" a new immigrant student with a classmate who is
expected to help the recent arrival understand the class. We did indeed
find this practice common among our respondents, several of whom
noted that other students were, in a sense, de facto teaching aides. For
example, when asked how she helped newcomers, a middle school
teacher in San Diego responded:

Well, usually I will put them next to a student who is kind and almost teacher-like.
I realize that they're my translator and that's what I expect that student to do . . . to

make that new student feel comfortable. . . . They're going to be talking more and I allow for that and that's okay. . . . I want them to keep conversing because it's constant translation. Sometimes a [newcomer] student will write a report in Spanish and then I'll have the translator work and we'll convert it to English and the student will rewrite it in English. Not only do I give credit to the student who is new for doing that extra . . . but the student who is doing translation is also doing extra work for me and so they get extra credit for that, too. And they're a language broker, you know, and that's something that I don't feel we give students—especially in California—enough credit for. . . . I'm not going to put the new student next to a student who could [not] care less. I'm going to put them next to a role model.

While it is possible to see how this practice could provide a beneficial educational experience for the more experienced student, it is also possible to see how there could be some unintended negative side effects. Consider this poignant vignette: An elementary school teacher reported that she places newcomers next to classmates who can translate needed information. She indicated that one student used the translating as a reason for not complying with an assignment, however. This type of resistance speaks to the burden that perhaps is felt by the child translators who perform these services. In addition, one could argue that these child translators are missing out on their own education by helping newcomer students. More research is needed about the effects of such practices. In addition, it seems reasonable that state and district programs, policies, and professional development opportunities should recognize and address such practices.

Teachers certainly do respond when the responsibility for handling recent immigrants is "left up to them." One Los Angeles elementary school teacher with significant numbers of newcomers felt it was important to involve their parents, which she did through making and enforcing her own policy:

When I have students who come from another country, they [their parents] . . . at first have to meet with me every morning at 7:30 . . . and then it's every week. . . . Yes, it's my rule.

Meanwhile, the principal of a charter middle school in southern California described the school's effort to incorporate recent immigrants into school life and captures the key tension over explicit newcomer practices—the potential segregation and isolation of recent immigrants:

I think our policy is that we treat them like any other student, and we meet their educational needs. Number one, we never call them "newcomer[s]," you know. They are students and we provide for the linguistic needs and the social needs. . . . They don't eat later than everybody else. They're just completely integrated.

This sentiment is echoed by one district administrator who indicated the importance of having schools with large numbers of new immigrants place their students in classrooms "purposely and intentionally, looking at language proficiency level [so that] they still have opportunities to integrate and to have lots of other native English-speaking models in their classroom."

The responses of those in favor of explicit newcomer programs, classes, and other policies show an understanding of both the current political environment and the inherent ad hoc and decentralized nature of the current practices. Lamenting the demise of a newcomer class, one elementary school teacher (a veteran with 32 years of experience) remarked, "It was very, very successful." As to the reason why the school no longer has the program, the teacher said,

> I think it changed because of the political climate in the country. Everybody wants everybody to achieve—and to a high academic standard—and for these children, it's a . . . double mountain to climb. . . . The thing that has been the most distressing is not recognizing that these children exist. . . . And not having a specific program for these children.

An elementary school principal, in favor of offering newcomer classes on a pullout basis, said that the teachers at her school would also be supportive, but the school could not afford such classes. She also stated that the bulk of newcomer support should not be placed on child translators or buddies:

> The biggest challenge is meeting [newcomers'] needs because, really, truly, what they need all day long is English language development support, and they don't get that. They get buddied up, they get partnered up, but they don't get what they need, which is ELD all day long. That's what they need. We don't have a newcomer class that does that here. We can't afford that at this point. . . . I mean, one of my greatest concerns is they're wasting their day. All day long, six hours, sitting there next to their partner or their buddy. . . . In my opinion, sitting in the class where you hear "wah wah wah" all day long, and you're buddied up with someone who is trying to support you, but certainly it's not their job, it's the teacher's. A fifth-grader is not a teacher, cannot teach the child.

We should note that there are neither credible studies of the effectiveness of newcomer programs or schools nor studies—quantitative or qualitative—of the effectiveness, benefits, and pitfalls of the wide range of classroom practices that schools and teachers are obviously developing and using on their own to educate recent immigrants. We do know, however, that beyond the classroom, schools and districts use many other ad hoc, de facto newcomer practices. Many of these involve or are targeted to the families of recent immigrants. It seems, however, that much of the tension around newcomer programs is based on politics and ideology, not pedagogy.

Ad Hoc Newcomer Practices beyond the Classroom

THE NEED FOR PARENTAL INVOLVEMENT

In the realm of school-parent relations, most educators and analysts will agree that parental involvement in a child's education can help improve a wide range of outcomes (Berger 1987; Epstein 1991; Henderson 1987; Lareau 1989). Increasingly, many believe that parent involvement at the school site can yield positive results, either through increasing parental involvement in a child's education or directly improving the accountability and governance of the school. Practitioners, scholars, and advocates have long called for increased parental involvement in minority and disadvantaged children's education and schooling.[10] The positive results from parental involvement in schooling appear to be taken as a given by nearly all of our respondents at both the district and school level, as is the challenge of achieving it with recent immigrants.

In addition, another recent trend involves incorporating minority and disadvantaged children's parents in the actual governance of public schools through membership on school-site councils, though there has been little exploration of the effect of such practices on educational achievement (Gershberg 2000). Many states (including California) mandate some form of formal governance structure or school-site council that includes parent members. California, in fact, mandates advisory councils specifically for its programs for English language learners: districts have a district English learner advisory committee (DELAC) and schools have English learner advisory committees (ELACs).[11]

OBSTACLES TO PARENT INVOLVEMENT

Most broadly, school and district staff we interviewed viewed school-parent interactions as a means for promoting the involvement of recent immigrants in their children's education. School and district staffs believe that school-parent interaction gives school staff an opportunity to explain the benefits of such parental involvement as well as to promote certain strategies for involving immigrant parents. Nevertheless, our respondents often indicated that encouraging immigrant parents to involve themselves in the traditional model of school participation is particularly difficult, more so than with native parents. According to most of our respondents, much of this difficulty is due to the inherent differences in U.S. public school expectations and immigrant parents' prior schooling experiences in their native countries. Some respondents elaborated specifically on the nature of parent participation in other countries. For example, two Los Angeles educators felt that U.S. schools inherently expect parents to be involved, whereas other schooling systems may not operate under these same expectations:

> [Many immigrant parents are] coming from a place where that kind of participation is not really required—it was not the parents' role to tell teachers what to do or to be actively involved in the school. Just getting over that feeling of "It's not really my role" [is a challenge].
>
> Many [immigrant parents] come from cultures where parental participation was not something that was stressed or pushed. The school was the school and parents raised their kids outside of the school . . . It's very different [here] . . . the expectations.

Those respondents who addressed the issue of parent participation felt it was critical to reach the parents and recent immigrant children early after their arrival to establish the most beneficial, long-lasting kinds of parent-school and parent-child relations. However, this was not always possible. In general, our respondents offered three main reasons for lower levels of parental involvement.[12, 13]

1. Schools and the school system are *inaccessible* to recent immigrant parents.
2. The "culture" of parental involvement is different for many immigrants.
3. Fear associated with undocumented status impedes parental involvement.

Inaccessibility of schools and the school system to immigrant parents. Most of our respondents implied that the school system itself is often generally inaccessible to immigrant parents. Before parents can even reach the point of considering or understanding parental involvement expectations at the school site, their experience in navigating the system as a whole can be overwhelming. Speaking of the biggest obstacles to immigrant parental involvement, a school psychologist in Los Angeles put this dilemma into perspective: "Navigating the system. . . . The bureaucracy here is just unbelievable! . . . How are they going to participate in the meetings if they can hardly enroll their kid [at the district office]?" A district official in San Diego went on to illustrate the critical stakes involved if recent immigrant parents do not learn how to find their way through the system:

> [Parents] who are new to this country need to know—to have their children not sacrificed by this change they've made in their lives—that they have to get on board almost immediately and begin to get the information and to get some footing in terms of figuring out what to do for their children.

Clearly, inadequate translation of basic school documents and important notices represents a major factor in school inaccessibility. The following comment from a teacher in a district with a central translation unit adds insight to the ad hoc nature of the translation process:

> The district is very poor about giving us very important notices in most of the languages, and that has gotten increasingly worse. As a matter of fact, retention letters went out in English only, and I mean, I was appalled. So last year, my bilingual aide and I sat down with all of them, and I had it written in Spanish [on our own] and in Hmong. I didn't have a Cambodian parent or aide to help me with that so it went out in Hmong and Spanish. But this year it's gone out in just English. And increasingly important notices are not being [translated].

Communication is an area where states could explore ways to encourage effective practices through regulation. As we discuss later, translation is important and basic, but immigrant parents also need help understanding such matters as (1) enrollment procedures, (2) available choices in schools and language programs, (3) their basic rights to educational and other related services, and (4) the causes and potential consequences of a variety of school disciplinary actions. While all districts we visited at least officially provide significant support in these areas, in practice we found the nature of "navigational" support parents receive rather scarce and ad hoc. In fact, the nature and quality of the front office and other nonteaching school staff members significantly determines the amount and quality of guidance parents receive. This factor emerged as a common theme in our interviews, yet we found no formal policies regarding nonteaching school staff and the support of immigrant parents and families. There is not much training for such staff—a need highlighted by several principals in particular.[14] The need for training to improve interactions with recent immigrant parents goes well beyond front office staff, however. Echoing the call for widespread cultural training, a Fresno district official stated:

> I would like to see ongoing training be available for teachers, for office managers, for custodians, for anyone who comes in contact with immigrant families or immigrant children . . . [training] to help the staff be more knowledgeable on cultural issues and . . . appropriately be welcoming to new students.

As much as respondents appear to believe in the importance of making school sites accessible and welcoming to immigrant parents, some also believe that schools and their staff members must go to the parents in their work and home communities in order to better foster parental involvement. A closely related concern, and one touched upon by most respondents, is that most immigrant parents' workloads are very high, impeding significant involvement either at their children's school or in their children's schooling. Obviously, schools need to adapt if they wish to succeed in reaching parents. One district official involved with improving parental engagement commented on the need for this link explicitly:

> [We need to] include parents, accept them as equal in the decisionmaking process, in the school—even if they do not know English. For example, many of our schools have received home visit funding for them [school staff] to go on weekends, or after school, to visit the homes. I think it's very important.

This official went on to explain that such trips help open teachers' eyes to the realities of their students' lives, not to mention that such trips help increase the number of parents who can experience a parent-teacher conference.[15] The district's outreach program also makes trips to agricultural fields or to "the motel row to serve the homeless parents." An elementary school principal in Los Angeles noted that state funds have been critical in funding such home visits. Alternatively, the district may provide a bus to bring parents to the school. Several teachers, however, reported conducting home visits unpaid on their own time, indicating that either (1) the state should increase funding for home visits or (2) the state should better target and encourage schools to apply for available funds.

The "culture" of parental involvement for immigrants. Although *culture* is a term that is both difficult to define and potentially contentious to discuss, its use among our respondents was so pervasive that we must both convey the way they used the term and discuss some implications. Respondents' use of the term *culture* most generally related to the roles of both public schools and parents, and their differing expectations about how parents do (or should) behave. The school-parent "culture gap" is based on the differing expectations of immigrant parents and the new school culture their children face in the United States.[16] When educators speak of this culture gap, there is some tension between their institutionalized belief in traditional parent-involvement activities and their empathy for immigrant parents' experiences.[17] A third grade Chinese bilingual teacher in San Francisco elaborated on this issue:

> I think one of the obstacles that parents encounter is the cultural conflict, the cultural expectation of them. I think here in America we want them to be involved in their child's education, and for many of my [students'] parents, they feel like that's the teacher's territory. They really should not overstep their bounds, and they say, "Oh, no, you take care of that, you teach my child, and I'll do everything else." So things like volunteering in the classroom, or working with their kids at home—to some extent they do work with their kids, but like, really supporting [and] working with them on their extracurricular activities, really supporting in that way—I think they're not really familiar with that cultural difference.

While this approach might have worked for immigrant parents in their sending countries, according to our respondents, implicit deference to teachers in California and other U.S. public schools will not usually be a successful strategy in school-parent relations. Nearly every respondent addressed some aspect of a culture gap. Among the key themes that emerged were (1) the time and effort needed to work with immigrant parents to foster greater parental involvement; (2) the important, if inconsistent, roles of PTAs, school-site councils, and bilingual/bicultural aides and liaisons in bridging that gap; and (3) the need for schools to be the initiators.

Beyond parental involvement in the schooling of immigrant children, many of our respondents discussed issues that arise from expectations that parents will be involved directly in school decisionmaking, school governance, and school-based management. In particular, there are often inherent tensions and challenges within a governance system that expects school staff to officially include parents in decisionmaking, yet these parents have potentially inadequate incentives and capacity to participate. An elementary school principal in San Francisco adds insight into immigrant parents' input to decisions involving educational practices:

> So [we] try and get them into this whole idea that, "We need your input, we need to know what you think," and they will tell us, but what they're telling us are things that totally touch them, or their child—how we discipline, is the school clean. You know what I mean? It's not necessarily the curriculum. And that's what's being asked. They [the district] want us to make huge site-based decisions on curriculum, on staffing, on programs. Now what's good is—I think that they [the parents] can. Parents can let me know that they feel . . . gee, they would really like a librarian, right? And so would the teachers.

A principal in San Diego gave a similar assessment of parental involvement in the English learner advisory committees (ELACs). Clearly, some key school-level staff have not bought into the ELAC concept, and the parents themselves may not always feel that the ELAC is an engaging and important place to be. This is not atypical for such advisory councils in urban districts across the country. A school psychologist in Los Angeles provided the following insight:

> The problem with these [ELAC] meetings is the stuff that they're really talking about or have power over. By the time they've paid the aides, paid the coordinator, and paid everybody else, they're not talking about any real money. There's nothing really they can make a decision over. They're making a decision over $50,000 out of millions and millions of dollars [in the] budget. $50,000—what are you going to do with that? You get to buy a few books, and maybe a TV set. So the decision that, you know, even though they're trying to get people to buy into these decisions, there are no real decisions to be made. . . . It's a farce that becomes real evident, real quickly. So the parents really can't discuss their concerns because nobody can do anything about their concerns. Their concerns are, "I don't want my kid on a bus for an hour to get to school." "Well, there's nothing we can do about it. Not here." . . . That's the real problem with those meetings. . . . They tell you that they're part of this big decisionmaking process, but you're not. Everything is already bought and spent before the meeting.

Given that many states and districts increasingly require and regulate such parental participation in governance, it would seem beneficial for all stakeholders if states would support and monitor such governance councils in fostering improved participation by recent immigrant parents. This is particularly poignant for state-mandated governance mechanisms impacting explicitly on immigrant populations, such as the ELACs, and our research indicates that any response needs to address the culture gap, albeit implicitly.[18]

Fear associated with undocumented status. Immigrant parents and the schools that educate their children face many of the same challenges and obstacles to parental involvement that disadvantaged native-born children and their families face. However, several issues make the challenges different, and arguably more difficult, for immigrant populations. Certainly, language is often an obstacle when immigrant parents have difficulty communicating with school staff and vice versa. A particular problem for recent immigrant parents, however, is the fear many parents experience as a result of their status as undocumented immigrants. This fear presents a challenge, too, for school, district, and state staff and policymakers. Often this fear stems from legal issues that many immigrant parents and students face regarding their immigration and residency status—although, by law, schools are required to serve undocumented immigrants and are not supposed to play any role in federal immigration investigations. A principal in Long Beach, for instance, found immigrant parents at his school did not "know that the schools have absolutely no connection with the Immigration and Naturalization Service" (INS).[19] In addition, recent immigrants may come from political situations that have instilled in them a more general fear of authority and, as discussed previously, they may view school staff as official authorities potentially connected to the INS. Such fear creates a particular obstacle for schools trying to foster parental involvement. A middle school teacher in San Diego commented,

> I think a lot of the parents are scared because a lot of them are illegal immigrants. They're illegal and they don't want to make trouble for [the] school or come in and talk to people because they're worried that, you know, somebody is going to find out that they're not supposed to be here. I think that cuts down your participation a lot.

In San Francisco, an elementary school parent liaison suggested,

> I would want parents to know that, so they're here as immigrants, so they have their child in the public school, so they should know that they have the right to make demands, and it's not going to cost them their job, their home.

An elementary school principal in Fresno discussed in detail the impact that fear of legal issues has on the many programs schools have implemented either to provide services directly to families or to link families to services available elsewhere:

> The other side is family services. And one of the things we [are doing is] helping families make application for either MediCal or Healthy Families. So all of [our staff] are trained to help the people do that. But the reservations among the folks that need that—they're afraid that they'll be reported to immigration once they become a part of the process. . . . ACCESS is a program for the homeless children. We used to run Saturday schools, and we have a teacher who coordinates all the children on campus who are actually designated as homeless. And there aren't as many immigrants in this program for good reason—they wouldn't want to draw attention to themselves.

Another elementary principal in San Francisco commented further:

> I have a child who was hurt here on the playground and the parents took him to the general hospital, but they don't have MediCal. They're afraid to apply for MediCal, you know, for all the reasons that you would expect.

For many reasons, one could argue that it is a role and duty of state and local governments to provide and promote the kind of information that could ameliorate some of these fears. First, such imperfect information is a market failure, and second, addressing this market failure could improve the effectiveness of a wide range of interrelated government programs and in doing so improve the schooling outcomes for recent immigrant students. Even if the schools and immigrant-oriented CBOs are best positioned to be the direct providers of this information, such efforts require time, money, and competent staff.

PROMOTING PARENTAL INVOLVEMENT, FORMALLY AND INFORMALLY

Schools, districts, and the state all have a wide array of programs and policies to promote parental participation. In addition, some schools and teachers do a great deal informally. These efforts are targeted at both immigrant and native parents, but, as many of our respondents indicated, the goal of involving immigrant parents has obstacles that require unique, tailored responses.[20] Given the discussion above, we consider these responses a form of de facto newcomer policy.

Several educators in each of the five districts mentioned their role in making parents feel comfortable at the school site. Principals were especially vocal on this issue. Using words such as *comfort, welcome,* and *trust,* our interviewees expressed concern in creating a receptive environment for immigrant families. The majority spoke of basic (but essential) elements in working with immigrant parents—such as greeting families in a personalized manner, accommodating parents' busy schedules, and providing translation services—but we highlight responses proposing efforts that go beyond these minimal gestures. These educators, in effect, call for schools to build trust and community with immigrant parents in order to promote meaningful and successful participation.[21] A Fresno principal commented that such efforts must surpass mere translation services. She emphasized that translation is indeed essential for home-school interactions; however, if school personnel have not made immigrant parents feel welcome, then efforts at securing on-site interpreters are obviated.

Several educators also indicated that district offices need to provide immigrant parents with more informative and welcoming assistance. Because immigrant students in all the districts we visited must visit some type of central placement office in order to enroll, their first contact with U.S. public schools often involves taking tests and negotiating a bureaucratic maze. Although some districts have gone to considerable lengths to personalize this process, immigrant families too often do not receive basic information that would greatly ease their transition into

U.S. schools. At no point do immigrant parents systematically receive an orientation to U.S. public schools (e.g., an explanation of the three types of schools [elementary, middle, and high schools], student report card systems, and parent-teacher conferences) nor do they systematically, across *all* districts in the state, receive an introduction to the purpose of different methods of language instruction.[22] Every district we visited, though, offers district-level programs specifically designed to promote parental involvement in schools (e.g., the parent involvement unit in Fresno and the parent university in San Diego).

Many immigrant groups use school facilities to offer Saturday or after-school classes geared toward teaching their native languages and cultures.[23] English as a second language, parenting skills, and/or computer classes for parents are also commonly offered at these sites. Sometimes these programs are supported by state or district funds, by monies from a principal's discretionary budget, or by teacher and school staff voluntarism. Teachers and school staff are indeed doing a lot of ad hoc, unfunded work with immigrant populations. Interestingly, these activities can positively influence other forms of parental involvement and lead to other types of on-site school participation. One principal reported, for example, that the parents in his school's adult ESL classes are the only parents he can call upon to serve on the school-site council. "The ESL teacher will [initially] recruit the parents," reported the principal, "So usually half of the parents that come are from the ESL class."

Schools also arrange for teachers to visit their students' homes and provide buses for parents to come to school. In addition, all districts have on staff some form of home-school liaison, parent liaison, or other kind of aide whose job it is to promote better communication between the schools and parents and increase parental involvement at a variety of levels. Sometimes these liaisons are certified teachers, while others are not teachers but immigrants from the countries that represent significant populations for the school. These liaisons received high praise from respondents for the role they play in fostering parental involvement—a task that includes such responsibilities as translating materials to be sent home, brokering effective meetings between parents and school staff, interacting with immigrant parents in their communities, and explaining the myriad ways these parents can become involved in their children's school and schooling.

In our interviews, some respondents cited the Nell Soto Parent/Teacher Involvement Grant Program as a state-funded option to support such home-school activities. Grants such as this one can play a substantial role in bridging the "disconnect" often felt between immigrant parents and school staff. The state could effectively encourage schools with high numbers of recent immigrant students to apply to these funds by expediting these schools' applications. Policymakers, however, need to reconsider the program's requirement that 50 percent of teachers and 50 percent of parents participate in home-school activities *before* the state can approve a first-time grant. Schools serving large immigrant populations that do not have half of their teachers committed to reaching out to parents (or half of their parents already involved) may benefit from a program such as this much more than school sites with already active home-school participation.[24] Two other state-funded grant programs also worth mentioning are the Teresa P. Hughes Family-School Partnership Award and Grant Program and the Tom Hayden Community Based Parent Involvement Grant Program.[25] Both provide financial support that directly impacts parental and community involvement in California's public schools.

SCHOOLS AS VEHICLES FOR HEALTH AND SOCIAL SERVICES

Public schools function as central outlets for or "connections brokers" to many family services that support poor and disadvantaged families. Our respondents mentioned health services most frequently, but also cited other programs such as welfare and child protection services. While this experience is true to some extent for many native families as well, it appears from our interviews that it is even more prevalent for immigrant and especially recent immigrant families who are living at or below the federal poverty level. Many school staff welcomed this role, while expressing concern over the strain it places on already scarce resources and staff. An elementary school principal in San Francisco remarked,

> [Parents] don't really know the community organizations . . . except for the school. . . . So if the school's going to operate as a focal point for the community, then the services have to be provided by someone other than the teachers and the principals. You've got to have health care providers here. You have to have counselors here. We have to know where the services are. It's not a problem to have the school as a focal point, the problem is not to have the resources to do it. And the teachers can't be the ones that do all this because their job is very difficult as it is and very much spelled out.

Parent centers emerged in interviews as important ways to foster parent-school relations and to support the school's role as a link to such social services. They literally create the space for parental involvement. Many individual schools have parent centers or neighborhood resource centers where the staff encourages parental involvement during parent-teacher conferences and many other events and activities at the school. Such parent centers help schools function as a link to many family services that support poor and disadvantaged families.

Respondents indicated that immigrant students have significant health issues and problems, which vary in both nature and intensity from those of native-born disadvantaged children. To begin with, our respondents reported, immigrants often do not have health records from their home country. Yet schools must ensure that students have received the required vaccinations. Furthermore, many new immigrants lack health insurance because they cannot afford it and/or they fear the application process for government-subsidized coverage, according to one San Francisco elementary school principal. As a result, the school nurse carries an additional burden, as described by a San Diego middle school principal:

> Sometimes what happens—and this is a *major* one in the issue of health—[is that] we have a significant number of our new immigrants without medical insurance. If a kid breaks their arm Friday night, the first treatment they get is Monday morning with our nurse.

Refugees present additional challenges in that they may be suffering from shock or posttraumatic stress.[26] Respondents mentioned a number of state and federal programs that help schools serve as links to health and other social service systems, Healthy Start being perhaps the most common.

One theme that arose occasionally with school staff, and more often in our CBO interviews, was the frequent need for schools to act as intermediaries between immigrant parents and Child Protective Services (CPS), a division of the California Department of Social Services. This situation stems from cultural differences in parenting practices. Referring to some Somalian parents, a San Diego elementary school vice principal noted:

> [One thing that] is different here in our culture is what we might call discipline. What I'm hearing through our interpreter again is in their home country . . . discipline is very physical . . . and very punitive and here they're told you do not discipline your child in a physical way that might result in a CPS visit. So I think the families feel—and again not all of them . . . very torn with their parenting skills and expectations here . . . because they want to discipline a certain way and they're told here in our country that you can't do that . . . and we're trying to— maybe through our parenting classes—talk about what are some ways that in our society you can talk through these parental ways of disciplining.

While the scenario presented here speaks to the role of parental authority in the context of physical discipline, Portes and Rumbaut (2001) also discuss parental authority in immigrant children's adaptation to the United States.[27] In their bicoastal, longitudinal study of over 5,000 immigrant students, diminished parental authority led to maladaptive student outcomes. Reduced parental authority in this case was fueled by immigrant students' embarrassment over their parents' ways, the students' preference for English and/or lack of understanding of their family's native tongue, and an overall level of dissonant acculturation where students and parents are adapting to the United States at different rates. Thus, in our work, diminished parental authority can also result from sources outside of the family, such as schools or "official" personnel who question the parenting practices of recent immigrants. These are turbulent waters that schools must navigate with care.

COMMUNICATION/LANGUAGE CHALLENGES (INCLUDING TRANSLATION ISSUES)

Translation issues are endemic in schools with large recent immigrant and ELL populations. Each case district has a delineated policy, and the California Department of Education (CDE) provides financial support through various sources, including the EIEP. Districts differ in the extent of centralized support they provide for translation (both for written communications and live interactions), but all schools conduct a great deal of on-site translation (or obtain it through outside contractors) with their own funds. It would seem that translation is one area where economies of scale could be present for some forms of services, and we believe the state should consider some centralized translation services. For instance, it is very costly to have a translator on site (at either a school or a district) for a language that is used by only a very small proportion of the school population. At the state level, however, nearly every language is represented by relatively large numbers of children and their parents. A Long Beach district administrator described the translation sources maintained in her district, including a database of employees in the district who speak various languages, sources of connections with people who speak another language, and connections with two major universities and many advocacy groups. Long Beach is a large district with resources for database building and maintenance, however. The impact of a newcomer who speaks an uncommon language on a small district could be overwhelming in the absence of such a database. The Long Beach administrator suggested that one of the services the EIEP office in Sacramento could provide or coordinate is a statewide, centralized database of translators for recent immigrants.

Describing Fresno's translation services, one district administrator said the translation unit helps connect the community with what goes on in the district.

> We have eight translators and we translate all district documents and site documents that go home to parents. And we translate into the five major languages. . . . And then if we have to, we'll call in part-timers or substitutes or something for other languages. And we also will provide two translators at the special ed building for special ed.

In addition, the district has five translators at the DELAC meetings and maintains a list of people to call upon who speak less well-known languages—sometimes these are community members not even involved in the schools. The district has also translated a parents' handbook into five languages. However, at least two principals and a teacher in Fresno indicated that what the district provides does not meet the schools' needs. One basic complaint from Fresno and other districts was that translations performed by the district take too long, so schools tend to take care of their own translation needs.

In San Diego, the district's Parent Involvement Unit also serves as a translation center, providing a variety of translation and interpreting services. However, one principal reported that, as is the case in Fresno, his school translates its own notices to be sent home regarding school-site meetings, as well as simultaneous translation at the meetings themselves. When asked whether his school gets any support from the district in these translations, the principal replied, "Yeah, if you had like ten weeks you could get [it]—no, we do it ourselves."

Moving beyond Ad Hoc Practices

This chapter has continued to explore the educational issues particular to recent immigrants, attempting to disentangle them from the issues of language proficiency and language instruction. We find that while there is no consensus as to how best to educate recent immigrants or how to train and support teachers for the task, educators do believe and understand that recent immigrants, or newcomers, present unique educational challenges.

Districts have a few explicit policies and programs, many of which—such as newcomer schools and pullout programs—have faded in the recent political environment in California, though other states appear more willing to experiment with them.[28] Schools and school staff, however, are in reality making newcomer policy every day. While much of their perception of these policies is tied closely to the nature of language instruction for ELL students, there are many ad hoc or de facto newcomer policies being designed and implemented daily by individual schools and individual teachers. There is neither consensus as to best practices for newcomers nor apparently any organized district or state attempt to begin to discern best practices or even understand what is happening in classrooms with many recent immigrants. Neither the policy research nor the policymaking community has focused on analyzing best practices or the effectiveness of either de facto or de jure newcomer programs.

School staff members are essential in helping (or hindering) immigrant students in their efforts to assimilate and become successful.[29] It also seems clear that there are particular challenges—academic and social—arising from teaching recent immigrants, and these challenges are distinct in many ways from the challenges of teaching ELL students—from translation to social welfare needs.

The challenges for fostering effective parental participation are particularly acute. Perhaps the greatest challenge both immigrant parents and school personnel face is simply understanding the different expectations each group has of the other. For example, educators want parents more involved in schools, while parents, for various reasons, often believe educators are fully responsible for children's formal schooling. Our respondents also expressed that this "disconnect" is exacerbated by structural issues, such as the inaccessibility of public schools and their processes, the differences between school systems in sending countries and those in the United States (described as "cultural" differences by respondents), and the undocumented status (and associated fear) of many recent immigrant families. Moreover, respondents described in detail how certain types of school involvement, such as participation in advisory or school-site councils, are not always meaningful or engaging places for immigrant parents.

It is important to note that schools and recent immigrant parents have much to gain in partnering, but effectively establishing these relationships requires tailored responses from schools. Connecting with immigrant families in a welcoming way and extending contact beyond the school walls is also critical. We would encourage policymakers working toward these ends to promote and support activities that bring teachers and administrators out into the communities they serve. Furthermore, in order to work effectively with recent immigrant parents, schools and districts need more support, especially support for the ad hoc activities and tasks personnel already perform as well as broader cultural and language training for local key stakeholders. Given that immigration policy is set nationally, there must be a federal role in providing such support.

NOTES

1. Much of the work in chapters 4, 5, and 6 is based on transcriptions from 86 of these interviews. Appendix C provides details on the methods employed. The need to reduce the number of transcriptions was driven in part by constraints in the project's transcription budget. The choice of which interviews to transcribe was made largely categorically (e.g., all district-level staff were included, but not CBOs). We also chose not to transcribe interviews for which we judged the interviewee had little to say. For instance, in one Fresno school, we interviewed a rookie teacher with fewer than two months' experience whose most common answer was some version of "I don't really feel I can say anything about that." Overall, we do not believe we added any systematic bias in our choice of transcriptions, although that possibility remains. Interviewers' notes from non-transcribed interviews were used in places, but not in any of the attempts to quantify our qualitative results.

2. Rubin and Rubin (1995). This text is not definitive or unique in the field of qualitative methods, but it provided a measure of uniformity in approach across the different researchers.

3. Recall that we put "bilingual" in quotes to indicate that these programs may use a language other than English but not be truly bilingual in any holistic sense.

4. We remind the reader that we did not conduct interviews with recent immigrant parents or students. The information provided here is based solely on responses from those who work with recent immigrant students.

5. Challenges were also mentioned in other parts of the interview. The protocol is available on the study web site at http://www.urban.org/pubs/bilingual. Figures in parentheses report the proportion of respondents who mentioned a given challenge at least once.

6. Because language curriculum is discussed in chapter 5, we include such issues as stigmatization and low prior schooling of students in that chapter as well.

7. The assessment center in Los Angeles offered medical facilities as well as academic services. However, it did not serve the entire district; it was geared to a sector of the district where disadvantaged immigrants tend to cluster. During the time we conducted

our interviews, the district decided to disband part of the center and require individual schools to perform certain services instead.

8. New York and Illinois both have active and apparently far less controversial policies to allow and, in some cases, encourage newcomer schools.

9. In terms of national origin, the largest numbers come from Mexico. However, Korean children tend to take part in EIEP to a greater extent than their proportion of the immigrant population would indicate, according to one district administrator who also noted that Chinese parents also want their children in the program.

10. See Cummins (1986) and Ada (1995). Galper, Wigfield, and Seefeldt (1997) report that parental expectations for Head Start children positively affect future math and reading performance. Keith and Lichtman (1994) found that parental involvement improved test scores of Mexican American eighth graders. They define parental involvement as "students' report of student-parent discussions about school activities, programs, high school plans (home-school communications), and things studied (home support of child as learner), along with students' report of parents' educational aspirations" (261–62). We use a working definition of *participation* derived from Shaeffer's (1994, 16) seven-rung "ladder of participation." Interested readers are referred to that source for more detail, but our working definition rests upon the concept that *participation* implies a relatively strong and active role on the part of parents and other stakeholders. *Involvement,* on the other hand, connotes "passive collaboration." We could not, however, guarantee that our interview respondents would make this same distinction, but an explanation was part of the protocol.

11. A summary of the regulations, functions, member composition, and guidelines for both ELACs and DELACs can be found in Fresno Unified School District (2000, section EL 9).

12. Not all respondents would categorize recent immigrant parental involvement as low in their school or district. We also heard instances of impressive parental involvement by immigrant parents. One middle school teacher in Long Beach said, "I'm inspired and very impressed with the parents of the ELD 1 [beginning-level English language learner] students. I had an open house. I want to say I had 15 or 18 of those parents show up—[a] much larger percentage of those parents showing up than any other class. The vast majority of those parents who showed up could not speak English and came into a school where the majority of the teachers are white and the majority of the teachers don't speak any Spanish whatsoever. . . . By and large, a lot of those parents have been very supportive." In this example, the parents are fulfilling the expectations the school has of them—all of this in spite of a language barrier.

13. In addition, when considering the following obstacles, it is important to remember that we did not hear directly from recent immigrant parents but from local stakeholders working with immigrant families; we would be remiss if we did not at some point state that the perceptions of school and district staff in this study may at times inaccurately reflect immigrant parents' views.

14. An elementary school principal in Fresno highlighted the role such staff can play in outreach to parents: "So we have a Spanish-speaking office staff, Spanish-speaking home/school liaisons. They're the ones who meet the families first, and help them register their children." And a middle school principal in San Diego noted, "When I first came here, there was no one in the front office that spoke a second language. Now you

tell me how you have a whole office staff who doesn't speak another language and over 60 percent of the parents speak another language. I think it's critical in schools like ours."

15. The state funds several grant programs that help support such activities: the Nell Soto Parent/Teacher Involvement Grant Program (grants of $25,000 or $40,000); the Teresa P. Hughes Family-School Partnership Award and Grant Program (grants of not more than $15,000 per school site); and the Tom Hayden Community Based Parent Involvement Grant Program (grants of not more than $40,000 per school site). For a fuller discussion, see pages 87–88.

16. Auerbach (1989) and Heath (1983) discuss the negative implications of home-school cultural differences and their potential for "deficit" thinking, which assumes parents inherently "lack the essential skills to promote school success in their children" (Auerbach 1989, 165). Noguera (2001) also asserts that "cultural theories" today play the same role as genetic theories—which polemically linked academic performance to racial and ethnic attributes—played at the beginning of the 20th century. We use quotations around "culture gap" to indicate that it is a term open to different interpretations by different respondents and readers. As with the term *assimilation,* we do not attempt to define it ourselves.

17. Auerbach (1989) describes traditional parental involvement as the "Transmission of School Practices" model where parents are expected (and trained) to "carry out school-like activities in the home" (168).

18. We recognize that it is difficult and, in some cases, illegal for policymakers to explicitly address such cultural issues. Still, if they do not do so implicitly, they will be unlikely to foster effective participation by recent immigrant parents.

19. It is important to note that in more than 120 interviews in California and nearly 60 interviews in New York City, the authors of this study have heard only one instance in which a respondent in any way implicated any school or school staff in playing a role in any INS issues faced by immigrant students or their parents. Note also that the INS has been renamed and relocated. Its duties are divided among various parts of the Department of Homeland Security.

20. A unique and tailored response to newcomer families was recently started by the University of Texas at Arlington. In this program, Maestros de la Comunidad, Latino immigrant parents attend a nine-session series dedicated to such issues as "Differences in the educational system here and in Mexico and other Latin American countries," "The role of parents in the public school system," "Student discipline in public schools: the rights and obligations of students and parents," "Getting help for public agencies and nonprofit organizations in Tarrant County," etc. For more information, please visit http://www.uta.edu/cmas/MdeC/EducInitiative.html.

21. Such efforts include embracing the skills or human capital their children bring to the school community, and have support in the education literature (Moll et al. 1992; Nieto 2002; Trueba and Bartolomé 2000).

22. A video orientation in San Diego is an exception.

23. For instance, in Fresno, the Khmer Emerging Education Program (KEEP) is a parent-initiated, grassroots program where parents volunteer to teach over 300 students two days per week. The self-funded program now receives some support from the district, and one district official has said, "This was an entirely grassroots effort, but it was done in such a professional way. The district would like to take the model and implement

it in other languages" (Kennedy 2000). Similar programs are offered in every district we visited for a wide range of cultures and ethnic groups.

24. This may be especially true, given our discussion regarding fear/legality issues among immigrant parents.

25. For additional information, see http://www.sbcss.k12.ca.us/legislation/chap99/ab33.htm.

26. See Padilla and Durán (1995) for a discussion on how this complicates the adjustment process. Furthermore, they find that many districts are unable to fully meet the challenges that refugee/asylum students present, primarily because they do not have enough bilingual staff who are adequately trained to provide specialized services to such students. Suárez-Orozco and Suárez-Orozco (2001) also address the psychosocial issues non–refugee/asylum students face as they adapt to the United States.

27. Though their work focuses on the second generation, they define this term broadly to include newcomer students who immigrated to the United States before age 12.

28. See, for example, Avila (2002) on Illinois or Gershberg (2000) on New York.

29. In addition, programs offered at school sites that demonstrate supportive institutional and cultural processes can promote school success for both immigrant and nonimmigrant youth and help address the generational decline in achievement. See Conchas (2001), Conchas and Clark (2002), Mehan et al. (1996), and Stanton-Salazar (2001).

5

The Debate over Language Acquisition

Caught between "Bilingual" Education and English Immersion

Our discussion in the previous chapters has broadened our understanding of challenges faced by recent immigrant and ELL students, eschewing a narrow focus on language instruction. We have argued that such expansion is likely to be an important component of an effective overarching strategy to better educate recent immigrants (and indeed all immigrant students). Nevertheless, we also recognize the centrality of the long-standing language instruction debate: "bilingual" education versus English immersion. Augmented in California by the passage of Proposition 227 (which curtailed bilingual education programs for non–English speakers in public schools), this debate remains important both in the political arena and in the practical challenges surrounding the effective education of recent immigrant and ELL students. While some argue that a discussion of language policy somehow deals less with recent immigrant students, we agree with those who see issues surrounding language policy and language minority students (such as Proposition 227) as part of a larger framework that encompasses the experiences of immigrants in this country. Proposition 227 was neither conceived nor passed as an isolated school reform effort. It erupted in a political context as part of a string of what many perceived as anti-immigrant, antiminority measures that swept California from 1994 to 1998 and spread to other states such as Arizona, Colorado, and Massachusetts.[1] Because of such political (and politicized) developments,

97

some educators in the field of language acquisition have begun to better address issues surrounding "bilingual" education within the larger context of immigrant rights.[2]

In our work, conversations with respondents indicated that in their view, most public school programs that affect newcomers—directly or indirectly—have to do with English language development. In fact, this perception was reflected by a substantial number of respondents who, at times, understood educating immigrant students as simply teaching them English. A middle school principal clearly exemplified this belief, "If you're talking about immigrants, we don't care if they're an immigrant—we care that they don't know the language." This perspective is unfortunate. This chapter focuses specifically on the issues surrounding language instruction and on the parameters of choice created by Proposition 227 (which includes the debate over "bilingual" education and English immersion).

Keys to Making the Choice

Educators, parents, and English language learners have often faced a web of choices about language instruction. Proposition 227 has altered the parameters and the ground rules for these choices, as well as the dynamics of the relationships among the different participants in the choice for each student. However, this legislation has not altered a basic tension inherent in the choice. On the one hand, professional educators are trained (or are at least expected) to understand the intricacies of the choice, and if they hold a credential in bilingual education, they are certified by (and in some ways "products" of) the state in this field of expertise. Thus, these educators operate from both a professional and a personal stance as experts able to provide guidance as to the best educational choice for each child. On the other hand, parents ought to have the right and the power to make the most important decisions for their children, including decisions about education. The keys to effective decision-making then, in a post–Proposition 227 era, are (1) healthy school-parent relations, (2) well-informed parents, and (3) the input of qualified professional educators. Reliable and trusted methods of accountability and assessment are also critical (see chapter 6).

The ongoing politicization of the debate, which Proposition 227 amplified, has resulted in a great deal of attention to the policymaking and administrative details, but has perhaps ignored the subtlety of the decision for each ELL child. At least, we argue, this may be the case for recent immigrant students, since the current system does not easily and transparently permit varying approaches for different kinds of recent immigrants (and English language learners who are not recent immigrants) with dissimilar educational histories and needs. In addition, it is evident from our interviews that, in many cases, the three keys for effective decisionmaking are not yet present in most school situations, and most of our respondents believed this situation is producing negative consequences.

We do not attempt to determine which method of language instruction is most effective for ELL students.[3] We simply highlight that, according to our research, current practices as implemented raise some red flags for recent immigrant students in California as well as in other states.

Current Issues in Language Instruction for ELL and Recent Immigrant Students

Proposition 227 Requirements

Many forms of English as a Second Language (ESL) instruction exist throughout California, though most can be categorized as either some form of "bilingual" education—in which at least some foreign language is spoken regularly in class—or some form of structured English immersion (SEI). Since the passage of Proposition 227, the type of instruction provided to students varies from district to district, school to school, and even classroom to classroom (Stritikus and García 2003).[4] The program at a given school depends on parent and staff preferences (often based on different ideologies regarding "bilingual" education),[5] staff size, the student body profile, and the kind of support the teachers receive. At least one sort of program is offered in every school with a minimum threshold of English language learners, and most schools with significant ELL populations offer more than one option for students. For example, one large elementary school in San Francisco offers some 12 Chinese "bilingual" classes and 10 Spanish "bilingual" classes, along with an almost equal number of SEI classes.

Proposition 227 requires ELLs to be placed in SEI unless parents choose to "waiver out" of SEI and select some form of "bilingual" education for their child. Before Proposition 227 in 1998, "bilingual" education was the default choice if it was available and if parents agreed to this placement. The only publicized result of Proposition 227 upon which all parties can agree is that the proportion of ELL students in "bilingual" education has fallen dramatically.[6] In addition, Proposition 227 requires that all new English language learners, regardless of any other factors, be placed for a minimum of 30 days in SEI "under observation," even if the student is going to waiver into a "bilingual" program. This policy affects recent immigrant students in particular, since they make up a relatively large proportion of the new ELL students each year.

Stigmatization of Recent Immigrant and ELL Students by the School System

Many respondents indicated that they believe their school system stigmatizes immigrant students.[7] And many felt this was also true before Proposition 227. We define *stigmatization* as the negative marking, labeling, or treatment of students with a shared characteristic—in this case, students who enter school not speaking English—that indicates a deviation from a set of norms. Respondents in our study primarily indicated that stigmatization occurs through the process by which students are placed in the "ELL" category. It includes not only the literal labeling, but also placement in a language curriculum different from that offered to native-born students—a curriculum that is often devalued locally by the school and generally by society at large. Stigmatization can also include physical separation or segregation either within or among schools, depending upon the particular language curriculum and school and district policies. It is, thus, difficult to separate this aspect of being a recent immigrant from that of being an ELL, although the initial "labeling" occurs upon a student's arrival in the education system—which is when immigrants are, in fact, newcomers.[8] The process of stigmatization or labeling by the assessment system begins when schools administer a home language survey (HLS) to new students.[9] If the HLS indicates that a language other than English is spoken in the home, students are required to take a language placement test to determine their ELL status. They remain ELL students until they are redesignated as fluent English proficient (FEP).

The educators we interviewed by and large believe the information schools do (or could) gather through the HLS is valuable, but they perceive the tracking it sets in motion as potentially, if not often, pernicious. It was typical for respondents to use phrases like, "I think it's a little unfair because that [process] labels the kids for the rest of their lives," or, "In the end, they're labeled something that stays with them through high school."[10] Another respondent suggested, "If it's a new student to the school, regardless of the language they have at home, they should be tested all the same. [Otherwise], it's almost a discriminatory measure."

In addition to labeling, the HLS assessment process can trigger a potentially marginalized school experience that, according to a San Francisco middle school teacher, physically separates English language learners from the mainstream:

> They're very separate. I'm going to be honest with you. At our school, our ESL program seems to be very separate [from] our regular program. They don't take classes together, really. Except for P.E., they don't interact much.

Therefore, even if recent immigrant and ELL students are not segregated between schools, they may still be segregated within schools. A teacher in Fresno who had previously served as a substitute teacher commented, "I got so that I didn't even ask where the [ELL] classes were. They were in the trailer or out in the field. That's always where they are, and it is true—that's what happens to newly arrived immigrants." Several respondents told us that they knew parents "gamed" the system by not telling the truth on the HLS: "So if [a] parent knows about that, they put 'English' even if they do not speak English—so that their children will not be labeled as [ELL] at the school."

Once placed in a particular "bilingual" class, a student's only possibility of exiting includes another series of language ability tests and other FEP redesignation criteria. Many respondents indicated that these tests are very difficult and measure more than language ability. Furthermore, and most important, respondents reported that many native-born students would be labeled as English language learners if the system required them to take the language ability tests! In fact, a native-born middle school principal in Fresno commented, "If I gave my own kid the test, he would have failed it, and he speaks English only." An elementary school teacher in San Diego recounted an experiment in which teachers administered the FEP reclassification test to native English speakers "and they didn't pass it." A middle school teacher in Fresno discussed using SDAIE (Specially Designed Academic Instruction in English) in the classroom with both ELL students and mainstream students and found that the SDAIE curriculum was tremendously effective for both groups of students in the school. The teacher explains, "[SDAIE] is really designed for the English language learner, but the mainstream kids are so low. In essence what I'm saying is all our kids are like immigrants from foreign countries." This same teacher said of the assessment system's impact on ELL students:

> It's holding them down, it's capping them. The [ELL] students are going through more criteria and more testing than the mainstream student and I would challenge anybody. . . . If we had to give those same tests to our mainstream students here at this school. . . . I see it as one more hurdle that adds on to students who need one less hurdle. We've added six inches to the wall and said, "Okay, now climb over this." And I think it's unfair.

Low Levels of Prior Schooling among Recent Immigrant Students

This tension over the HLS and subsequent language ability testing is particularly vexing given the prevailing sentiment among our respondents that proper information about school readiness is essential in properly placing and educating students new to the U.S. school system. One factor often mentioned was how the level of schooling immigrants receive in their home countries affects their academic success in the United States. Nearly half of our respondents discussed low levels of prior schooling as a challenge faced by recent immigrants and schools that educate them.[11] Nevertheless, many respondents discussed students coming from their home countries with higher levels and a higher quality of education. "We have some students who have higher levels in certain academic skills than our own students. So you have students who are even ahead of students who have only gone through our U.S. system," one San Francisco school district administrator commented. Indeed, several respondents observed that those educated in certain sending societies are significantly better educated than native-born Californians, pointing out that the math curriculum in Mexico is superior to that in California. One respondent reported: "I teach Algebra. . . . If the kids went to school in Mexico and had math, it's far superior to our students who receive math in our country. That was a real pleasure to get that."

This was not an isolated or rare sentiment among respondents, who generally believed that immigrant students with a history of regular school attendance in Mexico are better prepared in many ways than native-born students, especially by middle school. A San Diego middle school teacher said, "It's more rigorous [in Mexico]. And if you fail, you have to do the whole year over." A district administrator in Long Beach corroborated:

> The thing that's different in Mexico is that they have very stringent standards and expectations for students. If you have a fifth grade education in Mexico, you know a *lot* more than you do with a fifth grade education here—it's almost like what you should know at the end of an eighth grade education here. So they cram a lot

more into their education and their days are longer and their expectations are tough. And talk about benchmark! If you don't know something, you're retained—no ifs, ands, [or] buts about it. And they'll keep retaining you until you either drop out or until you get it. So it's very strict standards over there.

Immigrant students who have *not* attended school in Mexico—or any other home country—obviously present a greater challenge. California's school systems, however, are not particularly well prepared to assess school readiness. For instance, the state, the districts, and individual schools would benefit from knowing what proportion of a given school's recent immigrant students were consistently attending school at an age-appropriate level in their home country. This information is currently unavailable. As a consequence, the current process of designating language instruction methods does not allow for the kind of flexibility many respondents feel would best place children based on their previous schooling.[12]

In addition, when recent immigrants first arrive, they generally do not bring test scores from their home countries; if they do, the current system cannot translate or interpret these documents. A veteran ESL teacher at a middle school in San Francisco elaborated on intake information—in addition to the HLS—that would greatly benefit her in the classroom:

> Sometimes I wish I could have more information on the kids' schooling in their home country. I mean, I guess we're lucky—they will sometimes test students in their native language, and we'll get something that says they're at their grade level in reading Chinese or they're above fifth grade level in reading and writing Spanish, which is helpful. But you know, for some other relatively common languages in our district, like Arabic, Serb, or Croatian, I'll just get this notation, "Well, we weren't able to test it." If you've got people down there [at the Central intake office] that speak the family's language, you should be able to somehow get more information than that. I mean, can't you get some graded paragraphs in the language and have a non-teacher do it? Can the kid read or not read? . . . Some little checklist: Up to what grade did they go? Were they having trouble in school or were they doing well? Were they an above-average, average, or below-average student?—just based on their estimation. Oftentimes, especially when the kid is really struggling with their English—because that's when we want to go back and find out what the background was—I find that I have to go back to the kid. . . . "So, how were you doing in school?"

It should be noted, however, that while the intake process for all five case districts is not nearly as thorough as this teacher would like, some schools *do* offer tests in a student's primary language or that are not language-based. Overall, the processes by which school systems gather the information from new arrivals and assess these students for placement needs improvement.

The sentiment among educators that students with consistent school attendance in Mexico were better prepared than those with consistent schooling in the United States (especially in math) is surprising, given the popular perception of schools in Mexico. It is also a rather damning conviction of the quality of public schools attended by recent immigrant and ELL students in the five districts we visited. Nevertheless, we heard much more frequently of students who had had little or no schooling before arriving in the United States for later elementary and middle school grades. This was especially true in the case of immigrants from rural areas. In such situations, the issue is not just helping immigrant students catch up academically. Some arrive with no experience in schools whatsoever, which includes no experience interacting with teachers, holding a pencil, working at a desk, or sitting in a chair for long periods. In short, these newcomers need to learn just how to *be* at school—something most of their classmates have already mastered.

Placement of Immigrant Students

On the issue of placing recent immigrants in language classes, our respondents disagreed over what kinds of students benefit most from what kinds of curricula.[13] For example, an elementary school principal in southern California reported:

> We have a biliteracy program that's in and of itself going through lots of changes. But the children who come in literate, it's very easy to put [them] into a biliteracy program because then the teacher uses the Spanish to get into the English and move quickly. The children who are not literate . . . we're thinking that we would put them more into a structured English immersion class, especially if they come to us in the upper grades, because we need to allow the development of the language and the literacy at the same time. I don't know if that's the right decision or not, but that's where we are now.

Respondents also disagreed over the varying benefits and pitfalls stemming from the state requirement that all immigrant students must experience 30 days of an "English-only" curriculum upon arrival. Some felt that this practice works well for students who arrive with decent prior schooling, but not as well for those with little or no prior schooling. Recall the elementary school principal who believed that such newcomers were sitting in the class hearing, "'Wah, wah, wah,' all day long." Others felt differently (see The "30-Day Rule" in this chapter). Nevertheless, many respondents of both opinions expressed frustration that all students, regardless of prior schooling, must be treated the same upon their arrival as newcomers (i.e., all immigrant students are subject to the 30-day English-only requirement). Clearly, more research is needed about the effectiveness of different approaches as they are likely to be implemented. In the meantime, states need to consider carefully whether the initial decisions for and choices made available to arriving immigrant students are driven by politics or real pedagogy.

Issues Affecting the Choice of Language Instruction[14]

At the end of the initial 30 days of English immersion (and at the beginning of each new school year thereafter), parents of immigrant students who qualify as ELLs—in cooperation with school staff—choose the method of language instruction their children will receive. Broadly speaking, the choice is between some form of SEI and some form of "bilingual" education. Parents choose either directly, by completing a waiver form for their child to attend "bilingual" education, or indirectly, by not completing a waiver and letting the system run its course, automatically placing the student in SEI. Thus, parental involvement and parent-teacher/parent-school relations can play a critical role in the student's course of instruction.[15]

Two district officials summarized concisely the basic guidelines districts follow and touch upon some efforts to help parents make informed choices for their children:

> If [parents] want to enroll [their child] in an alternative program, either two-way[16] or bilingual, they have to request a parental exception waiver. And that's by state law. We have those waivers translated into five different languages, and we disseminate the waivers from here. A school calls us up and tells us how many waivers they want and in what languages. We send them out to the school site, and the schools are mandated to have contact with parents to provide that information. . . . They must make parents aware of their options.

> What we're directing [schools] to do is to use the information on those brochures and the district video for parent meetings in Spanish and in English [as a way of explaining] program options, but what we want is a real uniform, consistent message to go out there—that you have a right to choose, you have these options.

Quality of Information Given to Parents

As we will show below, it is very difficult to ensure any kind of uniformity in practice, in part because of the difficulty in getting sufficient information to parents and in part because of the tensions within the teaching profession over appropriate curriculum and parent-teacher interaction. On disseminating information to parents, a vice principal at a San Diego elementary school with over 800 students—82 percent of whom are English language learners—stated:

> We had a resource teacher from the Second Language Department in our district come out and co-lead [a parent] meeting with myself and the other vice principal. And so we had a parent meeting at 11:30 in the morning, at 1:30, and again at 5:00 o'clock in the evening. We made three different times available to parents. We had [the] expert from the [district] Second Language Department . . . so that [he] could answer any and all questions that could be beyond our scope. We explained the program options thoroughly. We also showed them [the parents] a district video. And then we had questions and answers. We probably had about seven parents attend all three meetings combined. Then we also sent home the information and [gave] the flyers to the children. . . . And it was again parents making this decision at home, either because they felt they knew the programs already or they did not come and really, really investigate the program but signed something that they thought was best for their child. So we wish that we would have had more parent participation. We've tried the same type of meeting for the same purposes for these "biliteracy" programs. We've tried to hold those meetings on Saturday mornings say at 10 o'clock. . . . We don't get any more to come out. So that's hard because you want the parents to be making well-informed decisions, and you hope that they do, but you're not sure that they have because, in my opinion, they didn't take full use of the informational meetings that they could have.

It is evident that a lot of time, effort, and other resources are being devoted to comply with the requirement to inform parents of their options. However, the relationship that this particular elementary school has with the population it serves is still unknown. Seven parents out of a student enrollment of 800 represent a dramatically low proportion. In addition, our study is limited because we were unable to gather parents' responses to this school's (or other schools') information campaign. The effectiveness, then, of such an expenditure seems questionable, especially if the goal is to have parents make informed and independent decisions for their children.

Advice from School Staff

Beyond the challenge of informing parents is another crucial concern in the current waiver process—namely the nature of the advice teachers and other professional staff provide to parents. An elementary school teacher in Fresno shared her impression of the process:

Recent immigrant[s] [will] probably do whatever they [are] told if it is recommended. They might ask a few questions. I guess it just depends on how it's presented to them. Many times, if they're recent immigrant[s], there's not a whole lot of understanding behind what we're doing here.

This teacher's comments highlight the potential for paternalism (Mehan et al. 1996) if parents are not given the opportunity to make choices for their children and educators exert excessive influence on the waiver process. Overall, we found two relatively evenly divided camps on the issue: those who try not to influence parental decisions (either directly or indirectly) and those who do. Interestingly, even the district official who called for a "uniform, consistent message" indicated that school staff are expected to inform and likely influence parental choices:

> Parents have the legal right to understand what those programs are and schools have an obligation to present it. Having said that, though, I think it's appropriate that if there is a child with a specific issue and the parent is requesting a program, teachers should sit down with the parent and say, "Our sense is that for your child, for these reasons, this program might be a better choice. The choice is still yours." They have to say, "The choice is still yours, but let's just talk about it and make sure that we're clear what the options are." I think that [process] varies from school to school. . . . We're trying to take away that element [of inconsistency between schools] so it really rests with the parent—that's why we have the videos and the brochures.

Yet a teacher in San Diego, who apparently tries not to influence parental decisions, commented:

> And many times the family will say to the teacher, "What do you think? Do you think my student is ready to be in an English class?" And the teachers are not allowed to give back advice, and we are not allowed to say anything about their choice. That's their choice. That's a difficult thing for the parents to make—sort of making a decision in a vacuum.

A Fresno teacher echoed this dilemma:

> If I were able to give my opinion, I would tell the parents not to sign [the waiver into bilingual education]. I would, but we're not supposed to. . . . They do ask, "What do you think is better?" . . . I [tell] them to talk to their husband—that I can't really give my opinion.

Teachers may find it difficult to prevent having an influence on parental decisions, however. The following excerpt from an interview with a "bilingual" kindergarten teacher in San Diego indicates the complexity of the tension:

> Interviewer: Do they generally ask you, and if they do, do you offer that advice and do they generally follow it?

Respondent: I think if they are placed in bilingual, for example—right now most of them want to stay in bilingual—I think the decision starts before they start school. That's when the big decision comes: "Will I place them in bilingual? Do I place them in sheltered [SEI]?" Right now we just turned in all the forms—the waiver forms so they could stay in bilingual—and you know, 100 percent signed them [authorizing their children] to stay in bilingual and probably about two parents asked me—because they were not sure and their child speaks a lot of English. And they're thinking, "What do you think we should do?" I just try to tell them, "This is what your child knows. And, really, if you place them in English or in bilingual, it's your decision really."

Interviewer: This is a sticky question, but do you think in general that parents make the best choice?

Respondent: No . . . because sometimes [they get] . . . the wrong information.[17]

On the other hand, many respondents were unabashed in conveying the influence school staff members impose on both parents' waiver choice. These responses not only reveal the sentiment that teaching professionals know what is best for most children, but also reflect teachers' commitment to "bilingual" education—dedication that may stem from training and certification and/or personal theories and beliefs regarding ELL students.[18] An elementary school principal in one district offered a typical response on this topic:

Most of our Spanish-speaking parents . . . when they come to school, they only speak Spanish, so we tell them, "We have an option for you. Would you rather have your child in an English classroom where they get support, or would you rather have the children in a bilingual classroom where they're getting instruction in Spanish while they're learning English?" And you know, we cheat. . . . We try to tell parents, "Think about it, you know, if we're teaching them in English, and they bring work home, can you help them? Can you help them in English? Can you read English enough to help your kids with their homework? They're going to have questions." . . . So we say, "You know what, if you choose bilingual, when the children bring their work home, you can help them, you can learn with them sometimes, also. . . . Then we'll be teaching [the parents] English; they'll learn English, too. And a lot of our immigrant parents, they have a lot of the same inclinations that our Hmong parents may have: "No, I want them to learn English." They don't know all the statistics and how long it takes to learn a language . . . they don't know that.[19] They just think [the children] can go to school, become immersed, and by golly, okay, fine. But there's a better way to do it. So you know, we encourage.

State and district policies cannot be made and reinforced without some honest recognition of (and consideration for) the depth of many education professionals' training, expertise, and commitment to "bilingual" education and their concomitant ability to influence parental choice. Two excerpts crystallize this point. An elementary school liaison in San Francisco asserted,

> Now the big one we're fighting is 227, you know, and really informing parents of what it means to be in a bilingual program, and why it's important to keep your child in a bilingual program despite a law.

Asked the kind of information parents are given in order to make an informed choice on the waiver decision, an elementary school teacher in San Diego answered,

> Not much. . . . For instance, every year they have to sign a reelection form so they can continue in the [bilingual] program. We just say, "This is so your child continues in this program—sign it."

Waiver Requirements

It is also important to note the official justification the waiver process gives for a child's placement in "bilingual" education: children who already know English (e.g., children from affluent or white monolingual, English-speaking middle-class families where the parents desire their children to learn a new language), children older than age 10 who school staff believe would be better off (e.g., older children who are recent arrivals and have had limited prior schooling), and children with special needs.[20] Yet almost never did we hear any respondent imply that the ultimate decision over the course of instruction was anything but the parents' choice (let alone the students'). The general consensus among respondents was that the waiver provides a choice for all students, not just those who already speak English or have a "special need." However, some school staff members do assert their authority in granting waivers, as is the case with this elementary school principal:

> The sticky part for me is [when] the parent elects the waiver and I don't feel that it's in the best interest of the child . . . I'll tell you, last year I approved all waivers. [However,] this year I'm playing around with not approving all of them because when our children go to middle school, there is no biliteracy program.

On the parental side, several respondents reported that many immigrant parents chose "bilingual" instruction so that they would be able to communicate with their child's teacher, thus positively influencing both the child's educational development and parent-school relations. Overall, however, most parents seem to follow the school's direct or indirect recommendation to the extent that they make an active decision; that is, parents must make "a personal visit to the school to apply for the waiver" (Fresno 2000). Particularly in the case of recent immigrants, our respondents indicated that this requirement presents a significant obstacle because of fear related to undocumented legal status issues (see chapter 4). Regarding the parental waiver, one teacher commented:

> I think because the parents won't come to complain, kids are stuck in classes they don't belong in. And sometimes it's really frustrating because we can push and push and push, but many times the parents won't come to complain because they don't have papers. They don't want to rock the boat.[21]

The 30-Day Rule

Our respondents often raised two additional specific concerns over placement: (1) the requirement that immigrant students receive an initial 30 days of English-only instruction and (2) the pattern of certain students who switch back and forth between "bilingual" and SEI instruction. Respondents expressed little support for the policy mandating 30 days of English-only instruction, but since we did not ask questions specifically about the policy, it is possible that some of our respondents felt positively about it. We did, however, hear some negative responses that give cause for concern. For instance, an elementary school principal complained:

> We're registering students all year long. Two first graders came today. . . . Two separate families but both from Mexico. I can't put them in a biliteracy class because they need 30 days of English, right? So I'm putting them in a[n English] class. They don't speak a word of English. They're with a sheltered teacher but the best thing . . . would be to put them in the biliteracy [class] so the teacher can communicate with them. These [sheltered-instruction] teachers can't even communicate with them. They have absolutely no language support. In some of our sheltered classes, there are other kids who speak Spanish, but in this other one [where I am placing the new students], there are none because they're all in the biliteracy class.

Asked about the kind of student most likely to benefit from the mandated 30 days of English-only instruction, a veteran elementary school teacher responded,

> Children who had already had school in another country. But we have a lot of children who come and they have never gone to school. And they come and, if they've never gone to school, and their teacher is speaking a foreign language. . . . They're really at a loss as to what they're supposed to do.

THE DEBATE OVER LANGUAGE ACQUISITION   111

After complying with the 30-day rule, a number of teachers and principals indicated that they suggested "bilingual" education for those children least prepared for school. Even some respondents who clearly did not favor "bilingual" education in general indicated that they felt differently about recent immigrants with little previous schooling, as did one biliteracy elementary school teacher:

> I think that the parents at the upper [elementary] grades are doing a disservice to the child [by choosing biliteracy] if the child has been here through their years because when they do hit middle school, there is no longer that biliterate program. I think if they are a newcomer child—for Spanish—biliteracy is there for them to help them get used to something. But if the child has been here, the parents are doing them a disservice.

Apparently, the current placement system does not always allow and, in the minds of many respondents, certainly does not ensure the placement of students in the course of instruction best suited to their needs. For instance, if the parents do not come to the school, it does not matter what the staff thinks is best for the child. Their hands are tied by a one-size-fits-all policy.[22]

Program "Switching"

Respondents universally indicated that alternating between "bilingual" and SEI instruction is detrimental to students.[23] Such switching appears to stem from (1) students switching schools, (2) the changing availability of program options in the same school from year to year, and (3) parental choice. Several school administrators also spoke of the difficulty that uncertainty from the waiver process creates for planning classes and curricula. An elementary school vice principal detailed planning and placement difficulties that arise from the waiver process:

> So every year we have to do the election ballot . . . count how many we have wanting it [a biliteracy class] for kindergarten, first, second, and third. . . . And that tells us whether or not we'll have a biliteracy class for that specific grade level. . . . That could be a disruption to programs. . . . For example, last year we only had enough parents "electing out" in K, grades one, two, and three. . . . This year we [are] very close to having the number [20 parents] electing it for fourth grade. But we never had it [a biliteracy class] last year in the fourth grade. Next year we might not have it [in] second grade. . . . So there could be gaps. Like this year we have . . . this year we don't.

Areas for Improvement

California now has several years of experience dealing with Proposition 227. It seems that improved accessibility of information and other aspects of parent-school relations could help ameliorate such planning difficulties. Improvement will likely include more nuanced approaches to student placement based on school readiness and other important factors. The California Department of Education appears to be performing an evaluation likely to lead to similar conclusions (Parrish 2001). And the California experience highlights issues that other states are also likely to face, especially with regard to the tension between parental choice and professional discretion.

Common Ground amidst the Divide

Just as academic and popular arenas are divided over the effectiveness of different language acquisition and instruction methods, so, too, are the school- and district-level educators we interviewed. While we do not advocate either "bilingual" education or English immersion for recent immigrants, this research has analyzed the choices that are likely to be made by parents (with input from teachers), given the current policy context. We have used qualitative interviews of school and district staff in five districts to illuminate the key dimension of the choice, the social dynamics surrounding the choice, and our respondents' impressions of ways to improve the quality of the choices made. Respondents do seem to agree that educators ought to be able to better inform parents of language instruction choices, that the school readiness of a recent immigrant student should largely influence that decision, and that one-size-fits-all policies are unlikely to serve all students well. Many respondents also identified some aspect of negative stigmatization fostered by the current treatment of English language learners. State and district policymakers can benefit from a deeper understanding of all of these issues.

The last two chapters have brought together the voices of teachers, principals, district officials, and other school-related staff who work with recent immigrant students and parents. In their experience, recent immigrant parents deal with many challenges when approaching school systems broadly and school sites specifically. When schools and parents find themselves in a weak partnership, the consequences can be deleterious—as in the case of the waiver process for "bilingual" education. Parents must be informed about the choice between SEI and "bilingual" education, but if schools cannot successfully transmit needed information, then parents may not necessarily choose the best course of instruction for their children. This situation has created tension in the teaching ranks, often leading to a gap between official district policies and actual school practices. The public debate over Proposition 227 in California, which has now been "exported" to other states, has often made any choices for parents and school staff difficult to implement and thus likely weakened the education provided to recent immigrant and ELL students.[24]

NOTES

1. California voters passed three major propositions in the past decade: Proposition 187, which eliminated health and educational services to undocumented immigrants; Proposition 209, which overturned affirmative action; and Proposition 227. In Arizona and Massachusetts, similar bills aimed at eliminating bilingual education also recently passed. However, Colorado's measure was defeated in 2002.

2. See Ovando (2003).

3. See chapter 1, note 15.

4. Stritikus and García (2003) cite others' findings on how schools and districts have responded to Proposition 227 in three major ways: "García and Curry-Rodríguez (2000) and Gándara et al. (2000) report that certain districts across the state have used the waiver clause of the law to pursue districtwide waivers, others have implemented the English-only provisions of the law, and a third group has left the primary decisions up to individual schools."

5. District administrators' "language ideology"—or the status accorded to the English language vis-à-vis students' home languages—is also a key indicator as to what type of educational program was implemented after Proposition 227. See Gutiérrez, Baquedano-López, and Asato (2000).

6. Prior to Proposition 227, 29 percent of English language learners were assigned to bilingual classrooms. Afterward, in 1998–99, only 12 percent of all English language learners were in these classes. See Gándara et al. (2000).

7. Over 20 percent of respondents discussed stigmatization in response to an open-ended question about challenges. Since we had no direct question regarding stigmatization, we consider this significant. Clearly, were we to have prompted respondents about the topic, a higher percentage would have said it existed.

8. The labeling occurs, too, when native-born children of immigrants (who are not recent immigrants themselves) and Puerto Ricans first enter the school system.

9. See appendix F for a sample HLS.

10. These statements may also reflect the wariness educators have of poorly implemented "bilingual" programs that water down academic instruction and do not fulfill their mission of teaching English. For a more detailed discussion of such a program at the middle school level, see Valdés (2001).

11. Limited schooling in a student's home country is also cited as a critical factor that language-acquisition programs need to assess and address (Ruiz-de-Velasco and Fix 2000). See also Jaramillo and Olsen (1999).

12. In fact, one challenge for immigrant students we explored in our interviews was getting access to gifted and talented programs (GATE) where students can make better use of their education. One elementary teacher in Los Angeles noted that the school takes too long to identify potential GATE students—she had recommended third-graders who didn't get tested until fifth grade. In general, respondents felt recent immigrant students do not have as much access to GATE programs as perhaps they merit. Language is often an obstacle if schools do not have—or do not know of—the appropriate bilingual personnel to do an evaluation.

13. This same disagreement carries over into the type of educational language program offered at each school. Several studies have found that if school and district administrators were not favorable toward "bilingual" education prior to Proposition 227, then this same ambivalence or lack of support carried over in their interpretation and implementation of Proposition 227. See Gándara et al. (2000), García and Curry-Rodríguez (2000), Gutiérrez et al. (2000), and Stritikus and García (2003).

14. It should be noted that the interview data for this section come heavily from two districts: San Diego and, to a lesser extent, Fresno. This is most likely due in part to the districts' pronounced efforts to consistently and emphatically adhere to Proposition 227's requirements. Employees in San Diego, for instance, appeared to feel the weight of the proposition's implementation decidedly heavier than did employees in other districts. For a discussion on the differences in implementing Proposition 227, see García and Curry-Rodríguez (2000) and Parrish (2001). In addition, this "choice" theme emerged late in our interview process, and San Diego was the last district visited. Thus, the interviewer sought greater depth in the responses in this district. We do not know what we would have found had we done so in other districts. Rubin and Rubin (1995) defend such evolving applications of an interview protocol for "interviews as guided conversations."

15. In practice, we should note, the choices are more available and more important at the elementary school level than at the middle school level. That is, many middle schools in California do not offer "bilingual" options—only ESL programs that do not use a language other than English for instruction.

16. Two-way immersion programs involve instruction in English and another language whereby students receive a certain percentage of instruction in each language on a daily basis in order to become bilingual.

17. Two additional points of note from this excerpt: This teacher next told a detailed story of two parents making what she perceived as the wrong decision to waiver their children into "bilingual" education, despite the teacher's subtle efforts to influence them otherwise. In the first example, the father's perception (as portrayed by the teacher) was that the choice lay between "bilingual" education and "learning English," as if the first choice would perhaps not in fact involve learning English. The second anecdote portrays the perception of the negative outcomes from students alternating between "bilingual" and SEI programs. Both of these themes were common among our respondents and are explored later in the chapter.

18. See Stritikus and García (2003) for a detailed analysis of how Proposition 227 complemented or contrasted teachers' theories and additive and subtractive conceptions

of schooling for culturally and linguistically diverse students. (Additive schooling builds on the students' home languages and cultures, while subtractive schooling attempts to erase them.)

19. A principal in Fresno said something similar: "The Hmong parents believe that their children will learn English better and faster if they are immersed in English. They believe that. And they have lots of success stories. Statistically, we know that's not true. But the success stories stand out."

20. "As per Article 3 of CA Ed. Code 300, English Only instruction may be waived by parent consent. . . . . [The District] will honor waivers whenever feasible, as per the terms of the law. Section 311 of CA Ed. Code 300 describes the three circumstances in which a Parental Exception Waiver may be granted: 1. Children who already know English. . . . ; 2. Older children: The child is age 10 years or older, and it is the informed belief of the school principal and educational staff that an alternate course of educational study would be better suited to the child's rapid acquisition of basic English language skills; or 3. Children with special needs: The child already has been placed for a period of not less than 30 calendar days during that school year in an English language classroom and it is subsequently the informed belief of the school principal and educational staff that the child has such special physical, emotional, psychological, or educational needs that an alternate course of educational study would be better suited to the child's overall educational development. . . . The existence of such special needs shall not compel issuance of a waiver, and the parents shall be fully informed of their right to refuse to agree to a waiver." This is from the Fresno USD (2000, section EL 8), but is typical of information available from other districts.

21. Another study found that students and parents actually do push very hard, often in vain, for high school students to "exit" out of the ESL program in order to have access to the college-preparatory curriculum. See Fuentes et al. (2000).

22. In the next chapter, we discuss the nature of the information that is gathered about immigrant children upon their entry into the school system. Many school staff members we interviewed believe that this information is very important for determining the best course of instruction for recent arrivals, and is currently insufficient.

23. This echoes conclusions in New York City that indicated that "consistency of programmatic approach (bilingual or ESL) appeared to be a particularly important determinant of program exit rates" (Board of Education of the City of New York 2000).

24. See Mendel (2002) for an example of the public debate.

6

Educator Evaluations of Language Assessment, Placement, and Accountability Systems

Accountability has become a cornerstone of our nation's education reform movement, and California is no exception. In fact, accountability and assessment have become commonplace in the education arena over the past half-century (Linn 2000). And now, such new elements as high-stakes testing and accountability[1] and challenging yet inclusive content standards have elicited renewed public interest. According to public opinion surveys conducted by the Public Policy Institute of California, the public in California appears to be solidly behind the ideas of testing and accountability (Baldassare 2001, 2002a, 2002b). More than 65 percent of all respondents, along with almost 80 percent of Latinos, 74 percent of Asians, and nearly 68 percent of African Americans, think that the "right amount" or "not enough" standardized testing exists in public elementary and middle schools. Furthermore, almost 77 percent of all respondents, in addition to 80 percent of Latinos, 74 percent of Asians, and 65 percent of African Americans, agree that students should have to pass statewide tests in reading and math before being promoted to the next grade—even if they have passing grades in their classes. Despite solid support for testing, however, only 36 percent of all respondents are satisfied with the way that test score accountability is being handled in California's public schools.[2] It should therefore come as no surprise that the implementation of accountability systems impacts immigrants and those who teach them in some unique ways—ways that we explore in this chapter.

The Purpose and Parameters of Our Interviews

Although testing and public school accountability enjoy both policy and popular support in California, it is important to examine how these concerns affect different groups of students. In this chapter, we address the implications and effectiveness of high-stakes accountability measures in California for recent immigrant and language minority students.[3] Our goal is not to judge the validity of tests and other instruments but to portray a range of responses from some key stakeholders and, drawing from their impressions, to derive some potential implications for state-level testing policies. Because of state mandates, the systems for identifying, placing, and assessing students are the result of the most universal policies and programs affecting recent immigrant and language minority students in California. Most other states use similar systems. Although there may be variation in the way these programs and policies are implemented, California districts and schools must still administer them in some form.

As noted in chapter 5, educators often might not distinguish students new to the U.S. school system from non–native English speakers who lack English proficiency but may in fact be native-born citizens. Indeed, the characteristic that most often gets the attention of educators is English language proficiency. Recall the response of one educator that illustrates this fact quite well: "We don't care if they're an immigrant—we care that they don't know the language." Although we asked respondents specifically about how the assessment and accountability system affects *recent immigrant* students, their answers show how difficult it is to separate recent immigrant students from English language learners, partially because language proficiency appears to be one of the most observable characteristics (if not the most observable) of many recent immigrant students.

While this chapter might seem to deal mainly with ELL students, our case study schools are those with some of the highest percentages of recent immigrants in each district. Therefore, our interpretation is that most if not all of the responses we received relate in some way to recent immigrant students—especially those who lack English proficiency. In a poignant example, one respondent described a newly arrived immigrant student taking a standardized test:

> It's a recent immigrant [situation], and I guess [the district and state education departments] discount the test results because of that, but in the meantime that

child is expected to sit down and take this test. And I had a student come from Thailand May 8th. It was her first time in the country, she knew not a word of English, and she was sitting there with the test in front of her on May 14th. And I was standing next to her, trying to help her as best I could, and she just looked so bewildered.

Clearly, students may find it quite challenging to face a standardized testing system when they enter U.S. public schools without English skills.

During the course of our interviews, we asked a series of open-ended questions designed to garner impressions of the process for student placement, the testing systems and instruments, and the system for ranking schools in California. These assessment systems and processes include (1) the home language survey (HLS), (2) the language placement system (LPS), (3) the English language learner (ELL) to fluent English proficient (FEP) redesignation process, (4) the Standardized Testing and Reporting (STAR) program (also called the SAT 9 or Stanford 9), (5) the Academic Performance Index (API), and (6) the High School Exit Exam (HSEE).[4] In semistandardized interviews, we asked respondents to give us their impressions of these systems as they relate to recent immigrants (Berg 2001).[5]

In this chapter, we analyze the responses (1) by district, (2) by level of employment (e.g., district, elementary school, middle school, or community-based organization), and (3) by position (e.g., district administrator, principal, teacher, or other) to see what kinds of variations might exist in different contexts. Because each district is represented by such a small number of interviews, and in order to preserve respondents' anonymity, we do not disaggregate by level and position within a district. Finally, we identify themes or topics in the conversations relating to each of the six placement or assessment processes detailed above using analytic coding (Lofland and Lofland 1995), and we give examples of respondents' explanations and thoughts on the various subjects.[6]

For several reasons, we cannot generalize the results to a whole district, across a particular level of employment, or across a particular employment position. First, our sample was not randomly selected; second, the number of interviews analyzed here totals 86; and, third, the number of respondents by district, level, and position is even fewer (see table 6.1). As such, we caution the reader not to generalize these results beyond these respondents. For example, when citing percentages of teachers who maintain a particular impression, we are referring to teachers we interviewed. Nevertheless, explanations provided by these respondents can help our understanding of some of the complexities of the processes of

Table 6.1. *Staff Interviews Transcribed, by District, Employment Level, and Employment Position, 2001*

	N	Share of total (%)
Overall	86	100.00
State EIEP	1	1.16
District (all personnel)		
Fresno	15	17.44
Los Angeles	19	22.09
Long Beach	17	19.77
San Diego	18	20.93
San Francisco	16	18.60
Total	85	98.84
Level (across all districts)		
District	16	18.60
Elementary	35	40.70
Middle school	31	36.05
Other (CBO)	3	3.49
Total	85	98.84
Position (across all districts)		
District	15	17.44
Principal	21	24.42
Teacher	32	37.21
Other	17	19.77
Total	85	98.84

Notes: EIEP = Emergency Immigration Education Program; CBO = community-based organization. One respondent works in a district office but is a part-time teacher. This person has a district level and teacher function. Figures may not add to totals shown due to rounding.

placing and assessing recent immigrant and language minority students, especially since we then supplement the results with their own words.

Emerging Themes—Accuracy and Fairness

The two most common themes to emerge from our interviews were the accuracy and fairness of the systems designed to identify, place, and assess immigrant and language minority students. Most respondents had positive impressions of the accuracy and fairness of the HLS, LPS, and redesignation systems. However, most respondents expressed negative opinions about the accuracy and fairness of the STAR, API, and HSEE—primarily because these assessments are not specifically designed to assess language minority students.

Other themes that arose less frequently include the importance or usefulness of these assessment systems, the purpose or use of assessment results, the stigmatizing effects of these systems, and consistency across districts and with state standards. Most respondents agreed that it is important to identify, accurately place, and periodically assess the progress of recent immigrant and language minority students. Respondents disagreed, however, as to how best to achieve these goals. This chapter presents interview analyses for the systems, including response frequencies and qualitative insights about the themes that emerged during our conversations.

Language Assessment Processes

The Home Language Survey (HLS)

When parents or guardians first enroll a pupil in a district, they must answer questions regarding the language spoken in the home (see appendix F for a sample HLS).[7] If a language other than English is spoken in the home, the student's English language proficiency is assessed (see next section). We asked respondents to give us their impressions of the home language survey and its possible consequences for students and the system.

IMPRESSIONS OF ELEMENTARY SCHOOL PERSONNEL
The majority of respondents (more than 60 percent) who gave an answer other than "no opinion" or "not covered" had positive attitudes about the items in the survey and the use of the information collected in the process of identifying non-native-English-speaking students. Analyzing the responses by level and function, however, reveals that elementary school personnel and teachers had more negative impressions of the HLS than did staff in the other levels and functions; in fact, there was a higher percentage of negative responses than positive responses among these two types of personnel when compared with other levels and functions. Among elementary staff voicing an impression, almost 55 percent

expressed a negative or somewhat negative opinion and, among teachers, 52 percent had a negative or somewhat negative impression (see table 6.2).

It is unclear from our interviews exactly why these response patterns exist among elementary personnel and teachers, but this greater discontent is in fact meaningful. These personnel initially handle any problems associated with students who have been inaccurately identified by the HLS and are arguably closest to the students being assessed and placed. Previous research (Betts, Rueben, and Danenberg 2000; Parrish 2001; Rumbaut 1995) shows a higher proportion of California's ELL students in elementary grades—particularly grades K–3—than in higher grades. Furthermore, research conducted by the New York City Board of Education (2000) suggests that if early interventions are made, it may be easier to transition a child from ELL to FEP instruction. Thus, our findings may reflect feelings of frustration that are connected both to the added burden of dealing with inaccurately placed students and to the sense that the longer students remain in the wrong program, the less likely they are to progress quickly to English fluency. However, it was more common to hear teachers give specific examples of children whose English fluency was higher rather than lower than expected based on what the HLS indicated it might be. An elementary school bilingual teacher in Fresno described an exchange about the HLS with a parent:

> She [the mother] put Spanish on the survey as a home language and I told her, "Your daughter doesn't belong in my class. This class is for the kids [who] are barely learning their English. She's far into English already."

Usefulness, Accuracy, and Stigmatization

Three themes arose from our interviews: the importance or usefulness of the HLS (58.9 percent), the accuracy of the process for identifying language minority students (39.7 percent), and the labeling of students (12.3 percent). Most of the respondents who spoke about the survey's importance or usefulness had positive impressions (83.7 percent), whereas most respondents who commented on accuracy (79.3 percent) and all respondents who talked about labeling had negative opinions.

In a typical positive response as to the importance of the information contained on the HLS, an elementary school principal in San Francisco remarked:

> Well, I think those [surveys] are important; they tell us a great deal, and I'm really glad that our district does it districtwide. [It's] part of the form for applying for a school here in the district, so it tells me a great deal.

Table 6.2. *Attitudes about the Home Language Survey, Language Placement System, and ELL to FEP Redesignation System, by Respondent District, Level, and Position, 2001*

	Home language survey			Language placement system			Redesignation system		
	N	Negative (%)	Positive (%)	N	Negative (%)	Positive (%)	N	Negative (%)	Positive (%)
Overall[a]	73	39.73	60.27	74	33.78	66.22	64	40.63	59.38
District (all personnel)									
Fresno	15	46.67	53.33	14	28.57	71.43	10	50.00	50.00
Los Angeles	18	27.78	72.22	16	18.75	81.25	15	26.67	73.33
Long Beach	13	38.46	61.54	16	31.25	68.75	15	33.33	66.67
San Diego	17	47.06	52.94	17	41.18	58.82	14	35.71	64.29
San Francisco	9	44.44	55.56	10	60.00	40.00	9	66.67	33.33
Level (across all districts)									
District	15	13.33	86.67	14	0.00	100.00	11	9.09	90.91
Elementary	31	54.84	45.16	32	56.25	43.75	27	51.85	48.15
Middle school	24	41.67	58.33	25	24.00	76.00	23	34.78	65.22
Other	2	0.00	100.00	2	50.00	50.00	2	100.00	0.00
Position (across all districts)									
District	14	14.29	85.71	13	0.00	100.00	11	9.09	90.91
Principal	19	42.11	57.89	19	42.11	57.89	15	26.67	73.33
Teacher	25	52.00	48.00	26	42.31	57.69	24	70.83	29.17
Other	14	42.86	57.14	15	40.00	60.00	13	23.08	76.92

Notes: ELL = English language learner; FEP = fluent English proficient. Figures may not sum to 100 percent due to rounding.
a. Although we interviewed the state's Emergency Immigration Education Program (EIEP) program director, we agreed to keep his responses confidential.

However, some responses suggest that based on the information in the HLS, some educators may also be making assumptions about the degree of English language reinforcement students receive outside the formal education setting. An elementary school teacher in Los Angeles told us,

> To me it helps, because you find out . . . if the kids and if the parents speak English or not, if they ever hear it, if they come with nothing. . . . [It] sort of gives you a little better feel of how much the child knows. . . . If the parents don't speak English, they can't help them with their homework. . . . I look at it [the survey]—not every time—but it helps.

These assumptions may sometimes be correct, but, in fact, the HLS poses no questions about the amount of English language reinforcement that a child receives outside the formal education setting (e.g., from parents, siblings, peers, or other sources). Often the information in the HLS does not reflect the amount of English proficiency a child actually has or the amount of English "community reinforcement" a child receives. This situation is reflected by a Los Angeles school psychologist's description of a scene at a school's registration desk where the HLS is given to a parent or guardian:

> But a clerk that's sometimes handing that [form] to [the parent or guardian to fill out], and [the adult who came to register the child that day] speaks Spanish . . . I mean, it's done very quickly, and somebody's just sort of filling it [the HLS form] out. And if there are any questions that the parents have, they're not really investigated. So sometimes you'll see something with Spanish [listed as the home language on the HLS] . . . and then the mother comes in [later], and everybody speaks English. And you're like, "How did this happen?" Well, obviously, some rushed clerk . . . the [Spanish-speaking] grandmother came in with the kids that first day, wrote down Spanish, and . . . If the clerk's going to administer it, there needs to be some very specific, concise questions as to why that's Spanish that you put on there.

Incorrect assumptions about the amount of parental or community support a student may be receiving—assumptions based solely on the family's home language—might influence teachers' expectations of the student's performance or unfairly contribute to stigmatization. Such assumptions may also inappropriately trigger an assessment process that will lead to the child's ELL designation, as we explore below.

Furthermore, many of the respondents who expressed positive views of the survey's importance or usefulness also expressed negative feelings as to its accuracy in determining what language a given student actually speaks. The following interview excerpt is typical of negative responses describing inaccuracies in the process of identifying language minority students. As one elementary school principal in Long Beach told us,

> It [the survey] figures out . . . what language is being spoken at home. . . . However, it can also be extremely misleading because if you just check one of those things—"every once in a while we speak Spanish"—you just put that on [the form] . . . it may help in incorrectly identifying a child.

Other respondents told of parents "gaming the system," indicating that only English was spoken in the home to avoid the LPS for their child. In fact, one community-based organization (CBO) reported that it actually arranged a campaign to encourage parents to do exactly that. These types of responses reflect the reality that students are improperly placed as a result of inaccurate HLS information. Therefore, the HLS can have unforeseen consequences for the new student. As such, the adult providing the information should at least receive a more complete explanation of how the information is going to be used if not a better instrument to begin with.

It is important to note, however, that the HLS generally triggers the LPS, so it is unclear how often the HLS itself can improperly place students in the absence of English language proficiency assessments. A teacher in San Diego provided a plausible explanation of how this might occur. Sometimes the HLS places the student in a particular program or classroom weeks before the LPS is given and the results are available. Thus, the HLS might label and stigmatize a child as an English language learner without test results to support the placement.[8] In addition, if there are problems with the language assessment tests, then the accuracy of the instrument that ultimately leads a child to those tests is key because a child who should not take the LPS tests in the first place may be forced to take them.

In sum, most respondents indicated that the HLS is an important or useful component in the process of identifying language minority students' needs. However, they also expressed considerable concern as to the improper placement of students because of inaccuracies in the identification process and, to a lesser degree, explicit concern that labels given to students may lock them into a particular program or track.

The Language Placement System (LPS)

Until the summer of 2001, California school districts could choose from among several instruments to test and place language minority students. Some respondents knew which instrument was used in their district and others did not; therefore, we do not focus on which instrument is used. However, the two assessment packages most commonly cited were the Language Assessment Scales (LAS) and the IPT-IDEA tests.[9] Again, most of the respondents who voiced an opinion had a positive impression of the assessment system used in their district.

Of those who expressed an opinion, over 66 percent were positive. However, disaggregating the analysis demonstrates again that more than half of elementary personnel who answered across all districts voiced negative impressions of their language placement system. District administrators, on the other hand, were overwhelmingly positive (87 percent), and the majority of principals and teachers were also positive, but by smaller margins (see table 6.2).

Test accuracy. Two main themes arose in conversations about the language placement system: (1) the accuracy of the tests and (2) the importance of proper student placement. The most common topic, the system's accuracy, was discussed by 46 percent of respondents who talked about the LPS. Almost 60 percent of these respondents thought that the LPS is not accurate, whereas approximately 35 percent thought the system to be accurate, and a few spoke of the importance of accuracy without taking a positive or negative stand. Respondents talked most about how often the LPS serves as a precise measure of the student's English language proficiency and the role that accuracy plays in the system's ability to deliver appropriate services to students.

District officials are generally more familiar with the testing protocols, but other staff members might deal with the outcomes of placement tests. A psychologist working in the Los Angeles district's placement office suggested a way in which the placement test could be subjective:

> The ratings system is very tricky. Two different people could take [administer] the test [to the same student] and give the student two different scores.

A Fresno middle school teacher explained that an objective test score might not reflect a child's ability in class, and a home-school liaison indicated that even after a student's English has been assessed, classroom space—rather than ability—might dictate placement. These responses suggest that a student's LPS score may be subjective or it may be ignored altogether in favor of other constraints, such as class size requirements or program availability.

Younger children are at a particular disadvantage. Shyness, nervousness, and fear of strangers may commonly account for test inaccuracy among elementary students. An elementary school principal in Los Angeles commented,

> Remember, they're babies if they come to us in kinder[garten]. . . . If they're shy and they don't talk enough on the assessment, guess what? They come out Limited English Proficient.

An elementary school teacher in Long Beach suggested that subjectivity in the test results might also be related to the individual administering the test:

> I've seen the difference [between students' low test scores and their higher ability], and so it didn't seem appropriate for them to get that score. But I'm not sure if maybe they were just shy with the individual that was testing them or they didn't understand the questions . . .

State functionaries are not unaware of these issues. A California Department of Education (CDE) official in the Language Policy and Leadership Office explained,

> For very young children, a lot of schools report that it's difficult to put them in the testing environment that way. They're not used to stimulus-response yet—they're too young, they don't want to participate, they get nervous—a lot of factors for the very little children.

Although these examples refer only to the youngest students, some respondents raised the question as to whether the LPS is, in fact, testing all students solely for English language proficiency or actually just testing their ability to navigate within a system that requires interaction with strangers and adequate test performance. (Remember that students whose parents identify English as the home language are *not* assessed in this manner.) However, other respondents were quite comfortable with the accuracy of the LPS and responded positively as to its accuracy. One San Diego middle school principal commented on LPS scores: "They're accurate enough for me to do the initial placement."

Appropriate placement. Many respondents spoke of the importance of placing students in the appropriate level of initial instruction. Of these, nearly all commented that appropriate placement is important or useful. A district official in Fresno stated,

> I think that, yes, we need to know how much English child[ren] know in order to place them appropriately, and, of course, know also what their skills are in their primary language, which we do.

Of course, these respondents assumed that the LPS is accurately assessing how much English a child knows—a topic over which we have already seen there is a certain amount of disagreement. Nevertheless, there can be little doubt that it is important to know a child's English proficiency in California today. So important, in fact, that the state has instituted a statewide, mandated test—the California English Language Development Test (CELDT).

ASSESSMENT USED SINCE 2001—THE CALIFORNIA ENGLISH LANGUAGE DEVELOPMENT TEST (CELDT)

At the time our interviews began in May 2001, CELDT, the new standardized language placement test for non–native English language students, was being implemented in public schools throughout the state. This test, developed by CTB McGraw-Hill and based on the LAS, replaces any one of several language placement tests that California public school districts could use under former guidelines. Presumably, districts already using the LAS would have fewer adjustments in transitioning to the new system than would districts using other LPS instruments.

Administration requirements. Our respondents obviously raised some concerns about the CELDT. The most common worry (expressed by 58 percent of respondents) is the time involved in test administration, especially that portion of the test administered on a one-on-one basis.[10] One district administrator in Fresno estimated that the individualized section would require at least one-half hour per child. A related concern surrounds the additional cost of administering such a time-consuming test, and there appears to be a certain amount of misunderstanding as to how CELDT test costs are shared by the state and by each district.[11] Finally, several respondents indicated that the only way for them to administer the test was to train their office staff (who are not trained educators) to do it. A middle school principal exclaimed:

> Do you know [that] if we really did this the way they wanted it, I'd have to pull every teacher out of the classroom for the first four weeks of school? . . . which is ludicrous because that's when they need to be with kids. I'm having every one of my support staff trained. I don't know how else to do it because I'm not about to have teachers compromise the other kids in the classroom to do this test. . . . All my aides, all my office staff—I'm even having my financial clerk trained. You name it! Anyone who doesn't work in the classroom as a teacher is going to be trained.

Timing. A district official in San Diego also questioned the timing of the CELDT testing period:

> The CELDT instrument might be a good one, but the window [of time]—also the fall test window—is problematic because we can't use the information in any realistic way. We can't use it for program placement because we get it [the test results] back in January. So halfway through the school are we going to shift programs for kids? Probably not. . . . So do we then use it for program placement the following year and have year-old information? That doesn't make sense to me either. So I'm not sure if it's going to require even more assessment for students because we're still going to need something in the spring to determine placement [for the following academic year].

In response to our inquiries, a state official explained that the CELDT is administered in the fall so as to avoid conflicts with STAR testing in the spring and promote consistency with other statewide data collections. The results of the CELDT are then available for the March annual language census (LC)—when counts of ELL and FEP students are reported to the state—and the CELDT data are more consistent with the annual fall enrollment census drawn from California Basic Education Data System (CBEDS) data. Still, the official conceded that for program placement purposes, test results from the previous fall might be out of date. This conflict may indicate differing state and district purposes—the state appears to be more concerned with accurate data collections, whereas districts may be more concerned with program placement and delivering appropriate services to students in a timely manner.

Costs. Despite CDE's position that the state's funding level for CELDT is adequate, the fact that CELDT testing requires more administrative time probably does imply a higher direct cost to districts or, at the very least, a higher concentration of resources directed at administering the new test to language minority students. Certainly if districts continue their current testing systems in addition to administering the CELDT, their costs will undoubtedly increase. The possibility of an enormous additional testing burden cannot be ignored and should be monitored by the state with significant input from school-level actors.

Calls for revisions. Since our interviews in 2001, CELDT implementation has gone forward amid a certain amount of controversy. The popular press has reported incidents of discontent with the new system based on individual district reports. The largest teachers' union in the state—the California Teachers' Association (CTA)—has called for revisions and the California Board of Education (CBE) has responded by approving several modifications.[12] However, it is too early to tell if the statewide CELDT is an improvement over the former English language and placement system. Given the impact that the test results can have on a student's entire educational trajectory (especially for recent immigrants entering school), it is critical to continue to monitor and evaluate CELDT's accuracy and validity.

English Language Proficiency Redesignation

One aspect of the English language assessment process involves redesignating students from limited to fluent English proficiency. The English proficiency of language minority students classified as English language learners is reassessed after they spend a certain amount of time in California schools.[13] Students meeting certain criteria are then reclassified as fluent English proficient (FEP). While there appears to be some variation in the criteria for ELL to FEP redesignation across the five case study districts, they are similar in that the process in each relies on multiple indicators—including the CELDT—rather than a single measure.

ACCURACY AND DIFFICULTY

Our respondents expressed three major concerns about redesignation: the accuracy of the process (35.9 percent), the level of difficulty in the assessments used for redesignation (28.1 percent), and the consistency of the process (12.5 percent). Most of the respondents who mentioned accuracy, however, were confident that the process is accurate. Respondents often mentioned the issues of accuracy and difficulty together, but the majority of respondents who talked about the difficulty of the process appeared to be satisfied that when a student is reclassified as FEP, that student really *is* FEP. Respondents who discussed the difficulty of achieving FEP designation reported that language minority students must meet very high standards before they are eligible for redesignation. Respondents in at least two of the districts mentioned that students must achieve at least the 36th percentile on the STAR test to be classified as performing at minimum grade level. The following interview excerpts suggest that students need to achieve not only English proficiency, but also subject matter proficiency in order to qualify for reclassification to FEP. One district official in Long Beach commented,

> I think that the 36th percentile on reading, language, and math is a high bar and that gives me comfort in knowing that we're going to provide support until they get there. It's fairly appropriate criteria at this point.

An elementary school principal in San Francisco mentioned multiple criteria for redesignation:

> The thing that kicks it off is that [the child] score[s] at the 36th percentile on the SAT 9, both reading and math. Then you start looking at the other criteria. Almost always, if the child writes well, if they have a high score on the oral language, if they have good grades [and] teacher recommendations, [but then] if they score [only] a '10' on the SAT 9 . . . It's really hard to redesignate.

Pointing out that students needed both writing ability and subject matter competency, an elementary school teacher in San Diego commented,

> Well, my experience has been [that] it's hard to get a student redesignated as fluent English speaking. On the written part, they have to really write good sentences and they have to know a lot of things that they would be learning; there has to be a good understanding of English and an understanding of what the words mean.

It is hard to argue with "a good understanding of English" as a criterion for redesignation; however, the results in practice are not so simple to interpret or defend. Respondents often questioned how successful native English speakers would be at taking the test if they were required to take it. In fact, many respondents in at least three districts who spoke about the difficulty of the process mentioned that many native English speakers either achieve Stanford 9 scores similar to those ELL students or would not be able to meet the criteria for redesignation if they took the English proficiency test. In fact, by definition there will be many native speakers scoring below the 36th percentile. A Fresno middle school teacher captured the feelings of many on this irony:

> Certainly they [ELL students being assessed for redesignation] are held to a higher standard than mainstream kids. Mainstream kids merely have to get through their classes and move to the next level. They [language minority students] can't pass that test downtown and yet they are more than capable than a lot of the mainstream kids who are already in those [regular] classes.

Other research suggests that these observations may reflect a broader pattern of FEP performance (Portes and Schauffler 1994; Schmid 2001; Stanton-Salazar and Dornbusch 1995). For example, Schmid cites empirical evidence from the Children of Immigrants Longitudinal Study (CILS) showing that FEP students perform better than ELL and English-only students on standardized reading and math tests, and that their grade point averages are higher.

CONSISTENCY

Finally, three topics surrounding process consistency arose: consistency with the Stanford 9, consistency between state and district content standards, and inconsistency of redesignation criteria across districts. Respondents suggested that, unless a certain amount of Stanford 9 content is emphasized in the classroom, students will not qualify for redesignation. Respondents speaking about the current redesignation process also raised the issue of inconsistency across districts—an issue similar to the consistency of the initial testing system. For example, a Fresno elementary school teacher described the problems associated with an inter-district transfer student who had been designated as FEP:

> [In the student's last district], they didn't have a bilingual program . . . they didn't have anything, so she was [classified as] FEP. But in our district—in my classroom or here in this school—she wasn't [FEP] because she didn't even speak the language. Either districtwide or statewide, we should all do the same thing or it's not going to work.

A state official showed clear understanding that inconsistencies in redesignation thresholds across the state have contributed to problems in providing effective services to students:

> What did seem to be a problem is when the student moved from one district to another, and had higher levels of English proficiency, but clearly still wasn't fluent in English. That caused a lot of difficulty. Or if a student was in one type of program, then . . . moved to a district with a different type of program—that also caused problems serving the student and assessing the student.

However, explained the same state official, inconsistency will still exist if the instruments used to redesignate students are consistent but the redesignation threshold varies across districts:

> I think conceptually it should be [the same across districts], but I don't know for certain that it will, because right now . . . the State Board is leaning toward giving districts a lot of flexibility, to the point of even setting their own cut-off score [on the CELDT]. So if this happens, I think you'll lose the standardization that was intended for that test.[14]

This flexibility and accompanying inconsistency may be one example of California's unusual education system, which combines local governance and state finance. Although schools are financed through a complex system of revenue redistribution by the state, governance decisions are most often made locally.[15]

In summary, overall responses about the redesignation process were positive (59.4 percent), with some variation (see table 6.2). District administrators (almost 91 percent) expressed positive impressions of the process more often than did elementary personnel (48.2 percent) and teachers (only 29.2 percent). Although only a few people raised issues about consistency, there appears to be consensus that consistency is important to a successful redesignation process in California. Many respondents thought that the ELL to FEP redesignation process is accurate and fair, although elementary school respondents were less confident. Respondents also agreed that redesignation holds students to a high standard, a standard that is perhaps higher than that for native English speakers.

High-Stakes Testing and Accountability in California

The Public Schools Accountability Act (PSAA) of 1999 laid the foundation for a new set of education reforms in California.[16] Although the PSAA comprises numerous components, we explore the implications of three in particular for recent immigrant and language minority students: the statewide Standardized Testing and Reporting (STAR) system, the Academic Performance Index (API), and the High School Exit Exam (HSEE).[17] These three assessment systems currently form the cornerstone of educational accountability in California.

Although federal and state policies have been moving toward including all students in performance assessment programs, some of the empirical research also suggests that standardized subject-area testing systems used in the United States may be unfair to language minority students because the tests use English. As such, the scores would not accurately assess students' subject-matter knowledge, but rather measure their English ability or lack thereof (Heubert and Hauser 1999). Given that California's accountability system so far relies mainly on STAR testing in English, the implications of the impact of assessments on language minority students should be of great concern for policymakers.

Standardized Testing (English Only)

The Standardized Testing and Reporting (STAR) Program

In the spring of 1998, California administered its first statewide test to students since the California Learning Assessment System (CLAS) (a test used during the early 1990s that ended in 1994).[18] The new testing system initially included only the Stanford Achievement Test Series, Ninth Edition, Form T (Stanford 9) (Harcourt-Brace, Inc.). Since 1998, however, new criterion-referenced, standards-based elements have been added to the testing system. Every California student in grades 2 through 11 is required to take this test each spring unless specifically exempted pursuant to Section 60640 of the California Education Code.[19]

In contrast with generally positive impressions of the procedures and instruments for identifying, assessing, and placing language minority students, the majority of respondents in all categories expressed negative opinions of the STAR test. In fact, in results not shown here, more than 83 percent of all comments about the STAR test were negative.

BIAS AND FAIRNESS ISSUES WITH STAR

Several themes emerged during our conversations about the STAR test. Among the respondents who voiced an impression, 50.7 percent commented on fairness or bias in making these students take the test at all, and 33.8 percent discussed accuracy. Other topics that arose less frequently were the use or purpose of the test (18.2 percent), the relationship between the test and curriculum or standards (15.6 percent), the time required to prepare for or give the test (13 percent), and cultural bias in the wording of the test questions (10.4 percent). Again, some respondents mentioned all the above subjects, whereas others mentioned only one or some of them. However, the overarching theme is fairness.

Over 80 percent of the respondents who mentioned fairness believe that it is unfair to administer the STAR test to recently arrived immigrants and language minority students, citing accuracy, use, relationship to standards or curriculum, or question bias. They also perceived the experience of taking the test itself as damaging for many ELL students, particularly recent immigrant students.[20] Several among these respondents expressed common sentiments about the degree of English language fluency required to take the tests—even for math questions. For example, a middle school teacher in San Diego told us,

> It's so literacy based . . . even the math portion is. . . . They're all very wordy problems where the students could actually know how to do the problem if they just knew what it was asking. So I think they [the questions] are definitely unfair for our English language learners.

This example suggests that if students do not understand the way a question is worded, they may be unfairly scored. In addition, some respondents who mentioned unfairness specifically expressed concern about cultural or socioeconomic bias in the wording of questions (25 percent). As one middle school principal in San Francisco suggested,

> I think there should be so many months in the United States exemption rule. I think if they've been here fewer than 24 months or 36 months—or whatever it was before they said we're not allowed to do that anymore—I think they should be exempt. First of all, the references on the test, most of them are *so American*.

In addition to addressing question bias, a principal in Los Angeles pointed out that the Stanford 9's norm-referenced population is quite different from the district's population: "I think some of the questions are biased—socioeconomically biased. And I know that the norms are not based on the population that we're serving." Indeed, the Stanford 9's sample consists of approximately 1.8 to 2 percent English language learners, whereas the Los Angeles district is nearly 44 percent ELL, and the state student population almost 25 percent ELL. The dramatic difference between California's ELL student proportion and the sample's ELL proportion should be a valid concern for researchers and policymakers alike.

Accuracy of STAR

The second theme arising within conversations about the STAR test is accuracy.[21] Most of the respondents who spoke of accuracy argued that the STAR test may be an accurate assessment for native English speakers, but because it is given in English, it may not accurately assess the knowledge and skills of immigrant and language minority students. Recall that more than 80 percent of the English language learners in California are Spanish speakers. In addition, educators *do* have an assessment tool for Spanish-speaking ELL students available—the Spanish Assessment of Basic Education (SABE/2).[22] The respondents who mentioned the SABE/2 thought that it is more accurate for Spanish speakers than the Stanford 9. However, some of these respondents also told us they do not usually receive the test results.

At this point, there is no such test for language minority students who do not speak Spanish. Therefore, a district with large concentrations of other languages, such as Fresno (41 percent Southeast Asian language speakers) or San Francisco (36 percent Chinese language speakers) may not have an accurate way of assessing the knowledge and skills of recently arrived and other non-Spanish language minority students. Responses in

Fresno and San Francisco suggest that testing inaccuracy is a greater problem for districts with large concentrations of non-Spanish ELLs. A district official in Fresno told us,

> What we need to do, if we really want to find out what students know, is test them in a language that they understand. Right now, I'm sure it's the same up and down the state, except for local creative assessment instruments—we don't know what those kids know. We have no way of finding out because we don't have the instruments; we have no standard instruments. I know we have a tremendous amount of different languages in this state, but there should be for the basic ones . . . some way of assessing those students, what they really know.

In addition, a little more than 19 percent of the respondents who discussed accuracy commented that the STAR test is not an accurate measure of what students learn in public schools because it contains items not included the curriculum or state standards. For example, an elementary school vice principal in San Diego expressed particularly strong sentiments, suggesting that because the test is inaccurate, it is unfair:

> I hate it [the system] for forcing our second language learners to take the test. This is an injustice. It's not an accurate portrait because what's tested is sometimes not even in the curriculum.

PURPOSE AND USE OF STAR TESTS FOR SANCTIONS AND REWARDS

Finally, although most respondents agreed that testing and assessment have a place in the educational system, slightly more than 18 percent expressed concern over the way in which test results are used to rank schools and provide monetary awards. They objected in particular to the fact that a single measure (the STAR test) carries such high-stakes rewards and sanctions for California schools and staff. Indeed, recent research suggests that program evaluation for the progress of ELL students compared with non-ELL students should not rely on a single achievement test administered in English (Thompson et al. 2002).

The Academic Performance Index (API)

The API is a system that ranks schools in California according to 10 deciles of academic performance, with "1" as the lowest and "10" as the highest ranking. At this time, the API relies solely on the Stanford 9 scores. However, in the future, the API is scheduled to include other school-level measures—such as attendance rates and High School Exit Exam (HSEE) scores. In addition, the API features a second ranking system—the Similar Schools Rank (SSR)—which attempts to control for such characteristics as student demographics and teacher qualifications by comparing schools "most similar" to each other. Thus, in any given year, a school could be in one of the lowest deciles overall, yet ranked a "10" in the SSR. Appendix E contains a general discussion of our findings about the API, many of which are interesting but not explicitly tied to immigrant issues.

ACCURACY

Accuracy in rankings emerged as the most important issue among our respondents. The concern expressed most often was that rankings may not be accurate because even the "similar schools" component may not be comparing schools that are truly "alike" despite having a certain number of similar student and teacher characteristics. Although the API considers a school's English language learner population, it considers neither the level of language proficiency among these students nor the percentage of recent immigrant students. And a district official in Long Beach specified a problem with the SSR's construction—it does not disaggregate English ability by ability level. Thus, two schools that may appear to be similar based on their total percentage of English learners may, in fact, be quite different from each other. For example, schools A and B might each serve the same percentage of ELL students, yet all of the ELL students at school A might demonstrate very low levels of English proficiency, whereas half of the ELLs at school B might exhibit low-level English proficiency, while 25 percent might operate at the middle ranges of English proficiency and 25 percent might demonstrate nearly fluent English proficiency. This hypothetical example illustrates problems with the SSR that could affect the ranking of and resulting resources allocated to schools with high proportions of recent immigrant and language minority students.

IMPROVEMENT STRATEGIES

If more school personnel—particularly the teachers we interviewed—better understood the "similar schools" component of the rankings, then some respondents would likely be more favorable towards the API. In the future, negative opinions of the API may decline as California incorporates more standards-based criteria and other elements not tied to the norm-referenced Stanford 9 (such as attendance rates and the HSEE) into the API.[23] The state needs to address the sense of lingering unfairness that ranking systems provoke among many educators working with recent immigrant and ELL students. This is certainly true for other states across the country.

Accentuate the Positive and Eliminate the Negative

Assessment and placement systems significantly affect recent immigrant and language minority students in California's public schools. Most respondents had positive opinions about the systems that specifically target language minority students—the HLS, LPS, and redesignation systems. However, educators expressed some difficult and poignant thoughts about these systems—opinions that policymakers should address. Most respondents have negative impressions of the assessment systems designed for all students—the STAR, API, and HSEE—because these assessments are not specifically designed to assess language minority students. Although some districts do use an alternative test for Spanish language students, results are often not available to educators. Furthermore, this test has no relevance to the academic assessment of English language learners who speak one of the other 54 specific languages tracked by the language census in California in 2001 and numerous "other" languages not tracked at all. Themes of inequity and inaccuracy in the processes emerge numerous times throughout the conversations about standards and assessment.

Respondents also called for consistency across the state and with the standards, suggesting that the system becomes dysfunctional if even one component is out of alignment with the others. Inconsistent information across schools and districts in the state may cause personnel to believe that particular systems are not working correctly or do not even exist. This "disconnect" was evident in conversations about the API, which is a cornerstone of California's recent focus on accountability and a policy instrument that affects the overwhelming majority of students, including recent immigrant and language minority students. The most worrisome issue is the potential for the language assessment system to hold English language learners and many immigrants to a higher standard than native speakers are required to meet. If this is true, the possibilities for stigmatization and unfair treatment of immigrant students are indeed troubling. States with high immigrant and ELL populations like California's have an obligation to ensure that tests of English ability are just that. How exactly to accomplish this goal is beyond the scope of this study, but this is certainly an area where the federal government could help fund states in evaluating their own assessments. A federal role is appropriate for several reasons: (1) immigration policy and much language minority policy are set federally, (2) general testing guidelines and goals are now set nationally by the No Child Left Behind (NCLB) legislation, and (3) enough states are affected that the issue could be considered national in scope. The national trends in accountability, spurred on by NCLB, have made testing high stakes for all public students, but as we have explored throughout this study, the stakes (and standards) may be just that much higher for immigrant students.

N O T E S

1. For example, some schools have received large monetary rewards for increasing test scores, while others have been sanctioned for not increasing scores.

2. Latino respondents (48 percent) appear to be more satisfied than Asians (38.5 percent) or African Americans (26 percent). See PPIC surveys for methodology, exact wording of questions, and error margins.

3. A language minority student is a non-native English speaker and can be an ELL or an FEP student.

4. We discuss our results for the HSEE very little because our focus is elementary and middle schools and because the number of respondents with opinions about it was low.

5. The semistructured nature of the interview allows interviewers to probe beyond the answers to the standard questions and topics in the interview protocol. It also allows respondents to contribute insights to the way that policies translate into practice and to explain why they have a particular impression. Although the responses were open-ended, we are also able to characterize them across a range of positive (very positive [VP], positive [P], and somewhat positive [SP]); undecided (U); or a range of negative (very negative [VN], negative [N], and somewhat negative [SN]) attitudes using a series of "trigger" words and phrases. Appendix figure D.1 contains words and phrases that compose the criteria used to make these characterizations. For example, a response of "I hate that" is VN, "I don't like that" is N, and "I guess I don't like that" is SN. We place respondents with no opinion, not familiar with a particular topic, or not asked about the topic in an eighth category. Tables with the full range of responses are available from the authors. Because the nature of qualitative analysis is often subjective, particular interpretations of the definitions of these categories may be subject to other characterizations. However, throughout this section the criteria are applied uniformly to all interview transcripts to obtain the highest degree of data consistency possible.

6. The three main types of analytic coding utilized in this chapter are *emergent and experimental posture, multiple coding of single items,* and *category saturation and subdivision* (Lofland and Lofland 1995). Generally, a theme or subtheme is identified as such if more than 5 percent of total respondents talk about it.

7. There is not a standardized survey form across the state; however, according to state guidelines, this information is supposed to be collected at the time the student enrolls in a district. In follow-up conversations with district officials, some districts collect this information on a separate form in the enrollment packet, whereas others include it as a line item on a broader form. Some districts ask for both the child's language and the parents' language and others ask only what language is spoken daily in the home.

8. See chapter 5 for a discussion about how the HLS may label and stigmatize students. In addition, because the HLS triggers language assessments, it is important to consider these insights with those in the next section on the LPS.

9. Published by CTB/McGraw-Hill (LAS) and Ballard and Tighe–IDEA (IPT).

10. Districts may use assessment instruments other than the CELDT, but if they choose to do so, the other instruments are used in addition to the CELDT and the district must bear any incremental costs.

11. Respondents who mention cost have different understandings of the per-pupil costs. For example, a district official in Fresno said, "The state hasn't given a whole lot of direction. They've given basically no money, like $1.50 a student, and you have to have a tape recorder to do it orally, and you know, whether you have a tape recorder or not, I'm sure secondary teachers don't have tape recorders. Elementar[y] [schools] tend to have them more than secondaries. And they're not giving you any money to buy them." Whereas in San Diego we heard from an elementary school principal, "Twelve dollars a kid isn't going to cut it unless I can hire college students to do it." Yet, information provided by CDE differs from both of these accounts—the state is paying for the statewide test contract plus $1.50 per student, ultimately spending approximately $9.75 per student in 2001 and approximately $10.25 per student tested in 2002. Information about the cost of the state contract and its estimated per-pupil cost comes from Mark Fetler, Standards and Assessment Division, California Department of Education (personal communication, October 5, 2001). Information about the estimated additional per-pupil apportionment cost comes from Spears (2001).

12. See Yi (2001) and *Oakland Tribune* (2001). Note that in February 2002, the SBE acted in response to requests by school districts for the state to reduce the administrative requirements of the test, which many school officials found difficult and time-consuming. The board approved the inclusion of "stop points" (that is, points at which the test will be stopped if a student does not have the ability to understand and continue the test). If a student reaches an "early advanced" or "advanced" level at any grade within specified grade spans, s/he will not be retested until s/he enters a new grade span. This provision would reduce testing time and costs for such students. Plans to develop a simplified scoring sheet were approved. The board expects this provision to lead to substantial administrative savings (California Department of Education 2002a, c).

13. Before our interviews, individual district policies set this time period. However, with the introduction of the CELDT in 2001, the state requires districts to assess students annually.

14. Redesignation guidelines from the state suggest that the above concerns are valid. Using multiple criteria, including the Standardized Testing and Reporting (STAR) system (described in the next section), each district may set its own range of scores for English proficient students in reading and math with which to compare the performance

of English language learners. For a full description of the reclassification guidelines, see California Department of Education ("Guidelines").

15. For a detailed history of California's education finance and governance system, see Sonstelie, Brunner, and Ardon (2000).

16. For a more detailed description of the PSAA and its implications for schools, staff, and students, see Betts and Danenberg (2002).

17. We use the terms STAR, SAT 9, and Stanford 9 interchangeably—as do many of our respondents.

18. For an overview of the CLAS test results and the policy debate that led to the cancellation of CLAS, see Kirst et al. (1995).

19. For more detailed descriptions of the testing system, see Betts and Danenberg (2002); Betts, Rueben, and Danenberg (2000); and California Department of Education ("Standardized Testing and Reporting").

20. An elementary school principal in San Francisco elaborated on the additional issue of stress for immigrant and language minority students, "I think it's really not fair for the few children who took it. . . . I just don't feel that we should put our children in such a situation that they're going to stress out. Because whatever score they get is not valid of what they know and what they are able to do because they don't understand the language."

21. Some of the reasons given in the responses about test fairness—particularly that the test measures students' English language ability rather than their knowledge of content—are also examples of inaccuracy in the testing system.

22. See CTB/McGraw-Hill ("About the SABE/2 STAR Program"). SABE/2: Scores based on normative data copyright © 2001 by CTB/McGraw-Hill.

23. Another concern about accuracy is that the rankings are based on a test that is not tied to state standards or a particular curriculum.

7

Mapping Recent Immigrant Students onto the Education Policy Landscape

Summary, Policy Recommendations, and Directions for the Future

Most states, including California, have no coherent education policy strategy for immigrants, particularly new immigrants. The same can be said for the federal government. Current policies are directed almost exclusively toward teaching immigrants English. So while this strategy addresses one critical issue relevant to immigrants and education, the real issues involved in educating recent immigrants are much broader. For example, California has virtually abandoned newcomer schools and programs while other high-immigrant states such as New York and Illinois have embraced them. Apparently, some of the political forces thwarting experimentation with newcomer policies in California also support the "English-only" movement.

To develop and explore the argument that current policies address only teaching English and its implications, we have examined several key sets of questions:

1. What is California doing to educate immigrant children, in particular recent immigrants and newcomers?[1] What are schools and individual teachers doing? How do state and district programs and policies help school and district staff in this endeavor?

2. How are these practices different from efforts to educate the much larger population of English language learners?
3. Should schooling policies direct specific attention to recent immigrants as opposed to assuming that policies aimed at the larger ELL population effectively serve both groups?
4. What are the characteristics of the schools attended by the typical recent immigrant, and how do they differ from those of the schools attended by the typical student and the typical English language learner? How well do schools with high proportions of immigrants perform on standardized tests? On average, do these schools have higher or lower levels of resources?
5. What are the primary challenges that recent immigrant students face as they enter the United States and its public schools? How are these challenges distinct from those faced by ELLs and/or disadvantaged native and native-English populations?
6. Are there social services that schools might (or do) provide or coordinate that would benefit recent arrivals?

We began answering these questions by offering a statistical profile of English language learners and recent immigrant students in California public schools and by then analyzing interviews with school and district staff in the five largest districts in the state: Fresno, Long Beach, Los Angeles, San Diego, and San Francisco. We highlighted the key obstacles to success that immigrant students must overcome, as well as the issues faced by the school and district staff charged with educating these students. We concentrated on elementary and, to some extent, middle schools because, in terms of the school system's influence, the opportunity for influencing lifetime outcomes is highest at these grade levels. In all, we have attempted to untangle the immigrant (especially the recent immigrant) student experience from that of the student in need of language assistance (the ELL). Sometimes that process is impossible; other times it is necessary.

The Differing Experiences of Recent Immigrant and ELL Students and Their Schools

There are approximately 1.5 million ELL students and 200,000 recent immigrants in California. These two student groups are often in schools with different average test scores and different resources; in many respects, however, they often share similar characteristics, test scores, and schools.

Compared with the typical student's experience in California, recent immigrants and English language learners attend schools where teachers are less experienced, have lower education levels, and are less likely to be fully certified. Future research should explore how expenditure per pupil compares in schools with these students. In particular, it would be helpful to know if the additional funds that follow immigrant students cover the additional costs of their education.

We find some segregation of ELLs and recent immigrant students across schools. This segregation is strongest at the elementary school level and is acute in some districts. However, blacks and free lunch–eligible students are generally more segregated, and it is difficult to argue that state policy should explicitly attempt to address the segregation of ELLs or recent immigrant students. In addition, the fear that newcomer programs will increase segregation seems uncompelling. The state could support more newcomer schools and programs without too much concern for augmenting segregation, which is the criticism most often articulated by critics of newcomer programs.

When we control for other student characteristics, our statistical analysis shows that being a recent immigrant student is significantly different from being an English language learner. While our qualitative analysis explores these differences in more detail, we can make some useful inferences from the quantitative work, which also sheds light on some of the issues raised in our interviews. Overall, at the school level, recent immigrants are apparently not attending schools with lesser resources, while ELLs are. All else being equal, recent immigrants are not associated with lower test scores, while ELLs are. In some cases, such as fifth grade math scores, recent immigrants are associated with higher test scores.

Like New York City (Schwartz and Gershberg 2001), California seems to have more of a "long-term ELL problem" than a "recent immigrant problem," suggesting a failure of the school system, not of immigration policy. The answer is not to seal our borders, but rather to better educate and support immigrant students once they do arrive. In addition, we challenge the notion that the so-called "immigrant problem" involves only Hispanics and Mexicans. However, schools with higher proportions of recent immigrant and Hispanic students do exhibit lower scores among their English language learners, suggesting that schools need to implement different approaches to educating different kinds of newcomer students. These findings suggest the need for more quantitative studies that could determine if recent immigrants actually have a positive impact on school test scores, controlling for the additional costs and resources needed to educate them. More quantitative work could also determine how the mix of immigrants, particularly the associated mix of different languages at a school, affects achievement. Finally, more quantitative work could determine the most effective school organization and curricula for educating newcomers.

School and District Practices and Programs for Recent Immigrant Students—Many Obstacles to Overcome

Whether or not districts or states choose to encourage even limited experimentation with newcomer policies and programs, newcomer policy *is* happening—every day in every school and classroom with significant populations of recent immigrants. Districts and schools have, in fact, explicitly developed formal (de jure) newcomer policies. In addition, informal (de facto or ad hoc) newcomer practices and programs have also arisen, and we find far more of the latter than the former. Teachers and other school staff are making daily decisions about how to educate newcomers. In other words, the state and most districts have essentially decentralized newcomer policy to the school level and, in many ways, to the classroom level. Here, policy development is idiosyncratic, even if it is often well thought out and tailored to the particular needs of the recent immigrant students. It is less clear if, as is, the practices developed are effective for all students in classrooms with significant numbers of recent immigrants.

Effective education of recent immigrants may require states and districts to develop more nuanced approaches—beyond language assistance—for supporting recent immigrants who enroll in elementary and middle school. California does sponsor several important programs that support schools' efforts to assist recent immigrants, even though such support is not the programs' explicit intent. Many schools have, for example, received home visit funding, enabling teachers to visit immigrants' homes. These visits appear to improve parent-school relations and increase the number of parents who can enter into a parent-teacher conference.[2] However, not all schools that apparently should take advantage of the programs do, and, of course, it is difficult to determine whether state programs are receiving the proper level of funding to be effective.

School personnel play a critical role in supporting recent immigrant students and their families, helping them make the adjustments and find the support services necessary to result in good educational outcomes. Nevertheless, most schools and school systems remain relatively inaccessible to recent immigrant parents, who struggle not only to navigate difficult bureaucracies while overcoming fear of legal difficulties but also to learn to advocate for their children's needs and rights. Many staff we interviewed expressed a desire for more and better training that would help them to improve interactions with recent immigrant parents.

Inadequate translation of basic school documents is a major contributor to school inaccessibility. Recent immigrant parents need help obtaining vital information. This is an area particularly where the California Department of Education and likely other state departments of education could serve an improved regulatory and policymaking function. In addition, immigrant parents need help understanding such issues as (1) enrollment procedures and school choice, (2) school and language program choices, (3) their basic rights to educational and other related services, and (4) the causes and potential consequences of a wide variety of school disciplinary actions. While all districts we visited officially provide significant support in these areas, we found that, in practice, the "navigational" support parents receive is often informal and inconsistent. Immigrant families, too, often do not receive basic information that would greatly ease their children's transition into public schools. At no point do immigrant parents systematically receive an orientation to U.S. public schools or to the types of and philosophies supporting the language instruction methods available to their children. Although we cannot provide empirical proof, the costs of teaching the parents of a recent immigrant student how to navigate and advocate for their child within the school system are likely lower than the value of the benefits (individual and societal) over the course of the student's entire academic career. All public school beneficiaries and stakeholders, therefore, should benefit greatly from successful efforts to foster improved parent-school relations for elementary school recent immigrant students—students who are likely to spend the most years in the system.

Schools clearly function as "connections brokers" to many family services that support poor and disadvantaged families, particularly health services. This role is especially critical for immigrants who have fewer connections to and knowledge of such services. Formalizing these relationships requires support, and though we have highlighted programs that provide such support, they are perhaps not as numerous or well funded as they ought to be. Many school staff welcomed this brokering role, while expressing concern over the strain it places on already scarce resources and staff. It is, essentially, unfunded work performed in no small part out of goodwill. The establishment and nurture of relationships between schools and community-based organizations (CBOs) are important in helping recent immigrants make effective connections for needed social services. Many schools offer parent centers, which appear to encourage parent-school relations and support the schools' role as a link to such social services and CBOs. Parent centers and school-CBO partnerships, therefore, merit consideration for additional state financial support.

Assessment and Accountability of School Outcomes for Recent Immigrants and English Language Learners

We examined six assessment systems and practices: (1) the home language survey (HLS); (2) the language placement system (LPS); (3) the ELL to fluent English proficient (FEP) redesignation process; (4) the Standardized Testing and Reporting (STAR) program; (5) the Academic Performance Index (API); and (6) the High School Exit Exam (HSEE) (see appendix table D.1). The two most common concerns to emerge from our school-level interviews were the accuracy and fairness of the systems designed to identify, place, and assess immigrant and language minority students. Impressions of the accuracy and fairness of the language assessment system were generally positive, although less so among elementary school staff. Our interview respondents' impressions of the accuracy and fairness of the STAR, API, and HSEE systems were largely negative, primarily because these assessments are not specifically designed to assess language minority students.

The potentially stigmatizing effects these systems produce for recent immigrant and language minority students were raised by many school and district staff. In particular, these interview respondents felt that the combination of the HLS and the language assessment system could either incorrectly or unfairly label students. More important, respondents believed that the assessment tests are difficult, that they test more than native language ability, and that many native-English-speaking students would be labeled as English language learners if they were required to take the same tests. Something is clearly very wrong if this is the case. In addition, there is considerable concern over state language assessment tests—particularly among school principals and district officials who worry that the level of time and resources needed to implement these tests correctly both strain school budgets and detract from other educational activities at their schools.

Interview respondents agreed that it is important to identify, accurately place, and periodically assess the progress of recent immigrant and language minority students. However, respondents disagreed as to how best to achieve these goals. Over 80 percent of our interview respondents who discussed the fairness of the state's high-stakes test (STAR) considered it unfair, uninformative, and, in some cases, counterproductive to administer the test to recent immigrants who are English language learners. They also expressed concerns of a poor match between the curriculum for ELLs and the contents of the STAR; that is, concerns that the curricula for ELL students are not properly designed to prepare students for the STAR test. The state of California and other states with similar issues need to recognize these sentiments in further developing policies about testing recent immigrants. This is particularly true given the emphasis on testing in the federal No Child Left Behind (NCLB) Act, and given that English language learners are a group specifically targeted by that legislation. Whatever state officials decide, they should seek "buy-in" from, or at least better communication of their goals to, the teachers who ultimately prepare the students for assessment. Allowing lingering dissatisfaction in a testing system resulting from a sense of its unfairness serves no one.

We found similar if somewhat more positive responses about the API, California's method for using the STAR system to rank and track school performance progress. While teachers clearly viewed the similar schools ranking (SSR) positively, some appeared not to understand how it works and how it helps to compare schools more fairly. Some respondents identified what they felt were flaws in the API's comparison of similar schools. For example, for schools in the lowest end of the lowest ranking, it may be difficult to show improvement because they can improve a lot without crossing the threshold to the next highest ranking. Moreover, since the API does not consider the level of language proficiency among ELLs, the SSR may be harsh on schools that educate the most recent immigrants with the lowest level of English language ability.

Tensions over Choices between English Immersion and "Bilingual" Education

Choices about language instruction are currently being made amid a basic tension between professional educators, who may have opinions about the best educational choice for each child, and parents, who have the right to make the decision for their children. Ultimately, effective decisionmaking requires (1) healthy school-parent relations, (2) well-informed parents, and (3) the input of qualified professional educators. Even if the debates before and after Proposition 227 had not politicized government's policy choices and individuals' private choices over "bilingual" education, there still would be friction. The current policy environment may not serve recent immigrant students well, since it often applies a one-size-fits-all approach to students with different educational histories and needs. It has also obscured the need and obstructed school systems' ability to achieve the conditions necessary for making effective decisions about what kind of education a child will receive. While we recognize the difficulties in devising educational plans specific to each child's needs, it may be that the current system is too constricting in its approach.

We did not find widespread agreement among school and district staff members as to the kinds of students who benefit most from various types of language curricula or the requirement that all students must have 30 days of English-only education upon enrollment. Some respondents felt that 30-day practice worked well for students who arrived with strong prior schooling, but not as well for those with little or no prior schooling. We were surprised at the number of interviewees who asserted that Mexican students who had consistently attended school in Mexico and arrived in the United States in, say, fifth through eighth grades were better prepared than their U.S.-educated peers, especially in math. This dismal assessment of U.S. schools has implications for the placement of students in different kinds of classrooms under the current set of rules and practices. Even those educators who disagreed often expressed frustration because they are required to apply the same policies to different students upon their arrival as newcomers. Recent developments in the public debate do not appear to be addressing this frustration.[3]

There is also considerable tension over the extent and nature of advice professional school staff can give to immigrant parents who are making the choice for their children. While many teachers are supportive of English immersion, we must recognize the depth of many others' commitment to "bilingual" education and their concomitant ability to influence parental choice. Teachers on both sides of the debate seem to feel their hands are tied in some key areas of decisionmaking over student placement, particularly in the choice between "bilingual" and English immersion.

Fostering a Productive Focus on Recent Immigrant Students in a Politicized World

While the political and policy debates resulting from Proposition 227—debates pitting "bilingual" education against English immersion—have been important, they have been overly narrow. In particular, this narrow focus has stymied the development of other programs and practices that might benefit recent immigrants. States with significant immigrant populations like California, along with their most immigrant-rich districts, should examine seriously—and likely support experimentation with—the range of potential school-level strategies and classroom practices for newcomers. In some instances, the state or districts may need to implement additional regulation. Well-designed quantitative studies and social experiments could determine the impact and effectiveness of newcomer schools and programs and other policies targeted at recent immigrants. This is an area where states could support program design and evaluative research to help determine the benefits and costs of such programs. So should the federal government.

Finally, the new federal NCLB legislation has wrought significant changes in funding allocation to school districts that is based on the number of recent immigrant students. The NCLB law channels monies to districts with high levels of *growth* in recent immigrants and away from districts with large but steady numbers of recent immigrant students (such as San Diego, Long Beach, and San Francisco). It is not at all clear that the latter group of districts has fewer relevant needs to address than those with (perhaps) small but growing numbers of recent immigrants. The changes in just a year or two are dramatic: federal funding for the program in California has fallen from about $33 million to under $9 million; annual per-pupil spending has dropped from over $150 to $67; and the number of qualifying recent immigrants has dropped by one-third. In fact, it is not clear that the reported numbers of recent immigrants are meaningful for policy or analysis anymore. Such changes will make it more difficult for districts with consistently large numbers of recent immigrants to meet the challenges of supporting these students effectively, even while the cost of failing to do so has never been higher.

School districts should be encouraged to explore ways of addressing the specific needs of newcomers in their schools. District officials need not only to understand what teachers and schools are currently doing, but also to incorporate this knowledge into an overall strategy for educating and supporting recent immigrant students and their families during their first few years in the school system. Positive achievements with recent immigrants pay dividends to a diverse range of stakeholders for as long as the students are in school, and beyond.

NOTES

1. Because we use data from the federal government's Emergency Immigrant Education Program (EIEP), we define *recent immigrant students* as those who have been in U.S. schools for no more than three years.

2. The state has several grant programs that help support such activities: the Nell Soto Parent/Teacher Involvement Grant Program; the Teresa P. Hughes Family-School Partnership Award and Grant Program; and the Tom Hayden Community Based Parent Involvement Grant Program. Given the idiosyncratic nature of such endeavors by schools, it is important that the state offer means for schools and districts across the state to share ideas and best practices.

3. For example, Brice (2002) reports on a State Board of Education action to delete a provision that would have allowed teachers to initiate the waiver application process. The board also dropped a provision that would have codified the current practice of a one-time, 30-day English assessment period before transferring to bilingual programs rather than an annual 30-day period.

Epilogue: Public Schools Caught in the Hypocrisy of Immigration Policy and Politics

I n our country we perpetuate a paradoxical reception of immigrants in general. During the past 10 years—especially in California, but also in Arizona and other states—ballot initiatives that can be interpreted as anti-immigrant and antiminority measures have swept through election polls.[1] Yet, most recently, California has enacted measures giving undocumented immigrants greater opportunities for participation in our society. For example, in January 2002, the state legislature passed legislation allowing undocumented college students to pay in-state tuition at all state universities and colleges. In addition, former governor Gray Davis signed a bill in September 2003 permitting undocumented immigrants to obtain driver's licenses. Governor Arnold Schwarzenegger on the one hand contested the latter legislation during his election campaign on the grounds that it compromised national security, but on the other hand stopped at opposing immigrant rights for children in public schools and public health programs.

The paradox is evident at the national level, too. In October 2002, the U.S. Treasury Department essentially approved the matricula consular card that Mexican consulates issue as a form of identification to nationals abroad. Undocumented residents from Mexico may open accounts at many U.S. banks and participate more fully in everyday life—all this while the Department of Homeland Security (DHS) tightens immigration controls at our borders. What was formerly the Immigration and

153

Naturalization Service (INS) has been folded into the DHS and divided among the Bureau of Citizen and Immigration Services (BCIS), the Directorate of Border and Transportation Security (BTS), and the Bureau of Immigration and Customs Enforcement (ICE). The Department of Homeland Security and, to some extent, the Department of Justice are charged with enforcing immigration laws and policies. Yet not much has changed since the days when the INS was described by a prominent immigration lawyer as "an organization designed *not* to find 6 million people"[2]—unless they clean floors at Wal-Mart! And while anyone who has ever given money directly to a child care provider with illegal immigrant status basically forfeits any opportunity to work in the federal government, anyone who has ever eaten in a restaurant has likely helped pay illegal immigrants for washing dishes and chopping onions, albeit with the restaurant as the middleman. In fact, most of the fresh fruits and vegetables that we eat in the United States have passed through the hands of an illegal immigrant (Rothenberg 2000).

The same paradox immigrants experience in the larger society is reflected in the public school systems newcomers attend. On one hand, state and federal governments support the credentialing of teachers certified to teach bilingual and culturally diverse students, yet California, for example, has severely constrained the very instruction programs wherein these teachers might best serve some groups of newcomer students. And this trend has spread to other states (e.g., Arizona and Massachusetts; Colorado, however, defeated a similar measure). In addition, younger immigrant students in our schools are often not supported to maintain proficiency in their family's home language, yet by the time they reach the end of high school, colleges require them to show proficiency in a foreign language. In sum, newcomer students and their languages, cultures, and families face an ebb and flow of policies and practices that can come in the form of an outstretched hand or clenched fist. It is no wonder that recent immigrant parents are often scared and confused and do not exercise their rights as parents of public school students, let alone serve as active advocates for their children. On the other hand, public schools also serve as rare immigrant bastions, places where the public sector is obligated to provide services to children regardless of their legal immigration status.

While the immigrant new to this country has historically been treated with ambivalence, what remains less ambiguous is that more newcomers will become a part of the fabric of life in U.S. schools and workplaces.

This trend is particularly powerful in California—the largest immigrant-receiving state in our nation—yet is also evident in New York, Illinois, New Jersey, Texas, and Florida, and increasingly relevant in many other states. Globalization of economic and social activities and markets will ensure this movement. Yet, immigration and the "new" wave of immigrant students in this country are increasingly part of broader processes that are often left out of discussions on public schooling and education policy. Instead of connecting this sudden influx of immigrant students to larger migration issues spurred by the new global economy (not to mention our voracious need for inexpensive labor), school officials explain demographic shifts in their districts with such phrases as "They just showed up."[3] What many educators do not realize is that globalization and its macrostructural forces have changed the places and modes of incorporation for many recent immigrants, thereby affecting the demographics of many school districts especially in large cities. Immigrant students and families are in our schools because our world economy has pushed them here, pulled them here, moved them here, and wanted them here. Newcomer students are the children of a highly desirable labor force that the United States needs for continued participation in the global market.[4] They are also the children of individuals who, all else equal, are highly motivated and future oriented, willing to take risks and make sacrifices for their children. And how U.S. schools receive, treat, and educate—or phrased more bluntly, "churn out"—the students of these immigrant workers will directly affect our country's continued economic and social health and progress.

NOTES

1. For example, Propositions 187, 209, and 227.

2. Interview with Lydia Tugendrajch, December 2000. The number is now likely well over 8 million.

3. Deputy Superintendent Jim Nelson of South-Western City Schools, a suburb of Columbus, Ohio, commented on the growing rate of Latino ESL students in the district: "It's not like they called us and told us this was going to happen. They just showed up" (Roebuck 2002).

4. For a discussion on the segmented labor force (elite/service sector) created by globalization, see Sassen (1998).

California State Programs Serving Immigrant and ELL Students

The state of California offers several programs that service immigrant students specifically and English language learner (ELL) students in general (or that did so at the time of our fieldwork). Programs that are designed for ELL students also impact many recent immigrants because of students' need to acquire English as a second language. Many other state programs and initiatives also affect immigrant students indirectly; that is, educational and social intervention programs help meet immigrant student needs even though the programs themselves do not require that the student be a recent immigrant to participate. Some of these programs are designed to improve parent-school relations and provide health, counseling, and other social services. Here, however, we describe four state programs that explicitly claim to serve immigrant and ELL students: the Emergency Immigrant Education Program (EIEP), the Community-Based English Tutoring (CBET) Program, the English Language Acquisition Program (ELAP), and the English Language and Intensive Literacy Program (ELILP).[1] Of these four, only EIEP is a federally funded program administered through the California Department of Education (CDE). The other three programs are exclusively state funded and administered.[2]

Emergency Immigrant Education Program

The Emergency Immigrant Education Program (EIEP), first authorized in 1984 and specifically designed to serve recent immigrant students, is now part of Title III (Language Instruction for Limited English Proficient and Immigrant Students) of the No Child Left Behind Act. (We discuss throughout this book the significant policy changes wrought by the new legislation, but unless otherwise specified, all references are to the program as it existed at the time of our fieldwork.) The program's primary goal was to provide supplementary programs and services to eligible immigrant students. An eligible immigrant student is defined as any pupil between the ages of 3 and 21 who was born outside of the United States and its territories and who has been enrolled in any school in the United States and its territories for fewer than three full academic years. EIEP itself was administered collaboratively by the U.S. Department of Education (USDE) and the CDE.

Each year the program was in effect, local educational agencies (LEAs)[3] in California applied for federal funds through the state's EIEP office. An LEA was eligible to participate in EIEP if its (1) enrollment of eligible immigrant pupils was at least 500 or (2) eligible immigrant pupils constituted at least 3 percent of its total enrollment.[4] During fiscal year 2000–2001, California districts received $172.50 per eligible immigrant student to provide supplementary programs and services. Out of Congress' $150 million EIEP appropriation, California received $33.5 million to be distributed to 347 eligible school districts that served 192,540 immigrant pupils. Districts did not have to distribute these funds to schools on a capitation basis.

Based on CDE and federal guidelines, school districts receiving EIEP funds could use this money for any of the following:

1. Family literacy, parent outreach, and training activities designed to assist parents to become active participants in the education of their children.
2. Salaries of personnel, including teacher aides specifically trained, or being trained, to provide services to immigrant children and youth.
3. Tutorials, mentoring, and academic or career counseling for immigrant children and youth.

4. Identification and acquisition of curricular materials, educational software, and technologies to be used in the program.
5. Basic instructional services directly attributable to the presence in the school district of immigrant children, including the costs of additional classroom supplies, overhead, construction, acquisition of rental space, transportation, or such other costs directly attributable to such additional basic instructional services.
6. Such other activities related to the purposes of EIEP, as authorized by the U.S. Secretary of Education.

As discussed in chapters 4 and 5, most districts did not have an EIEP program per se, though Los Angeles was the exception. That is, the Los Angeles district actually hosted an EIEP office and coordinator, while school staff in the other districts had hardly even heard of the program even if EIEP funds were being used to finance programs within their districts.

Community-Based English Tutoring Program

Through the Community-Based English Tutoring Program (CBET), the state of California provides English tutoring for parents of English language learners and for other community members who then "pledge" to subsequently provide English language tutoring to English learner students. This program was established in 1998 as a result of Proposition 227 and is intended to help LEAs provide free or subsidized adult English language programs. Local educational agencies receiving CBET funds may use monies to provide direct programs to adult ELLs, notify the local community of such programs, offer transportation services to and from programs, and conduct background checks required of volunteer tutors who work in public school settings. Funding for this program is determined yearly based on the number of English language learners enrolled in LEAs participating in that year's CBET program. For fiscal year 2000–2001, participating LEAs in California received a $35 per-pupil allocation, based on a total of 1,422,907 English language learners and $50 million in state allocations.

Participating LEAs must demonstrate the enrollment of one or more ELL students the previous school year in order to be eligible for

CBET funds. The CBET program allows LEAs to subcontract with community-based organizations to implement English tutoring and related services if necessary. Recipients of CBET funds must maintain documentation that adult participants have pledged to provide English language tutoring to California school students categorized as English language learners.

English Language Acquisition Program

The English Language Acquisition Program (ELAP) began in 1999 and was created to "improve the English proficiency of English language learners and to better prepare them to meet the state's academic content and performance standards." Monies from this program may be used "to supplement regular school programs that support . . . English learners in grades four through eight. Funds may be used to provide . . . newcomer centers, tutors, mentors, special materials, or any other supplemental activity that meets the objectives of ELAP" (California Department of Education, "English Language Acquisition"). Recipients of funds must be LEAs that enrolled one or more English learners in grades 4 through 8 in the previous school year. Each participating LEA receives $100 for each ELL in these grades. When there are more requests for funding than money available, the law stipulates that priority be given to schools with the highest proportion of ELLs.

Districts may also receive an allocation of $100 per pupil—on a one-time basis—for K–12 students who are reclassified as fluent English proficient (FEP) and for those in fourth through eighth grades who did not receive program funding. To receive funding for reclassified students, LEAs must have used as part of their reclassification criteria the California English Language Development Test (CELDT).

English Language and Intensive Literacy Program

Initiated in October 2000, the English Language and Intensive Literacy Program (ELILP) became California's most recent effort to increase the English and literacy skills of ELL students who are experiencing difficulty learning English. This program allocates $400 per pupil for K–12 English language learners. Instruction is intended to occur four hours per day for six continuous weeks (for a total of 120 hours of instruction) during off-peak school hours, such as before or after school, on Saturdays, or during summer/intercession periods. Teachers in this program must be credentialed and/or hold appropriate authorization to teach ELL students. In addition, LEAs that apply for these funds must provide information on the process and indicators used to determine the pupils to be served. These indicators may include results of state-approved language proficiency assessments, the CELDT (as available), the Stanford Achievement Test 9 (SAT 9), and the Spanish Assessment of Basic Education 2 (SABE 2). Local educational agencies with the largest percentage of English language learners may receive priority funding.

NOTES

1. The California Department of Education (CDE) is sponsoring an ongoing evaluation of ELAP and CBET as part of an evaluation of the effects of Proposition 227 (Parrish 2001). We hope that this study can provide some insights for that comprehensive evaluation effort. For instance, in our qualitative interviews, few respondents mentioned EIEP, CBET, ELAP, or ELILP as "programs" when asked to describe the programs in their schools/districts that serve recent immigrant students. These programs seem to be considered more as funding sources than programs, as suggested by Parrish (2001, 45–46). Note that we use the names of all programs as they were when we carried out our fieldwork.

2. In addition, there is an array of federally funded programs, such as the Migrant Education Program, and a number of smaller, often-localized programs receiving state support, such as the Local Library Language and Literacy Intensive Program and the English Language Development Professional Development Institute, operated by the University of California to provide professional development to teachers of English language learners. Of course, the federal government's large compensatory programs (most notably Title I) impact disadvantaged immigrant and ELL children. However, the Board on Children and Families (1995, 80) asserts that such programs "could serve low-income immigrant children, but has failed to do so in a systematic way."

3. Local educational agencies in California are defined as school districts, county offices of education, and charter schools.

4. Private schools could participate in EIEP by requesting that their immigrant student counts be included with those of the school district within whose geographical jurisdiction they were located.

Data Sources, Descriptive Methods, and Additional Quantitative Analysis

T his appendix contains (1) information about data sources used for our quantitative analysis, (2) analytic methods for descriptive statistics, (3) coding schemes for nationalities and language groupings, and (4) additional data and analysis related to chapters 2 and 3.

Data Sources

Much of the challenge of analyzing immigrant students in California schools stems from inadequate data collections for at least three important student characteristics. Because individual-level student data are not reported to the state, any overlaps among immigrant and English language status, immigrant and poverty status, and immigrant and ethnic/racial status cannot be reliably calculated. However, we can use school- and district-level data collections to analyze the distribution of single characteristics, such as recent immigrant and English language learner (ELL) status across districts and schools in California.

Emergency Immigrant Education Program (EIEP)[1]

DISTRICT-LEVEL DATA

Data collected each February from applications that local educational agencies (LEAs) submitted to the Emergency Immigrant Education Program (EIEP) included counts of eligible students (Part II—Eligible Immigrant Student Enrollment by Grade Level, and Part IV—Student National Origin Report [SNOR]).[2] This census of immigrant students was conducted as part of the requirements LEAs had to fulfill in order to receive federal funding for eligible immigrant students under the Improving America's Schools Act, Title VII, Part C. Both public and private school students (through a public LEA) were eligible for funding if the LEA met the following conditions: (1) an enrollment of at least 500 eligible immigrant pupils and/or (2) the number of eligible immigrant pupils represented at least 3 percent of the LEA's total enrollment. If an LEA had eligible immigrant students under the student eligibility described in chapter 1, but did not have enough students to qualify under the threshold described above, it did not participate in the census. Students from U.S. territories such as Saipan, Mariana Islands, Guam, Marshall Islands, Samoa, and Puerto Rico were also excluded from the census. Therefore, the recent immigrant student count in California (and nationwide) was likely to be understated. A table listing total enrollment, the percentage of EIEP enrollment, the percentage of ELL enrollment, and the change in the latter two measures between 1997–1998 and 1999–2000 in districts for which we had data in all three years by county is available at http://www.urban.org/pubs/bilingual.

SCHOOL-LEVEL DATA

Although the EIEP data were collected each year under the federal guidelines, there were no requirements for data collection at the school level. Because the data were submitted by district rather than by school, we discovered some variation across districts in exactly what level of data collection existed—some districts aggregate directly from individual student data in a centralized data system without regard to which school the EIEP student actually attended, whereas other districts collected data on a school-by-school basis. We were unable to obtain school-level data from districts that used the former data collection method. And even in cases where districts collected data by school, the school-level data we received varied—some districts provided us with national origin counts, some with grade-level counts, and in one case, only counts for grades 2 through 11. Some districts provided us with 1999–2000 counts, whereas others provided us with 2000–2001 counts. Because of this inconsistency, we used only the total count at each school to create percentages of EIEP students and EIEP enrollment weight variables. In the case of the district that provided data for grades 2 through 11 only, we calculated the percentage of EIEP students using a denominator that was the sum of grade 2 through 11 enrollment at the school, and the EIEP-enrollment weight as the sum of grade 2 through 11 EIEP enrollment. Because the dataset with which we merged the EIEP data was for 1999–2000, the EIEP percentages and weights should be considered estimates. We refer to all data in the database we created as "EIEP data."

California Basic Educational Data System (CBEDS)

The California Basic Educational Data System (CBEDS) is an annual data collection system maintained and supported by the Educational Demographics Unit in the California Department of Education (CDE). It contains individual-level, credentialed-personnel data and summary-level student and program data at the school and district levels. These data are collected through three report forms each October: the Professional Assignment Information Form (PAIF), the School Information Form (SIF), and the County/District Information Form (CDIF).

The PAIF collects individual data on credentialed personnel in California's public schools for such variables as gender, ethnicity, education level, experience, and types of credentials held. The PAIF also collects information on specific classes taught and student counts per section for each teacher. In 1997, this dataset included over 307,000 individual observations and over 100 variables. By 1999, the number of observations had increased to over 322,000.

The school-level data (collected on the SIF) contain variables of two general types: staff and student counts, and program types. Staff and student counts consist of classified staff counts and student enrollment, including student counts in specific types of programs (such as college preparatory and vocational education curricula), as well as graduate and dropout counts. These variables are enumerated by gender and ethnicity. Program types also include such variables as technology, educational calendar, and alternative education. In 1997, the SIF contained over 500 variables reported for each of the 8,179 public schools in California. By 1999, the SIF included 8,563 schools. Likewise, the CDIF is used to collect county and district data for the CBEDS.

Cal-Works (Formerly Aid to Families with Dependent Children [AFDC])

This school-level dataset contains counts and percentages of California children in families receiving Cal-Works funds and children enrolled in free and reduced-price meal programs. According to the CDE, these data are collected each October through the cooperative efforts of the schools, districts, county offices of education, and the county offices of health and welfare. Schools report their meal program enrollment data annually, based on their October meal program enrollment files.

The Language Census (LC)

The language census is a school-level summary that each March collects four types of data elements for the current school year. First, it enumerates the number of ELL and fluent English proficient (FEP) students in California public schools (K–12) by grade and primary language other than English. Second, it counts the number of ELL students enrolled in specific instructional settings or services by type of setting or service. Third, it summarizes the number of ELL students from the prior year who have been redesignated to FEP during the current year. Fourth, it tallies the number of bilingual staff providing instructional services to ELL students by primary language of instruction. Our analysis uses only the first of these elements to calculate an overall ELL percentage for each school. For the district-level analyses, we aggregate the data in each of the latter three data collections and match them to district-level EIEP data.

Standardized Testing and Reporting (STAR) Test Results

The Standards, Curriculum, and Assessment Division of the California Department of Education maintains the Standardized Testing and Reporting (STAR) file. This file contains results from the Stanford Achievement Test Series, Ninth Edition, Form T (Stanford 9) administered by Harcourt Brace Educational Measurement. These results are reported at the school level in two ways for each subject area and grade level (grades 2–11 only): first, for all students tested in the subject area or grade level, and second, for ELL students tested. From these two measures, we also calculated non-ELL students' test scores.

The Stanford test covers six subject areas: (1) reading, (2) math, (3) language (written expression), (4) spelling, (5) science, and (6) history/social science. Students in grades 2 through 8 are required by California Senate Bill 376 (1997) (California Department of Education 2001) to take tests in the first four subject areas above. Students in grades 9 through 11 are required to take tests in areas 1, 2, 3, 5, and 6 above. Our analysis focuses on the first two subject tests.

The following six statistics were reported at the school, district, county, and state level: total number of scores valid in each subject and grade, the mean scaled score (MSS), the percentage of normal curve equivalency, the percentage scoring above the 75th percentile (based on national norms), the percentage scoring at or above the 50th percentile, and the percentage scoring above the 25th percentile. We focus principally on the MSS in our analysis.[3]

Descriptive Methods

Exposure Index

Exposure indices measure the degree of contact between immigrants and other types of students. For example, the exposure of immigrant students X to students of type Y is calculated as:

$$E_{XY} = \sum x_i(y_i/t_i)/\sum x_i = \sum [(x_i/\sum x_i)(y_i/t_i)]$$

Where t = total number of students,
x = number of immigrants,
y = number of students in the comparison group,
i indexes the schools.[4]

In other words, E_{XY} measures the percentage of the students of type Y in the school attended by the "average" X student.

Dissimilarity Index

Dissimilarity indices measure the proportion of all immigrants (or other group) who would have to change schools in order for the group to be evenly distributed across schools. The dissimilarity index is calculated as:

$$D = \sum \left| x_i / \sum x_i - y_i / \sum y_i \right| / 2$$

Where x_i = number of immigrants in school i,
y_i = number of non-immigrants in school i.

D ranges from a low of zero (when immigrants and non-immigrants are distributed identically) to a high of one (when immigrants are completely segregated). For comparison purposes, we also calculate dissimilarity indices for ELL students and other demographic groups. Although the index is typically calculated on a scale of zero to one (White 1986), we discuss the indices in terms of the percentage of students that would have to move to eliminate segregation—in other words, we multiply the value that this formula yields by 100.

Methodology for Pupil-Teacher Ratio, Average Class Size, and Weight Variable Calculations[5]

Pupil-Teacher Ratios

Pupil-teacher ratios are calculated at the school level as number of students divided by number of full-time equivalent (FTE) teachers, where full-time equivalency is calculated by CDE as the percentage of a full-time job the teacher holds. FTE is, thus, similar in California to other states—an approximation that standardizes what it means to have a full-time employee, so that counts of the workforce can be compared across schools and districts.

Average Class Sizes

Average class sizes for each teacher are calculated based on up to eight classes or sections per teacher as:

$$\frac{\sum_{s=1}^{8} a_s b_s}{\sum_{s=1}^{8} a_s}$$

Where a = 1 or 0 values coded for whether a teacher teaches that section
or not,

b = the number of students in the section,

s indexes the eight sections.

These teacher-specific averages of class size are then aggregated to school or statewide averages by taking a weighted mean, where the weight is each teacher's proportion of full-time equivalency.

For specific grades and subjects, the teacher-specific average class size was calculated by replacing the a_s variables in the above formula with a variable that equals 1 if the given section s corresponds to the subject area or the grade level being analyzed, and 0 (zero) otherwise. To aggregate the resulting measures of average class size for a given subject or grade level for each teacher to school-level or statewide averages, these teacher-specific measures are averaged using weights. In this case, the weight variable is the proportion of the teachers' time devoted to the given subject or grade level multiplied by the teachers' FTE proportion. For example, if a teacher teaches two sections of science and two sections of math, her full-time equivalency is 100 percent, and she spends 25 percent of her time each day in one of the four classrooms, then the class size for each subject would be weighted as:

proportion of teacher's time · proportion of FTE = $(2 \cdot 0.25) \cdot (1) = 0.5$.

This formula gives smaller weight to part-time faculty members. For example, consider a second teacher, working three-quarter time, who teaches two math courses and one science course, each taking up 33 percent of her time. The weight for math would be:

$(2 \cdot 0.33) \cdot (0.75) = 0.5,$

whereas the weight for science would be 0.25.

In effect, by weighting the teacher's full-time equivalency in the specific subject or grade, we are calculating average class sizes weighted by the time that the teacher spends on the given subject or grade level.

School-Level Teacher Characteristic Means

We take weighted means of overall teacher characteristics, such as the proportions for ethnicity, experience, education, and credentials at each school. These means are weighted by the teacher's percentage of full-time equivalency. When taking means for teacher characteristics, such as education, experience, and specific subject authorizations, we weight the means by the teacher's full-time equivalency *in that subject,* as described in the section above.

EIEP National Origin and ELL Language Categories

EIEP National Origin Groupings

Using geographic criteria along with information from the International Monetary Fund (IMF), the World Bank, the U.S. Department of State, and the U.S. Department of Justice, Immigration and Naturalization Service, we identified 16 categories of national origins (table B.1).

ELL Language Groupings

Using the Ethnologue, we identified 13 language categories based on geographic distribution and similarities of the languages in the language census (table B.2).

These two categories allow us to aggregate what we argue are groups sharing similar cultural characteristics and facilitate the analysis in tables B.3, B.4, and B.5, as well as in chapter 2.

Additional Detail on Methods and Groups

Tables B.3 through B.6 provide data useful for readers of chapters 2 and 3 who want additional detail. They also provide examples and applications of each of the statistical methods and groupings discussed above. For example, the columns labeled "Recent immigrant–weighted mean" contain simply the exposure indices for RI students. That is, they tell us the characteristics in percentage terms of the school attended by the average RI student. Tables B.4 and B.5 use the language groupings described in table B.2.

Additional Discussion of Outcome Models with Recent Immigrant*Hispanic Interaction Term

Tables B.7 and B.8 specify models similar to those in tables 3.1 and 3.2 but use an interaction term for the proportion of recent immigrants with the

Table B.1. *National Origin Groupings*

Country group	Countries or nationalities
Mexico	Mexico
Central America	Belize, Costa Rica, El Salvador, Guatemala, Honduras, Nicaragua, Panama
Other Latin America, Portuguese or Spanish speaking	Argentina, Bolivia, Brazil, Chile, Colombia, Cuba, Dominican Republic, Ecuador, Paraguay, Peru, Uruguay, Venezuela
Caribbean, non-Spanish speaking	Antigua and Barbuda, Aruba, Bahamas, Barbados, Bermuda, Cayman Islands, Dominica, Grenada, Guyana, Haiti, Jamaica, Netherlands Antilles, St. Kitts and Nevis, St. Lucia, St. Vincent and Grenadines, Suriname, Trinidad and Tobago, British Virgin Islands
Philippines	Philippines
Southeast Asia	Brunei, Cambodia, Indonesia, Laos, Malaysia, Myanmar, Thailand, Vietnam
Northeast Asia[a]	Hong Kong, Japan, Singapore, Taiwan
China	People's Republic of China (Mainland), Macau, Mongolia
South Asia	Afghanistan, Bangladesh, Bhutan, India, Maldives, Nepal, Pakistan, Sri Lanka
Western Europe and developed Western economies	Australia, Austria, Belgium, Canada, Cyprus, Denmark, Finland, France, Germany, Greece, Greenland, Iceland, Ireland, Israel, Italy, Luxembourg, Monaco, Netherlands, New Zealand, Norway, Portugal, Spain, Sweden, Switzerland, United Kingdom
Eastern Europe and former Soviet republics	Albania, Armenia, Azerbaijan, Belarus, Bosnia and Herzegovina, Bulgaria, Croatia, Czech Republic, Estonia, Georgia, Hungary, Kazakhstan, Kyrgyzstan, Latvia, Lithuania, Macedonia, Moldova, Montenegro, Poland, Romania, Russia, Serbia, Slovakia, Slovenia, Tajikistan, Turkmenistan, Ukraine, Uzbekistan
Africa	Algeria, Angola, Benin, Botswana, Burkina Faso, Burundi, Cameroon, Cape Verde, Central African Republic, Chad, Comoros, Congo (Democratic Republic of), Côte d'Ivoire (Ivory Coast), Djibouti, Equatorial Guinea, Eritrea, Ethiopia, Gambia,

(*continued*)

Table B.1. *Continued*

Country group	Countries or nationalities
	Ghana, Guinea, Kenya, Lesotho, Liberia, Libya, Madagascar, Malawi, Mali, Mauritania, Mauritius, Morocco, Mozambique, Namibia, Niger, Nigeria, Rwanda, São Tomé and Príncipe, Senegal, Seychelles, Sierra Leone, Somalia, South Africa, Sudan, Swaziland, Tanzania, Togo, Tunisia, Uganda, Zambia, Zimbabwe
Middle East	Bahrain, Egypt, Iran, Iraq, Jordan, Kuwait, Lebanon, Oman, Palestine, Qatar, Saudi Arabia, Syria, Turkey, United Arab Emirates, Yemen
Pacific Islands	Fiji, Kiribati, Malta, Micronesia, Palau, Papua New Guinea, Samoa (Western), Solomon Islands, Tonga, Vanuatu
Other	Any other country not listed
Korea	North Korea, South Korea

Sources: Authors' analysis of data from Grimes and Grimes (2001), the World Bank Group ("Countries and Regions"), and Hudson and Espenshade (2000).
   a. Excluding Korea.

proportion of Hispanic students (EIEP*Hispanic). This interaction has potentially less statistically worrisome correlations with other key variables of interest. The correlations (all significant) of EIEP*Hispanic with recent immigrant, ELL, and Hispanic percentages are, respectively, 0.62, 0.55, and 0.56 (not shown). Note, however, that the results for these models, especially as to the coefficient on the EIEP*Hispanic interaction, indicate that multicollinearity may in fact be more of a problem with these regressions than with those in chapter 3 (tables 3.1 and 3.2). Together, however, all the results indicate support for the major conclusions we draw from the interaction terms in chapter 3. For second grade test scores (table B.7), the interaction term is positive and significant for the models of all student test scores and non-ELL student test scores. As with the ELL*Hispanic interaction term used in chapter 3, we can interpret this to mean that, having controlled for the other student characteristics (which include the recent immigrant and Hispanic percentages independently), schools with higher proportions of Hispanics among their recent immigrant populations have higher test scores than schools

(*text continues on page 186*)

Table B.2. *Composition of Language Groups in California,*
1997–98 to 1999–2000

Language group	Language(s) from the California Department of Education language census
Spanish	Spanish, Mixteco
Filipino	Filipino (Tagalog), Ilocano, Cebuano, other Filipino language
Southeast Asian	Vietnamese, Khmer (Cambodian), Lao, Burmese, Hmong, Indonesian, Thai, Lahu, Khmu, Toishanese
Northeast Asian[a]	Japanese, Chaozhou (Chaochow), Taiwanese
Chinese	Cantonese, Mandarin (Putonghua), Mien (Yao), other Chinese language
South Asian	Hindi, Punjabi, Pashto, Gujarati
Western European[b]	Portuguese, Dutch, French, German, Greek, Hebrew, Italian
Eastern European	Armenian, Croatian, Hungarian, Russian, Serbian, Ukrainian, Polish, Rumanian, Serbo-Croatian, Albanian *(new 1999)*
African	Triginya *(new 1999)*
Middle Eastern	Arabic, Farsi (Persian), Turkish, Urdu, Assyrian, Kurdish, Chaldean
Pacific Island	Chamorro (Guamanian), Samoan, Tongan, Marshallese
Korean	Korean
Other	All other non-English languages

Source: Grimes and Grimes (2001).

Notes: Language codes were collapsed into 12 categories and an "other" category based on geographic regions, ethnic categories, and shared culture or history. Mixteco was combined with Spanish, as most Mixteco-speaking peoples are either bilingual in Spanish, or speak Spanish as a second language. Filipino languages were coded separately from other Southeast Asian and Pacific Island languages because of the unique relationship between the Philippines and the United States, including a history of military bases in the Philippines, trade and other relationships between the two countries, and political involvement. Toishanese was coded with Southeast Asian languages because most Toishanese speakers are from the Southeast Asian peninsula area.

a. Excluding Korean.
b. Excluding Spanish.

Table B.3. *Resources for 329 Districts Submitting EIEP Student Counts, 1999–2000*

	Mean	Pupil-weighted mean	EIEP-weighted mean	ELL-weighted mean	Min.	Max.
1999–2000						
District size (total enrollment)	12,273.59	150,772.10	144,584.87	197,563.90	42.00	710,007.00
Student-teacher ratio	20.42	21.17	21.13	21.12	11.72	29.68
Average class size	25.64	27.40	27.29	26.57	13.00	73.50
Average teacher experience (y)	12.56	12.53	12.53	12.31	3.95	25.74
≥ 10 y (%)	50.36	49.95	49.60	48.98	8.20	100.00
≤ 2 y (%)	16.13	17.40	17.74	18.29	0.00	60.00
Teachers not fully credentialed (%)	13.21	15.65	16.85	18.32	0.00	59.19
Teachers with language credential[a] (%)	32.88	31.70	32.82	35.38	0.00	85.47
Teachers with at least a master's degree (%)	26.31	30.95	30.37	29.71	0.00	65.88
Teachers with at most a bachelor's degree (%)	17.45	24.03	24.03	27.08	0.00	74.91
Change, 1997–98 to 1999–2000						
District size (total enrollment)	1,001.35	15,052.52	5,398.90	7,163.58	3.00	29,577.00
Student-teacher ratio	-0.44	-0.35	-0.41	-0.46	1.64	1.51
Average class size	-0.70	-0.30	0.23	-0.30	9.62	-12.03
Average teacher experience	-0.62	-0.92	-0.93	-0.92	2.29	2.00
≥ 10 y	-2.86	-4.18	-4.10	-4.18	8.20	0.00
≤ 2 y	-2.71	-0.68	-1.07	-0.50	0.00	-23.33
Teachers not fully credentialed (%)	3.48	3.16	3.41	3.80	0.00	-40.81
Teachers with language credential[a] (%)	9.09	7.28	7.27	6.94	0.00	3.38
Teachers with at least a master's degree (%)	-0.98	-1.26	-0.69	-1.26	0.00	-6.11
Teachers with at most a bachelor's degree (%)	2.78	2.96	2.01	2.63	0.00	-18.92

Source: Authors' calculations from CDE, CBEDS, and EIEP datasets.

Notes: EIEP = Emergency Immigration Education Program; ELL = English language learner.

a. BCC, ELD, SDAIE, bilingual, language specialist.

Table B.4. *ELL Student Languages in Schools in California's Five Largest School Districts Pooled, by School Level, 1999–2000*[a]

	Unweighted mean (%)	Enrollment-weighted mean (%)	Recent immigrant-weighted mean (%)	ELL-weighted mean (%)
All schools[b] (*N* = 1,092)				
ELL students who speak				
Spanish	76.35	79.89	81.79	86.68
Filipino language	2.22	2.05	1.91	1.18
Southeast Asian language	7.75	7.06	4.89	5.42
Japanese	0.46	0.34	0.23	0.14
Korean	1.62	1.51	1.87	1.00
Chinese language	4.52	2.94	3.13	1.85
South Asian language	0.50	0.42	0.38	0.24
Western European language[c]	0.53	0.43	0.36	0.18
Eastern European language	2.20	2.14	2.50	1.54
African language	0.03	0.02	0.01	0.01
Middle Eastern language	1.48	1.21	1.11	0.58
Pacific Island language	0.53	0.43	0.36	0.18
Other language	1.82	1.54	1.47	1.01
Total	100	100	100	100
Elementary schools (K–6)[d] (*N* = 748)				
ELL students who speak				
Spanish	76.76	81.32	85.15	88.35
Filipino language	2.20	1.94	1.58	1.04
Southeast Asian language	7.10	6.62	4.10	4.69
Japanese	0.57	0.45	0.28	0.16
Korean	1.77	1.52	1.84	1.01
Chinese language	4.56	2.63	2.14	1.67
South Asian language	0.50	0.38	0.35	0.20
Western European language[c]	0.59	0.44	0.31	0.14
Eastern European language	2.01	1.71	2.16	1.30
African language	0.03	0.02	0.01	0.01
Middle Eastern language	1.62	1.22	0.97	0.49
Pacific Island language	0.59	0.44	0.31	0.14
Other language	1.71	1.31	0.80	0.80
Total	100	100	100	100

(*continued*)

	Unweighted mean (%)	Enrollment-weighted mean (%)	Recent immigrant-weighted mean (%)	ELL-weighted mean (%)
Middle schools (6–8)[d] *(N = 138)*				
ELL students who speak				
Spanish	75.87	81.84	81.51	85.77
Filipino language	2.33	1.72	1.78	1.18
Southeast Asian language	9.29	6.21	4.61	5.71
Japanese	0.21	0.18	0.14	0.09
Korean	1.12	1.24	1.68	0.79
Chinese language	4.38	2.79	3.53	1.91
South Asian language	0.42	0.35	0.37	0.26
Western European language[c]	0.48	0.43	0.36	0.22
Eastern European language	2.07	2.14	2.76	1.93
African language	0.04	0.02	0.02	0.01
Middle Eastern language	1.26	1.10	1.10	0.67
Pacific Island language	0.48	0.43	0.36	0.22
Other language	2.07	1.53	1.77	1.24
Total	100	100	100	100
High schools (9–12) (N = 127)				
ELL students who speak				
Spanish	72.60	75.40	75.49	79.98
Filipino language	2.53	2.47	2.59	1.75
Southeast Asian language	9.80	8.58	6.51	8.05
Japanese	0.23	0.25	0.20	0.12
Korean	1.15	1.60	1.86	1.20
Chinese language	5.45	3.89	4.92	2.85
South Asian language	0.47	0.50	0.44	0.39
Western European language[c]	0.41	0.45	0.46	0.31
Eastern European language	3.51	3.03	3.18	2.42
African language	0.04	0.02	0.03	0.02
Middle Eastern language	1.26	1.37	1.43	0.92
Pacific Island language	0.41	0.45	0.46	0.31
Other language	2.14	1.99	2.44	1.68
Total	100	100	100	100

Source: Authors' calculations from CDE, CBEDS, and EIEP datasets.

Notes: ELL = English language learner. "Recent immigrant" students are foreign-born students with fewer than three years in U.S. public schools. Figures may not total 100 percent due to rounding.

a. California's five largest school districts are Los Angeles, San Diego, Long Beach, Fresno, and San Francisco.

b. The "all schools" category includes all the elementary, middle, and high schools plus those schools that do not fit neatly into the three grade spans.

c. Excluding Spanish.

d. Some districts include grade 6 in elementary school, while others include it in middle school.

Table B.5. *ELL Student Languages in Schools in California's Five Largest School Districts, All Schools, 1999–2000*

	Unweighted mean (%)	Enrollment-weighted mean (%)	EIEP-weighted mean (%)	ELL-weighted mean (%)
Los Angeles (N = 626)				
ELL students who speak				
Spanish	88.11	89.85	89.40	93.24
Filipino language	1.09	0.98	0.93	0.69
Southeast Asian language	1.20	1.01	1.00	0.78
Japanese	0.33	0.21	0.18	0.11
Korean	2.27	1.94	2.27	1.26
Chinese language	0.90	0.78	0.80	0.69
South Asian language	0.48	0.39	0.35	0.22
Western European language[a]	0.53	0.41	0.35	0.16
Eastern European language	2.37	2.26	2.74	1.79
African language	0.00	0.00	0.00	0.00
Middle Eastern language	1.54	1.20	1.07	0.55
Pacific Island language	0.53	0.41	0.35	0.16
Other language	0.63	0.57	0.58	0.35
Total	100	100	100	100
San Diego (N = 174[b])				
ELL students who speak				
Spanish	71.36	68.04	60.58	76.94
Filipino language	5.46	7.05	9.10	3.74
Southeast Asian language	10.95	12.25	16.27	10.67
Japanese	0.68	0.72	0.55	0.33
Korean	0.83	0.89	0.75	0.37
Chinese language	1.29	1.43	1.68	0.76
South Asian language	0.07	0.10	0.14	0.04
Western European language[a]	0.85	0.82	0.63	0.36
Eastern European language	1.03	0.98	0.87	0.43
African language	0.00	0.00	0.00	0.00
Middle Eastern language	1.40	1.42	1.42	0.76
Pacific Island language	0.85	0.82	0.63	0.36
Other language	5.24	5.48	7.37	5.23
Total	100	100	100	100

(*continued*)

Table B.5. *Continued*

	Unweighted mean (%)	Enrollment-weighted mean (%)	EIEP-weighted mean (%)	ELL-weighted mean (%)
Long Beach (N = 84)				
ELL students who speak				
Spanish	76.95	76.60	80.40	80.88
Filipino language	2.21	2.43	2.61	1.93
Southeast Asian language	17.35	17.91	14.82	15.27
Japanese	0.19	0.16	0.07	0.07
Korean	0.17	0.11	0.06	0.07
Chinese language	0.40	0.36	0.26	0.25
South Asian language	0.04	0.04	0.05	0.03
Western European language[a]	0.22	0.21	0.16	0.15
Eastern European language	0.30	0.19	0.09	0.08
African language	0.00	0.00	0.00	0.00
Middle Eastern language	0.50	0.38	0.18	0.19
Pacific Island language	0.22	0.21	0.16	0.15
Other language	1.45	1.38	1.12	0.95
Total	100	100	100	100
Fresno (N = 94)				
ELL students who speak				
Spanish	52.35	51.49	53.95	54.99
Filipino language	0.18	0.26	0.21	0.12
Southeast Asian language	39.02	39.62	39.72	41.35
Japanese	0.05	0.03	0.02	0.01
Korean	0.30	0.25	0.16	0.06
Chinese language	0.35	0.40	0.31	0.26
South Asian language	1.49	1.44	1.11	0.69
Western European language[a]	0.16	0.17	0.13	0.05
Eastern European language	3.12	3.33	2.43	1.32
African language	0.08	0.07	0.05	0.06
Middle Eastern language	1.55	1.47	0.90	0.47
Pacific Island language	0.16	0.17	0.13	0.05
Other language	1.18	1.30	0.90	0.57
Total	100	100	100	100

(*continued*)

Table B.5. *Continued*

	Unweighted mean (%)	Enrollment-weighted mean (%)	EIEP-weighted mean (%)	ELL-weighted mean (%)
San Francisco (N = 114)				
ELL students who speak				
Spanish	38.69	34.04	33.76	37.61
Filipino language	5.17	4.91	5.63	5.20
Southeast Asian language	5.97	5.95	5.78	5.58
Japanese	1.38	1.64	0.65	0.68
Korean	1.39	1.76	0.88	0.84
Chinese language	35.81	38.70	39.90	38.46
South Asian language	0.75	0.84	0.76	0.77
Western European language[a]	0.57	0.54	0.54	0.43
Eastern European language	3.69	4.67	3.60	3.11
African language	0.23	0.23	0.21	0.18
Middle Eastern language	1.89	1.78	2.10	1.85
Pacific Island language	0.57	0.54	0.54	0.43
Other language	3.89	4.40	5.66	4.86
Total	100	100	100	100

Source: Authors' calculations from CDE, CBEDS, and EIEP datasets.

Notes: ELL = English language learner; EIEP = Emergency Immigration Education Program. Figures may not total 100 percent due to rounding.

a. Except Spanish.

b. The EIEP-weighted mean in San Diego used 173 observations. Because our qualitative analysis revealed African-language students in San Diego Unified School District, we suspect that the district coded any African languages as "other" in the 1999–2000 language census.

Table B.6. *Performance in Eighth and Eleventh Grades in California's Five Largest School Districts, Pooled, 1999–2000*[a]

	N	Mean	Student-weighted mean	Recent immigrant-weighted mean	LEP-weighted mean	Min.	Max.
Eighth grade							
All students							
MSS reading	139	677.34	675.32	672.32	669.29	650.50	726.00
P-50th reading	139	35.97	33.64	30.17	26.85	9.00	93.00
MSS math	139	671.51	669.32	667.07	664.17	645.80	726.00
P-50th math	139	34.63	31.94	29.30	25.97	6.00	92.00
ELL students							
MSS reading	135	650.04	648.37	648.01	646.67	630.40	673.30
P-50th reading	135	6.24	5.46	5.11	4.54	0.00	31.00
MSS math	135	654.29	652.22	652.53	650.49	634.90	700.90
P-50th math	135	13.93	11.65	12.28	9.78	0.00	73.00
Non-ELL students							
MSS reading	139	686.38	684.85	683.01	680.82	659.10	726.70
P-50th reading	139	45.14	42.87	40.43	37.61	15.00	94.00
MSS math	139	676.86	675.06	673.33	671.03	647.70	726.00
P-50th math	139	41.11	38.72	36.62	34.07	8.00	92.00

Eleventh grade

All students							
MSS reading	131	689.65	692.66	690.07	687.79	653.20	746.30
P-50th reading	131	26.24	28.46	25.34	23.02	0.00	95.00
MSS math	131	694.88	699.79	697.77	695.02	661.20	767.70
P-50th math	131	35.85	41.41	39.40	35.86	0.00	98.00
ELL students							
MSS reading	87	664.18	663.06	661.84	661.32	646.50	705.60
P-50th reading	87	3.95	3.38	2.69	2.32	0.00	33.00
MSS math	86	685.95	684.20	683.89	681.65	670.20	743.60
P-50th math	86	24.09	21.41	20.98	17.98	3.00	83.00
Non-ELL students							
MSS reading	127	695.52	699.41	698.07	696.12	656.40	746.30
P-50th reading	127	30.85	33.69	31.32	29.18	0.00	95.00
MSS math	126	698.14	703.19	701.43	699.07	661.20	768.10
P-50th math	126	39.90	45.94	44.39	41.42	0.00	98.00

Source: Authors' calculations from CDE, CBEDS, and EIEP datasets.

Notes: For each type of student (all, ELL, non-ELL), MSS is mean scaled score for the given grade's scores at the school; P-50th is the percentage of students in the given grade scoring at or above the national 50th percentile of scores. MSS scores can be compared across grades but not between subjects. ELL = English language learner. "Recent immigrant" students are foreign-born students with fewer than three years in U.S. public schools.

a. California's five largest school districts are Los Angeles, San Diego, Long Beach, Fresno, and San Francisco.

Table B.7. *School-Level Outcome Equity OLS Regressions with District Fixed Effects and Recent Immigrant*Hispanic Interaction Term, Second Grade, 1999–2000*

| | Dependent variable (mean scaled score on SAT9 test) | | | | | |
| | Math scores | | | Reading scores | | |
Independent variable = student characteristic	(1) All scores	(2) ELL scores	(3) Non-ELL scores	(4) All scores	(5) ELL scores	(6) Non-ELL scores
Intercept	633.39301** (10.9421)	596.89097** (15.1554)	629.97921** (11.7122)	634.8143** (9.2123)	602.15122** (11.8917)	629.10182** (10.3844)
Eligible for reduced-price lunch (%)	-0.09144** (0.0391)	-0.02571 (0.0558)	-0.13874** (0.0406)	-0.07687** (0.0329)	0.00765 (0.0437)	-0.14434** (0.0360)
English language learner (%)	-0.27124** (0.0534)	-0.08789 (0.0655)	-0.40331** (0.0618)	-0.40516** (0.0449)	-0.18951** (0.0512)	-0.32947** (0.0548)
Recent immigrant (EIEP %)	-0.59752 (0.4051)	0.75545 (0.6322)	-1.02175** (0.4333)	-0.83468** (0.3410)	0.11098 (0.4966)	-1.13441** (0.3840)
Asian (%)	0.15356** (0.0724)	0.33195** (0.1017)	0.19965** (0.0793)	0.10313* (0.0610)	0.27739** (0.0798)	0.13052* (0.0702)
Hispanic (%)	-0.38333** (0.0628)	-0.1588* (0.0913)	-0.30971** (0.0689)	-0.43398** (0.0529)	-0.2447** (0.0717)	-0.37654** (0.0611)
Black (%)	-0.49886** (0.0484)	-0.17825** (0.0800)	-0.52044** (0.0477)	-0.51073** (0.0407)	-0.2832* (0.0628)	-0.49444** (0.0422)

	(1)	(2)	(3)	(4)	(5)	(6)
Filipino (%)	-0.19598**	0.08244	-0.19055**	-0.15589**	0.1989*	-0.21145**
	(0.0815)	(0.1515)	(0.0755)	(0.0686)	(0.1189)	(0.0669)
Other race (%)	-0.91172**	-0.0407	-1.21933**	-0.73252**	-0.30036	-0.84445**
	(0.3686)	(0.5968)	(0.3590)	(0.3103)	(0.4669)	(0.3181)
EIEP*Hispanic	0.01046*	-0.00975	0.02752**	0.01197**	-0.0027	0.02546**
	(0.0056)	(0.0081)	(0.0069)	(0.0047)	(0.0064)	(0.0061)
Female (%)	-0.25778	-0.33987	-0.08345	-0.07371	-0.31433	0.12085
	(0.2214)	(0.2886)	(0.2385)	(0.1864)	(0.2266)	(0.2114)
San Diego dummy	0.72539	-0.52339	2.40093	-1.08532	-5.82638**	2.39885
	(1.7385)	(2.3257)	(1.7984)	(1.4641)	(1.8204)	(1.5938)
Long Beach dummy	7.35956**	5.79342**	9.5849**	3.53613**	4.71001**	3.30666*
	(1.8899)	(2.5136)	(1.9877)	(1.5914)	(1.9653)	(1.7614)
Fresno dummy	-20.60133**	-21.22353**	-19.6147**	-22.77333**	-23.18907**	-21.97768**
	(1.8431)	(2.8007)	(1.8065)	(1.5522)	(2.1948)	(1.6010)
San Francisco dummy	-7.07703**	13.81173**	-16.38415**	-8.6273**	6.70065	-16.55066**
	(2.8521)	(5.2814)	(3.2777)	(2.4013)	(4.2337)	(2.9114)
Adjusted R-square	0.666	0.352	0.6735	0.8	0.5037	0.7245
Number of observations	708	575	690	707	568	687

Source: Authors' calculations from CDE, CBEDS, and EIEP datasets.

Notes: OLS = ordinary least square; ELL = English language learner. "Recent immigrant" students are foreign-born students with fewer than three years in U.S. public schools. Figures in parentheses are standard errors.

* = significant at 10% level, ** = significant at 5% level.

Columns (1) and (4) are weighted by total enrollment; (2) and (5) by ELL enrollment; (3) and (6) by non-ELL enrollment.

Table B.8. *School-Level Outcome Equity: OLS Regressions with District Fixed Effects and Recent Immigrant*Hispanic Interaction Term, Fifth Grade, 1999–2000*

	Dependent variable (mean scaled score on SAT9 test)					
	Math scores			Reading scores		
Independent variable = student characteristic	(1) All scores	(2) ELL scores	(3) Non-ELL scores	(4) All scores	(5) ELL scores	(6) Non-ELL scores
Intercept	679.4202**	638.23433**	684.28197**	688.39343**	635.78177**	690.47568**
	(8.5822)	(10.1752)	(9.5489)	(7.3450)	(8.6298)	(8.2472)
Eligible for reduced-price lunch (%)	-0.10392**	0.02962	-0.13615**	-0.10958**	0.03228	-0.13436**
	(0.0309)	(0.0388)	(0.0340)	(0.0265)	(0.0330)	(0.0293)
English language learner (%)	-0.35687**	-0.13916**	-0.20784**	-0.45054**	-0.0715*	-0.25656**
	(0.0424)	(0.0444)	(0.0518)	(0.0363)	(0.0376)	(0.0447)
Recent immigrant (EIEP %)	-0.11542	1.41506**	-1.05017**	-0.2036	1.06505**	-0.81712**
	(0.3230)	(0.4312)	(0.3723)	(0.2765)	(0.3657)	(0.3214)
Asian (%)	0.22942**	0.1543**	0.21247**	0.03868	-0.0782	0.03843
	(0.0573)	(0.0687)	(0.0663)	(0.0490)	(0.0584)	(0.0573)
Hispanic (%)	-0.25159**	-0.10879*	-0.31273**	-0.28439**	-0.17381**	-0.32222**
	(0.0496)	(0.0622)	(0.0574)	(0.0425)	(0.0528)	(0.0496)
Black (%)	-0.49364**	-0.26102**	-0.53835**	-0.49243**	-0.28737**	-0.52159**
	(0.0385)	(0.0549)	(0.0401)	(0.0329)	(0.0467)	(0.0346)

	(1)	(2)	(3)	(4)	(5)	(6)
Filipino (%)	-0.17133**	0.04894	-0.18674**	-0.15433**	0.16858**	-0.1988**
	(0.0645)	(0.0988)	(0.0633)	(0.0552)	(0.0838)	(0.0547)
Other race (%)	-0.26547	0.79587**	-0.57408*	-0.64311**	0.16316	-0.84931**
	(0.2927)	(0.4040)	(0.3011)	(0.2505)	(0.3426)	(0.2602)
EIEP*Hispanic	0.00736	-0.01177**	0.02389**	0.00588	-0.01239**	0.01865**
	(0.0045)	(0.0055)	(0.0058)	(0.0039)	(0.0047)	(0.0050)
Female (%)	0.054	-0.14386	0.08905	0.04737	-0.15169	0.10346
	(0.1733)	(0.1930)	(0.1942)	(0.1483)	(0.1637)	(0.1677)
San Diego dummy	0.67987	4.97226**	1.05733	0.20352	2.83822**	2.37024*
	(1.3957)	(1.6298)	(1.4999)	(1.1945)	(1.3817)	(1.2960)
Long Beach dummy	1.09125	6.41402**	0.61279	-1.676	5.05147**	-1.58856
	(1.5244)	(1.7539)	(1.6717)	(1.3046)	(1.4868)	(1.4435)
Fresno dummy	-20.36967**	-8.17808**	-20.19644**	-21.47465**	-7.53534**	-20.04428**
	(1.4645)	(1.9362)	(1.5220)	(1.2534)	(1.6434)	(1.3141)
San Francisco dummy	-8.27335**	9.25966**	-8.76199**	-9.11019**	10.02531**	-8.25576**
	(2.2595)	(3.1434)	(2.7313)	(1.9338)	(2.6826)	(2.3582)
Adjusted R-square	0.7471	0.4395	0.681	0.8338	0.418	0.75
Number of observations	696	542	694	696	539	693

Source: Authors' calculations from CDE, CBEDS, and EIEP datasets.

Notes: OLS = ordinary least square; ELL = English language learner. "Recent immigrant" students are foreign-born students with fewer than three years in U.S. public schools. Figures in parentheses are standard errors.

* = significant at 10% level, ** = significant at 5% level.

Columns (1) and (4) are weighted by total enrollment; (2) and (5) by ELL enrollment; (3) and (6) by non-ELL enrollment.

with lower proportions of Hispanics among their recent immigrant populations. In general, the interaction term has two other effects in these models—it greatly reduces the effect of the recent immigrant percentage variable (often reversing the sign from positive, or insignificant, to negative) and it reduces the size of the coefficients on ELL and Hispanic percentages.

Math scores for all students (table B.7, column [1]) further support our conclusion. Overall, in the models in chapter 3 (table 3.1), we found that while ELL second graders attended lower-scoring schools, recent immigrant students were neither in higher- nor lower-scoring schools, all else equal. According to table B.7, however, the impact of the recent immigrant percentage is now negative and nearly significant, while the EIEP*Hispanic interaction term is positive (0.010) and significant (at the 10 percent confidence level). Once again, the implication is that Hispanic recent immigrants may fare well, all else equal, or at least attend higher-scoring schools than non-Hispanic recent immigrants; Hispanic recent immigrants, therefore, fare well from an equity standpoint, although we must remember that this result is conditional upon (controls for) other characteristics, such as race, poverty, and most importantly, ELL status. The opposite is true overall for ELL students.

In the models of ELL scores only (table B.7, columns [2] and [5]), very few non-race variables are significant for math scores, while for reading scores, the association of ELL is now negative and significant. Neither the recent immigrant percentage nor the interaction term appears to have much effect at all. The interpretation of the race variables is largely unchanged.

Table B.8 presents the same model for fifth grade test scores. The effects are similar to those for second grade, if not more pronounced. For math scores, the coefficient on the interaction term (EIEP*Hispanic) is positive for all scores combined and non-ELL scores and significant for non-ELL and ELL scores, indicating that schools with relatively high numbers of Hispanic recent immigrants are associated with higher test scores. All else equal, chapter 4 presents qualitative interview data in which many teachers reported that Mexican students who had been to school in Mexico were stronger math students than their counterparts schooled entirely in U.S. schools.[6] For reading scores, the results are similar though not as statistically significant. For non-ELL math and reading scores, the impacts are even stronger and more statistically significant. Non-Hispanic recent immigrants attend lower-scoring schools.

Finally, for fifth grade scores of English language learners, the association of recent immigrant students is positive and significant, though the EIEP*Hispanic interaction term is negative and significant. This implies that higher levels of non-Hispanic and recent immigrant students are associated with higher math and reading scores among ELL students. Higher levels of Hispanic and recent immigrant students are also associated with higher test scores among ELL students, although these scores are not as high as those associated with non-Hispanic recent immigrants.[7] These preliminary conclusions merit additional research.

NOTES

1. This section relies heavily on a data description provided by the State Education Agency (SEA) that administered the federal EIEP program in California.

2. The data we obtained from the State Education Agency (SEA) are the latter.

3. Due to the varied nature of school district organization, the relatively low number of observations in each type for the participating EIEP districts, and the problems associated with comparing different districts (e.g., comparing an elementary school district with a high school district), we do not analyze test scores at the district level.

4. The first term ($x_i/\Sigma x_i$) represents the share of the total pool of immigrants in school i and the second term (y_i/t_i) represents the percentage of students of type Y in school i. Thus, E_{XY} is the weighted average of the percentage of students of type Y across schools, where the weight is the share of the total number of immigrants in the schools.

5. This methodology is the same one used in Betts, Rueben, and Danenberg (2000).

6. Our results here would coincide with such insights. Non-Hispanic recent immigrants are not associated with higher or lower test scores, although ELL, Hispanic, and black students are all in lower-scoring schools. This interpretation, however, would have to be reconciled with the perhaps contradictory results presented next for the scores of ELL students. Clearly, more research is needed in this area.

7. Remember that to examine the impact of the proportion of recent immigrant students on Hispanic math scores, we calculate $1.415 + 100 * (-0.0118) = 0.235$, which is positive.

Selection Processes and Methods for Interviews

General Analytic Guidelines

The qualitative work in this study was designed to describe and analyze important school governance trends in California as they relate to immigrant and recent immigrant students. This work was done in five case districts (Los Angeles, San Diego, Long Beach, Fresno, and San Francisco), which are the largest districts in the state and for which we obtained school-level data on the number of recent immigrants. We were primarily concerned with several overarching questions:

- What are the primary challenges that recent immigrant students face as they enter California schools? How are these challenges distinct from those faced by all English language learner (ELL) students and/or disadvantaged native populations?
- What are districts and schools doing to help recent immigrants surmount these challenges?
- What newcomer programs are schools and districts pursuing? What other programs and policies significantly affect recent immigrant students?

Appendix C presents and discusses the general methods employed by the research team for all qualitative analysis presented in the study. Additional methods related specifically to the work presented in a given chapter are discussed in that chapter.

- Besides newcomer programs, are there other relevant policy responses (perhaps even informal responses) by local districts, individual schools, or even individual teachers and/or other school staff?

We examined these questions through a series of purposive interviews with three sets of stakeholders at the state level and in five selected districts: (1) district- and state-level government officials charged with operating immigrant and ELL programs; (2) school-level actors, primarily principals, teachers, guidance counselors, and English as a Second Language (ESL) program coordinators; and (3) the growing number of community-based organizations that have determined as part of their mission to support immigrant parents in negotiating the school system. In a typical case district, we met with three to five district staff and then interviewed three to six school principals. We then selected two to three schools for school-level interviews—including at least one elementary school and one middle school. At each school, we interviewed the principal, two to six teachers, and a selection of appropriate guidance counselors, ESL coordinators, home-school liaisons, school nurses, and other staff identified by the principal as having significant contact with and impact on recent immigrant students. Within each district we also interviewed appropriate individuals in three to five community-based organizations (CBOs) concerned with different immigrant groups.

School-Level Case and Interview Selection

We began the interview process in each district by talking with key district-level officials involved with programs and policies for recent immigrant and ELL students. After (or in some cases during) these discussions, we asked these officials to recommend for interviewing other district-level staff and principals of elementary and middle schools with significant recent immigrant student populations. We suggested that these schools could be ones that, in the officials' opinion, (1) were "doing good things" or "being innovative" with this student population and/or (2) were struggling with issues related to this student population. In general, we asked for names of principals at both kinds of schools (recognizing, however, that a given school could in fact fit both criteria). We verified that the schools mentioned indeed demonstrated significant levels of recent immigrant students (not only ELL students) and then interviewed their principals.

After interviewing the principals, we selected two schools in each district (one elementary school and one middle school) to visit and at which to perform school-level interviews. We made these school selections based on (1) the principal's willingness to participate (though in most cases this was not an issue) and (2) the researcher's assessment that the school had significant recent immigrant student populations and appeared to be working explicitly to serve these students. We also attempted to pick a group of case schools that together served a range of recent immigrants. For example, in Los Angeles, we chose one school serving primarily Latino students and another serving Latino and Korean students. In San Diego, we chose one school serving primarily Latino students and another with significant African populations. In San Francisco, we chose one school serving primarily Latino students and another with a significant Chinese population. In San Diego we selected three case schools because one was a charter school and thus exempt from many of the state and district regulations governing the education of ELL and recent immigrant students. We also chose schools with relatively disadvantaged students among both their immigrant and native student populations.[1]

Tables C.1 through C.3 provide statistical profiles of the 11 case study schools, whose names we have suppressed. While most of the schools demonstrated relatively low overall performance (e.g., low Academic Performance Index [API] scores), many showed relatively high API rankings when compared with similar schools. This outcome was partly by design and partly because we requested the opportunity to visit schools that were "innovative," which the district officials clearly associated with relatively high performance. It is interesting to note that some of the schools considered innovative by district staff scored poorly on both API measures (e.g., the Fresno elementary school, which was also categorized by the school district as a "failing school"). District and school staff members explained this phenomenon by spelling out that these schools serve among the most disadvantaged and low-scoring immigrant and ELL student populations, and the API is perceived as particularly inaccurate and/or unfair to schools serving mostly the lowest-scoring students.

We asked the principals to set up interviews with a range of instructors, teaching different subjects and different grades, who also represented a variety of experiences and teaching curricula (e.g., bilingual and structured English immersion [SEI]). We also requested interviews with other school staff members recommended as relevant by the principals, such as counselors, school administrators, home-school liaisons, and nurses. Obviously,

(*text continues on page 196*)

Table C.1. *Descriptive Data for Case Study Schools, 1999–2000*

	Fresno Elementary	Fresno Middle	Los Angeles Elementary	Los Angeles Middle	Long Beach Elementary	Long Beach Middle	San Diego Elementary	San Diego Middle #1	San Diego Middle #2	San Francisco Elementary	San Francisco Middle
Grade level	K–6	7–8	K–5	6–8	K–5	6–8	K–5	6–8	7–9	K–5	6–8
Year-round	No	No	Yes	Yes	Yes	Yes	Yes	Yes	Yes	No	No
Enrollment	948	524	1,424	3,008	898	1,064	982	1,463	1,385	504	557
2000 API rank	1	1	5	1	3	1	3	1	2[a]	2	5
API similar school rank	1	1	6	4	10	8	7	7	10[a]	3	8
Student characteristics (%)											
EIEP	7.1	5.0	18.8	6.4	5.7	6.5	5.9	2.6	8.4	8.7	11.0
ELL total	61.4	39.1	72.4	52.5	88.6	65.1	75.3	57.7	63.3	73.2	36.1
ELL Spanish	51.1	21.2	42.6	49.6	85.3	58.4	54.3	47.0	62.7	46.0	5.4
ELL Hmong	9.0	9.7	0.0	0.0	0.2	0.4	0.0	1.2	0.0	0.0	0.0
ELL Khmer	0.0	6.9	0.0	0.0	2.0	4.1	7.1	1.2	0.1	0.6	1.3
ELL Lao	0.5	0.0	0.1	0.0	0.0	0.0	0.5	0.4	0.1	0.0	0.0
ELL Vietnamese	0.4	0.0	0.1	0.0	0.0	0.0	0.5	0.4	0.1	0.0	0.0
ELL Cantonese	0.1	0.0	0.0	0.0	0.0	0.0	0.5	0.0	0.0	19.4	13.1

ELL Korean	0.0	0.0	27.8	1.2	0.0	0.0	0.0	0.0	0.0	0.0	0.0
ELL other	0.3	1.4	1.8	1.8	1.0	1.8	6.1	3.8	0.4	7.2	13.6
Eligible for reduced-price lunch	48.7	85.5	72.5	84.3	98.8	95.6	99.2	97.1	90.5	64.4	73.5
CAL-Works	49.2	49.6	19.7	29.2	39.5	46.8	33.4	29.0	22.4	14.9	26.4
Hispanic	80.1	54.6	53.2	87.8	85.3	67.0	62.8	60.7	87.4	51.4	11.8
Asian	11.3	26.5	41.6	3.4	2.6	10.3	20.0	11.3	0.6	33.3	62.7
Black	6.1	10.1	3.3	2.4	8.1	17.0	15.3	19.5	8.1	7.5	7.9
White	2.3	7.4	0.5	0.7	2.3	1.5	1.6	6.8	3.5	4.2	6.5
Filipino	0.0	0.4	1.4	5.7	0.8	1.4	0.2	0.7	0.2	3.0	10.1
Other	0.2	1.0	0.1	0.1	0.9	2.7	0.1	1.0	1.6	0.6	1.2
Teacher characteristics (%)											
Fully credentialed	73.7	63.0	80.3	72.3	47.0	73.8	83.6	78.8	81.2	63.6	90.0
White	38.8	81.8	39.4	50.0	28.6	52.4	58.5	74.6	41.5	16.7	69.0
Hispanic	51.0	18.2	8.5	14.4	59.2	33.3	32.1	6.0	50.8	46.7	3.4
Asian	4.1	0.0	42.3	12.7	6.2	2.4	1.9	0.0	1.5	26.7	20.7
Black	4.1	0.0	4.2	14.4	2.0	9.5	5.7	13.4	3.1	6.7	3.4
Other	2.0	0.0	4.2	3.3	4.1	2.4	0.0	3.0	1.5	0.0	0.0

Source: http://www.ed-data.k12.ca.us/dev/District.asp. (Accessed November 21, 2001.)

Notes: API = Academic Performance Index; EIEP = Emergency Immigration Education Program; ELL = English language learner; CAL-Works = California Work Opportunity and Responsibility to Kids program. Figures may not add to totals shown due to rounding.

a. 1998–99 API.

Table C.2. *API Rankings for Case Schools, 1999–2000*

Case study school	API rank	API similar school rank	Growth target	Met growth target?	Subgroups met target?	Eligible for GPA?[a]	Percentage tested, 2000[b]
Fresno Elementary	1	1	20	Yes	Yes	Yes	98
Fresno Middle	1	1	15	No	No	No	99
Los Angeles Elementary	5	6	8	Yes	Yes	Yes	100
Los Angeles Middle	1	4	17	No	No	No	98
Long Beach Elementary	3	10	12	Yes	Yes	Yes	100
Long Beach Middle	1	8	16	No	No	No	97
San Diego Elementary	3	7	13	No	No	No	97
San Diego Middle #1	1	7	16	Yes	No	No	100
San Diego Middle #2	2[c]	10[c]	n.a.	n.a.	n.a.	n.a.	n.a.
San Francisco Elementary	2	3	13	Yes	Yes	No	75
San Francisco Middle	5	8	8	No	No	No	89

Source: http://www.ed-data.k12.ca.us/dev/District.asp. (Accessed November 21, 2001.)
Notes: API = Academic Performance Index; n.a. = not applicable.
   a. Governor's Performance Award (Distinguished School). For further information, see http://www.cde.ca.gov/ta/sr/cs/basis00.asp.
   b. Percentage of students in the school who took the STAR test.
   c. 1998–99 API.

Table C.3. STAR Test Results, Two Most Relevant Grades Available for Case Schools, National Percentile Rankings, 1999–2000

School	Grade	Reading			Math			Language			Spelling		
		All	Non-ELL	ELL	All	Non-ELL	ELL	All	Non-ELL	ELL	All	Non-ELL	ELL
Fresno Elementary	2	21	27	18	31	40	26	19	27	16	25	29	23
	5	14	19	11	24	24	24	17	20	15	18	21	15
Fresno Middle	7	20	30	11	28	35	20	28	38	18	26	37	16
	8	23	35	10	29	35	21	27	34	16	22	31	10
Los Angeles Elementary	2	44	55	41	59	71	56	55	70	51	61	71	58
	5	35	48	18	56	65	40	50	62	31	46	61	23
Los Angeles Middle	6	22	37	12	30	45	18	30	48	17	21	37	10
	8	24	37	12	27	35	18	28	40	14	21	32	10
Long Beach Elementary	2	37	37	37	59	38	62	30	28	30	47	39	48
	3	23	29	22	37	39	37	29	36	27	37	43	36
Long Beach Middle	5	21	38	14	36	50	30	27	41	22	28	52	20
	8	22	34	15	35	46	28	26	39	19	22	36	15
San Diego Elementary	2	28	37	27	39	29	40	23	24	22	33	49	31
	5	28	50	18	36	57	26	27	51	17	27	53	16
San Diego Middle #1	5	18	31	14	25	35	22	28	41	24	24	41	19
	8	27	44	18	33	42	26	32	45	24	26	44	16
San Diego Middle #2	7	21	30	15	25	32	21	26	33	22	23	36	16
	8	30	37	21	30	34	25	34	40	25	26	33	16
San Francisco Elementary	2	22	22	22	54	24	73	27	24	29	25	32	21
	5	26	30	23	47	51	43	30	33	28	37	45	29
San Francisco Middle	6	40	56	23	61	71	49	56	67	43	52	65	36
	8	35	47	15	55	66	34	48	59	27	34	46	15

Source: http://www.ed-data.k12.ca.us/dev/District.asp. (Accessed November 21, 2001.)

Notes: STAR = Standardized Testing and Reporting System; ELL = English language learner. In addition to the "All" category, which includes every student tested, data are also shown for subgroups of students who are proficient in English (non-ELL) or who have limited English skills (ELL). For the small number of students not identified during testing as part of either group, their scores are only included in "All."

the selection of schools and individuals was a somewhat idiosyncratic process guided loosely by our goals and these principals, so our results cannot be taken as representative of those in any given school or district. Nevertheless, the range and number of individuals we interviewed, along with the structure and method of the interviews, allows a rich set of issues to emerge.

Interview and Coding Methods

These interviews followed a set of methodological guidelines from Rubin and Rubin (1995) called "interviews as guided conversations." This method of interviewing calls for the development of a protocol for each group interviewed. Each protocol contains a list of topics to be covered and specific questions to be asked. However, the interview takes the form of a free conversation, which both inspires confidence and trust on the part of the interviewee and allows for a richer level of detail to emerge.[2]

Our interview research team consisted of four individuals who together developed the protocol and discussed ways to make the interview approaches employed by the different researchers as uniform as possible. Nevertheless, in performing "interviews as guided conversations," there is clearly an element of idiosyncratic difference in the manner in which each interviewer performs interviews. The team discussed ways to resolve issues arising from the time constraints of the interviewees, and agreed upon certain questions that would always be asked ("must ask") and others that would be asked time permitting. Interviews in each case district were performed by a single researcher, with one of the four researchers visiting two districts.

We used the interviews to better define the policy issues for both immigrant and ELL students. We allowed the interviewees themselves to define the governance trends they viewed as most important and attempted to have them define issues that go beyond language instruction. In all, we performed (and recorded) 122 official and 6 informal interviews. The interviews lasted on average about an hour; the interviews with teachers took less time, while the interviews with district staff and CBOs often lasted considerably longer than one hour.[3]

Of the 86 interviews used in our detailed coding and analysis (see table 6.1), 84 were transcribed from the tape recordings. Two interviews were not recorded because of the interviewee's preference; for these, the interviewer prepared detailed notes. We did not generally transcribe interviews with CBO representatives or school nurses.[4] Additional interviews were not transcribed if either (1) the interview was in Spanish,[5] in which case interviewer notes were used, or (2) the interviewer decided the interview should not be transcribed for some substantive reason. For instance, two interviews with teachers were not transcribed because the teachers had very little experience (one to two months). A few teacher interviews were not transcribed because they were performed at schools that were not eventually chosen as case study schools. Some of the remaining interviews that were not transcribed were with district-level officials and were not selected because (a) they were deemed repetitive and/or (b) the team gave school-level staff priority in its transcription budget. We do not believe that significant elements of bias relevant to the themes we analyze were introduced as a result of our decisions as to which interviews to prioritize for transcription; however, we cannot assert this definitively. Information from interviews not transcribed was still gleaned from interviewer notes and could be used, for example, in the open coding process described below.

"Simple" Coding of Challenges

The research team then performed two different coding techniques with the interview data. The first was a simple coding of the different challenges immigrant students and their parents face inside and outside of school. This was done in order to be able to catalogue and list the various challenges and determine the frequency with which respondents mentioned them.[6] We discerned 27 different challenges (some of which we divided into subthemes) and coded all interviews for these challenges. The list of themes and subthemes of challenges for which we coded are listed below,[7] where the figures in parentheses report the proportion of respondents who mentioned a given challenge at least once.[8]

1. Health issues for children (20 percent)
2. Lack of health benefits and difficulty navigating the health system (21 percent)[9]
3. Legal issues, immigration/INS issues/related fear (24 percent)
4. Children not living with their parents (25 percent)
5. Children reuniting with parents after a long separation (12 percent)
6. Lack of documents (e.g., birth certificate, school records) (5 percent)

7. Child care to assist parents (25 percent)
8. Parents' working hours (45 percent)
9. Children working (13 percent)
10. Stigmatization by the school system, school staff, or others[10] (21 percent)
11. Poverty (54 percent)
12. Housing (28 percent)
13. Teen pregnancy (8 percent)
14. Domestic violence between parents (4 percent)
15. Corporal punishment by parents (15 percent)
16. Substance abuse by children and parents (11 percent)
17. Navigating the school system: understanding school and school system policies (46 percent)
18. Parental participation/involvement at school[11] (26 percent)
    18a. Parental participation is mentioned positively (9 percent)
    18b. Parental participation is mentioned negatively (15 percent)
19. Parental participation/involvement with children in their schoolwork[12] (28 percent)
    19a. Parental participation is mentioned positively (8 percent)
    19b. Parental participation is mentioned negatively (21 percent)
20. Assimilation/culture[13] (67 percent)
    20a. How well children acclimate to their new environment (16 percent)
    20b. Opinion of importance immigrant parents place on education[14] (31 percent)
        20b(1) Opinion of importance placed on education is mentioned positively (25 percent)
        20b(2) Opinion of importance placed on education is mentioned negatively (7 percent)
21. Communication/language[15] (89 percent)
22. Parents' low educational level (years of schooling) (31 percent)
23. Students' low prior schooling (46 percent)
24. Gangs (25 percent)
25. Isolation[16] (15 percent)
26. Transportation (21 percent)
27. Trauma (e.g., coming from a war-torn country) (12 percent)

In our interviews, we prompted respondents to discuss how immigrants face these challenges differently from the way disadvantaged native students and parents face such challenges—or how the nature of these challenges was different for immigrants and natives.

"Complex" Focused Coding, Theme Development, and Analysis

We also employed a second, more complex coding technique on the interview data. We used a process of focused coding, which included developing subcategories within the themes established earlier, and then wrote more extensive integrative memos prior to the final written analysis. Our research team began a process of open coding (Emerson, Fretz, and Shaw 1995) in which each member was asked to review field notes, interview notes, and available interview transcriptions from case site(s). We reported upon and continued this process in an extended team meeting. In open coding, we simply coded or labeled in the information in our gathered data. We shared this initial coding in order to hear what others had found in their case site fieldwork. We then developed some preliminary themes as a means for analyzing our data as a whole. After our meeting, each team member worked to expand these preliminary themes into more analytic and detailed categories. This process resulted, in part, in the development of the primary and secondary themes, as well as additional themes.

PRIMARY THEMES

1. Challenges immigrant students face
2. Newcomer policies and practices used by districts, schools, and teachers and how they relate to policies and practices for ELL students. Policies and practices that substantially impact recent immigrant students, even those not specifically designed to serve them or target these students.[17]
3. Teachers' classroom practices for newcomers and how they relate to the overall job teachers must do and the learning experience of other students.
4. Stigmatization of ELL/immigrant students, including how assessment, placement, and other aspects of the system are different for non-ELL students.
5. Choices parents and school staff members have regarding the form of language instruction recent immigrant and ELL students receive, including the choice among bilingual/biliterate education, structured English immersion, and other forms of instruction.
6. Improvement of participation by immigrant parents

SECONDARY THEMES

1. Translation issues for districts, schools, and parents
2. Differences among different kinds of immigrant groups based on country of origin or other categorization
3. Inaccessibility of the school system (its people, processes, and literature)
4. Adjustments immigrant parents must make to be considered "good" parents in our school system (and how schools may help or hinder this process)
5. Schools' responses to immigrant parents' work overload
6. Reworking discipline strategies: School and immigrant family differences (especially regarding corporal punishment)
7. Differences in immigrant challenges as students move from elementary to middle school
8. Discernable differences in the ways schools treat or think about recent immigrants as opposed to other ELL students

Our analytic treatment both considered the case districts individually and sought to draw inferences across the cases by examining the attitudes and responses of various groups of stakeholders: teachers, principals, district officials, guidance and other support staff, and members of community-based organizations (CBOs). Where appropriate, our analytic treatment also considered school-level analysis at several of the 11 schools visited most intensely by the research team.[18]

Focused Coding and Integrative Analysis

The next step of analysis involved reading all of our transcribed interviews and coding these in a focused manner, unlike our initial process of open coding. During this step, we read through each interview and coded it with the primary and secondary themes and categories mentioned above.[19] During this focused coding phase, subcategories emerged within the themes.[20] In the process of integrative analysis, we combined sets of interview data that had been themed together, weaving in quotations and relationships that emerge from the dataset. The goal here was to develop theoretical connections with our interview data excerpts and expand the analysis initially written to develop the themes mentioned above.[21] We sought to make extensive use of the interviewees' own words to allow the voices of the stakeholders to emerge.

Once coded and categorized, we quantified some of the data analysis where appropriate, and this was accomplished by analyzing the frequencies of given characteristics (primarily in chapter 6 and in the simple coding described above) (Dey 1993). Where this quantification was either not possible or inappropriate, the interview data were described, although less precisely, in terms of the degree to which interviewees in a given unit of analysis (whether school district or type of school employee or type of school) responded in a given way. For example, we described categories in terms of whether "the vast majority," "many," "some," or "a few" of the respondents fell into a category. This is, in fact, the dominant form of description used in our analysis. We also sought to discern policy recommendations for state-, district-, and school-level staff and policymakers, as appropriate. These emerged from our analysis as well as from the interviewees themselves.

NOTES

1. A more in-depth description of school selection processes is available from the authors.

2. A copy of the protocol is available from the authors.

3. These interviews consist of 1 state-level official; 21 district-level officials; 26 school principals (17 elementary and 9 middle school); 38 teachers (18 elementary and 20 middle school); 5 nurses; 14 other school staff (including psychologists, counselors, staff developers, bilingual coordinators, home-school liaisons, and instructional aides); and 17 representatives from CBOs.

4. We did transcribe three very rich CBO interviews, but then realized that we would not have the time or resources to transcribe them all, particularly since these were among the longest of our interviews. We thus relied mainly on notes and conversations between researchers to glean insights from our discussions with CBOs. Nevertheless, these interviews remain a rich resource that we could explore further, though we do not do so in this study.

5. We did complete two Spanish transcriptions, however.

6. Most of these themes emerged in response to two questions on the protocol, but we used the entire interview for coding purposes.

7. We consider the definition of a theme to be self-explanatory unless explicated in a footnote.

8. We also counted the total number of times each challenge theme was mentioned (repeated) in an interview to get an additional rough measure of the intensity with which respondents perceive each challenge. We do not report those results in their

entirety though we make reference to them occasionally. Themes were considered to be "repeated" in the same interview in three cases: (1) If the topic was mentioned as a challenge by the interviewee, and then, if the interviewer asked a question or made a comment that did not relate directly to the topic and the interviewee returned to the topic to emphasize the challenge; (2) if the interviewee mentioned the topic, then changed the topic but later returned to it to emphasize it as a challenge; or (3) if the interviewee mentioned the topic and repeated it later in the interview after other topics had been discussed.

9. Note that 29 percent of respondents mentioned some form of "health" issue or challenge (either theme 1 or 2). In chapter 4, we refer to this theme as "general health issues."

10. In some cases, the respondents themselves used some term using the word "stigma." In many cases, the word they used that triggered us to code for this theme was "label," as in "the language assessment system labels kids." In general, we attempted to discern when respondents were describing ways in which immigrant students are set apart from non-immigrant students in a negative way or in a manner that has, in the opinion of the respondent, negative consequences or connotations.

11. This theme and the next were coded in this round only if they were mentioned during the early section of the interview in which respondents were asked generally about challenges, and if the themes were not provoked by the interviewer. A later section of the interview discussed parental participation directly; thus all respondents were, in a sense, forced to discuss the issue (though they did not necessarily have to view it as a challenge). The "positive" and "negative" subthemes relate to whether the respondent mentioned parental participation in a way that portrayed either (1) the "positive" aspects and/or benefits from immigrant parental participation and/or their willingness or propensity to do so or (2) the "negative" aspects and/or lack of parental participation by immigrant parents. The two subthemes added up to a little less than 26 percent because one answer was deemed neutral.

12. Subthemes do not add up to 28 percent due to rounding.

13. Note that we did not attempt to discern a definition of "assimilation" or "culture." In most cases, the respondents themselves used these terms. In some cases, we interpreted phrases such as "difficulty in adjusting to a new country" to fit under this theme. The subthemes are not mutually exclusive. In addition, there were many instances where we coded responses as pertaining to "assimilation/culture" even though they did not relate to any of that category's subthemes.

14. Subthemes do not add up do 31 percent due to rounding.

15. Note that while "communication/language" is clearly related to "assimilation/culture," we coded for each separately.

16. "Isolation" was described by respondents most often as being caused by poverty, lack of social connections in the community, parents' working hours, and issues in assimilating to a new culture. In general, interviewees described immigrants from Latin America as being less likely to be isolated because many of them live in communities with immigrants with similar origins who share the language, and some have extended family in the area.

17. This should include, but in no way be limited to, the use of instructional aides, home-school liaisons, primary academic liaisons, and other paraprofessional and fully credentialed school staff in similar areas.

18. In future work, it would be useful to classify case schools and seek to draw inferences about the underlying conditions at different schools that lead to different outcomes relevant to the primary and secondary themes.

19. Different research team members coded for different themes across all of the interviews. While coding the hard copies of our interview data, researchers often also electronically cut and pasted the coded quotes into themed electronic documents. When these data were maneuvered electronically, we labeled each pasted quote with its corresponding interviewee number and case. We followed shared guidelines for keeping track of interview sources and confidentiality developed by the team.

20. As these subcategories emerged, we coded them on the hard copies and within the themed electronic documents in order to more finely organize data analysis.

21. See Rubin and Rubin (1995); note that this book in general was considered a guide to our qualitative analysis.

Coding Criteria for Language Assessment and Accountability Analysis

This appendix contains information about criteria used to characterize responses regarding standards, testing, and accountability in chapter 6. Not all respondents used these *exact* words or phrases; however, if the essence of their statement was synonymous with an example in figure D.1, the response was characterized as belonging in that category.

Figure D.1. *Response Categories and Characterization Criteria*

Response category	Trigger words or phrases
Very negative	Terrible; horrible; awful; *very* bad; *very* unfair; *very* wrong; disastrous; totally/completely against it; hate it; can't stand it; *big* waste of time; doesn't tell us anything; not *at all* helpful; ridiculous
Negative	Wrong; dislike it; against it; unfair; bad; waste of time; inaccurate (not accurate); doesn't tell us (very) much; problem; not realistic results; not necessary; not useful; not helpful
Somewhat negative	Lack of consistency; I guess . . . (followed by negative comment); not used very well; not very accurate; doesn't serve its purpose very well; not very useful; not very helpful
Undecided or mixed impressions	This characterization is given if the respondent states that he has mixed feelings or voices an argument on each side, but doesn't give a personal opinion
Somewhat positive	Don't mind it; I guess . . . (followed by positive comment); gives some measure; serves its purpose; somewhat useful; tells us a little; necessary; somewhat helpful
Positive	For it; good; fair; like it; useful; accurate; tells us something; no problem; helpful; nice; important
Very positive	Great; wonderful; *very* good; *very* fair; totally for it; love it; *very* useful; tells us a lot; *very* accurate; *very* helpful; *very* important
No opinion or not covered	This characterization is given if the respondent states that he has no opinion or is not familiar with the topic, or if the topic wasn't covered in the interview

APPENDIX E

Additional Discussion on General Impressions of the Academic Performance Index (API)

Our research revealed interesting insights about the API that, while not directly relevant to our discussion of immigrant students, could prove of interest to our readers. Thus we include a discussion of those insights here. We found a slightly more positive impression of the API than we found of the Standardized Testing and Reporting (STAR) system—only 60 percent of respondents overall had a negative impression of the API, compared with an 83 percent negative impression of the STAR. Given that the ranking system until the 1999–2000 academic year was based on the STAR, it is incongruous that impressions of the API were more positive. However, this finding may reflect respondents' generally positive attitudes toward accountability even though they lack information about exactly how the API is constructed. It also may be that the Similar Schools Rank (SSR) places the STAR results into a context that made respondents more comfortable with the results (see table E.1).[1]

Among all respondents who had impressions of the API, three themes arose: use of the rankings (65.3 percent), fairness of the index (31.9 percent), and accuracy of the rankings (26.4 percent). Often, respondents combined these three themes. The majority of people who talked about using the API to make comparisons had favorable impressions of this use—particularly the similar-schools comparisons and gains (or losses) for a given school over time. A middle school principal in San Diego

Table E.1. *Attitudes about the Standardized Testing and Reporting (STAR) System, Academic Performance Index (API), and High School Exit Exam (HSEE), by Respondent's District, Level, and Position, 2001*

	STAR			API			HSEE		
	N	Negative (%)	Positive (%)	N	Negative (%)	Positive (%)	N	Negative (%)	Positive (%)
Overall[a]	77	83.12	16.88	72	59.72	40.28	48	58.33	41.67
District (all personnel)									
Fresno	15	73.33	26.67	12	50.00	50.00	14	78.57	21.43
Los Angeles	17	76.47	23.53	17	58.82	41.18	11	54.55	45.45
Long Beach	16	81.25	18.75	16	68.75	31.25	6	50.00	50.00
San Diego	15	93.33	6.67	15	46.67	53.33	12	50.00	50.00
San Francisco	13	92.31	7.69	11	72.73	27.27	5	40.00	60.00
Level (across all districts)									
District	12	91.67	8.33	14	64.29	35.71	10	80.00	20.00
Elementary	33	84.85	15.15	30	56.67	43.33	16	37.50	62.50
Middle School	29	75.86	24.14	26	61.54	38.46	19	57.89	42.11
Other	2	100.00	0.00	1	0.00	100.00	3	100.00	0.00
Position (across all districts)									
District	11	90.91	9.09	13	61.54	38.46	9	77.78	22.22
Principal	20	80.00	20.00	21	42.86	57.14	15	53.33	46.67
Teacher	30	83.33	16.67	26	76.92	23.08	14	57.14	42.86
Other	15	80.00	20.00	11	45.45	54.55	10	50.00	50.00

Source: Authors' coding data.

a. Although we interviewed the state's Emergency Immigration Education Program director, we agreed to keep that individual's responses confidential. We do not report these here because that individual would represent a category with only one person.

explained more about using the school's SSR to evaluate the school's performance,

> The API? I don't have a problem with those kinds of things as long as you realize it's only one measure of growth. The problem with API is—I consider "like" schools' information more important to me. When you look at the state, of course we're not going to do well. When you have 800, almost 900 of our kids speaking a second language out of 1,500, of course we're not. You can't expect second language students to be at the same level as native English speakers—and then the poverty issue comes into that. But we're at Level 8 when you talk about "like" schools. Now that tells me we're on the road.

Given that the majority of the school staff we spoke with worked in schools with a higher SSR than API rank, it is not surprising that we find the majority of respondents who mentioned the SSR were positive about it. We would naturally expect these remarks to be more positive than the remarks of a respondent from a school with both a low API ranking and a low SSR.

We also found, however, that some personnel in schools that rank poorly on the API and SSR had generally positive impressions of the API's use for comparison purposes, despite their schools' low ranking. In such instances, respondents tended to refer to comparison within a school over time rather than across schools. For example, a middle school principal in such a school told us,

> So we need to be able to look—and that API gives us that chance—because it puts you under the gun, and makes you say, "How can I show you what I'm doing?" But also, it says, "Every group at your school should be growing," and before, I don't think we really did a lot of that. I think we've looked globally. Has the school globally grown? But the API asks you to look at every ethnic group at your school. The part that I don't like is that they say it has to be 15 percent of the population before you say, "That's the group you have to change." For example, my African American and my white population at this school are not 15 percent, but they need to grow. So it gives you a chance to really start talking data, and really start talking to your kids, and really start talking, "Why is this group not growing, how do we make it grow?"

Most respondents who talked about publicizing the rankings, putting the districts, schools, and staff on notice, and creating accountability were also positive about that process. Although the idea of accountability was acceptable to virtually everyone we interviewed, there was some disagreement about what constitutes accountability and then how to accomplish it.

A few respondents explained that the API is used to identify low-performing schools so that resources can be directed toward them. Once identified as such using the API, the school receives an increase in resources through the Immediate Intervention/Underperforming Schools Program (II/USP) component of the Public Schools Accountability Act (PSAA) of 1999. The II/USP refers to schools in the lowest API deciles as underperforming, which also brings negative results. An elementary school principal in Fresno pointed out that despite efforts to be optimistic, a school's ranking in the lowest deciles and the resulting "underperforming" label have a demoralizing effect:

> We feel very optimistic that we're going to meet our targeted growth numbers, but you know, it's very difficult for a community, and for a staff, to be labeled "underperforming." There's no way about it, that's a negative—there's a negative connotation to it. And you're in need of immediate intervention because, in effect, you're failing.

The second, less-common theme among respondents who had impressions of the API was fairness. Some of the people raising the issue of fairness were concerned that the API relies solely on the Stanford 9—in fact, respondents often spoke of the Stanford 9 and the API interchangeably during the conversations. Most respondents thought that a ranking system is fair as long as it contains multiple measures and adequate controls, such as the SSR strives to achieve. For instance, a district official in San Diego told us,

> We still have teachers say it's not fair, but at some point there has to be a way to weigh this up and to have parents have the ability to look across schools and say, "Given the demographics, [how does one school look compared with another?]"

Many respondents suggested that the state had taken adequate steps to develop a fair ranking system; however, some teachers appeared to be unaware of the attempts to control for demographic and other school characteristics using the SSR and this misinformation negatively impacted their impressions.

NOTE

1. When we analyze the responses by level and function, elementary personnel have the lowest percentage of negative impressions for API (56.7 percent), whereas district-level personnel have the highest percentage of negative impressions (64.3 percent). Principals have the lowest percentage of negative impressions (42.9 percent), whereas teachers have the highest percentage (76.9 percent).

Sample Home Language Survey

FOR STAFF COMPLETION TO BE COMPLETED FOR ALL NEW STUDENTS			
ESL File Opened ☐ Yes ☐ No	ESL Test Date	Today's Date	Test
ESL Evaluator		ESL Level	Placement

PARENT/GUARDIAN HOME LANGUAGE SURVEY	
Student's Name	Grade

Relationship of Person Completing Survey

☐ Mother   ☐ Father   ☐ Guardian   ☐ Other *Specify*

Directions: Check the correct response for each of the following questions and indicate other languages if appropriate

	English	Other	Other Language(s)
1. What language did the child learn when she or he first began to talk?	☐	☐	
2. What language does the family speak at home most of the time?	☐	☐	
3. What language does the parent(s) speak to her/his child most of the time?	☐	☐	
4. What language does the child speak to her/his parent(s) most of the time?	☐	☐	
5. What language does the child hear and understand in the home?	☐	☐	
6. What language does the child speak to her/his brothers/sisters most of the time?	☐	☐	
7. What language does the child speak to her/his friends most of the time?	☐	☐	

	Yes	No	
8. Can an adult family member or extended family member speak English?	☐	☐	
Can they read English?	☐	☐	
9. Do the parents/guardians request oral and/or written communication from the school to be in English?	☐	☐	☐ Oral ☐ Written If no, in what language

SIGNATURE	
Signature of Person Completing Survey ➢	Date Signed

Source: Wisconsin Department of Public Instruction, Bilingual English as a Second Language Program, http://www.dpi.state.wi.us/ell/pdf/homelang.pdf. Adapted from: *Sample Survey, Institute for Cultural Pluralism,* Lau General Assistance Center, San Diego State University, San Diego, CA 92182, 1976.

References

Ada, Alma F. 1995. "Fostering the Home-School Connection." In *Reclaiming Our Voices,* edited by Jean Frederickson (163–78). Ontario, CA: California Association of Bilingual Education.

Auerbach, Elsa R. 1989. "Toward a Social-Contextual Approach to Family Literacy." *Harvard Educational Review* 59 (2): 165–81.

August, Diane, and Kenji Hakuta, eds. 1997. *Improving Schooling for Language-Minority Children: A Research Agenda.* Washington, DC: National Academy Press.

Avila, Oscar. 2002. "New Centers Try to Soften Immigrants' School Shock." *Chicago Tribune,* February 26.

Baldassare, Mark. 2001. "PPIC Statewide Survey: Californians and Their Government." San Francisco: Public Policy Institute of California, December.

———. 2002a. "PPIC Statewide Survey: Californians and Their Government." San Francisco: Public Policy Institute of California, January.

———. 2002b. "PPIC Statewide Survey: Californians and Their Government." San Francisco: Public Policy Institute of California, February.

Berg, Bruce L. 2001. *Qualitative Research Methods for the Social Sciences,* 4th ed. Needham Heights, MA: Allyn and Bacon.

Berger, Eugenia Hepworth. 1987. *Parents as Partners in Education: The School and Home Working Together,* 2nd ed. New York: Merrill.

Berne, Robert, and Leanna Stiefel. 1984. *The Measurement of Equity in School Finance.* Baltimore, MD: Johns Hopkins University Press.

Betts, Julian R. 1998. "Educational Crowding Out: Do Immigrants Affect the Educational Attainment of American Minorities?" In *Help or Hindrance? The Economic Implications of Immigration for African Americans*, edited by Daniel S. Hamermesh and Frank D. Bean (253–81). New York: Russell Sage Foundation.

Betts, Julian R., and Anne Danenberg. 2002. "School Accountability in California: An Early Evaluation." In *Brookings Papers on Education Policy: 2002,* edited by Diane Ravitch (123–97). Washington, DC: Brookings Institution Press.

Betts, Julian R., and Magnus Lofstrom. 1998. "The Educational Attainment of Immigrants: Trends and Implications." NBER Working Paper 6757. Cambridge, MA: National Bureau of Economic Research.

Betts, Julian R., Kim S. Rueben, and Anne Danenberg. 2000. "Equal Resources, Equal Outcomes? The Distribution of School Resources and Student Achievement in California." San Francisco: Public Policy Institute of California.

Board of Education of the City of New York. 2000. "ELL Subcommittee Research Studies: Progress Report." New York: Board of Education, Office of Assessment and Accountability.

Board on Children and Families. 1995. "Immigrant Children and Their Families: Issues for Research and Policy." *The Future of Children, Critical Issues for Children and Youths* 5 (2): 72–89.

Boehner, John. 2001. "Committee on Education and the Workforce, H.R. 1 Conference Report Highlights: Bilingual Education Reform." December 10. http://edworkforce. house.gov/issues/107th/education/nclb/bilingualfactsheet.htm.

Borjas, George J. 2001. *Heaven's Door: Immigration Policy and the American Economy.* Princeton, NJ: Princeton University Press.

Brice, Jessica. 2002. "Education Board Adopts Rules for English-Only Education." Associated Press, May 30.

California Department of Education. 2001. "2000 STAR Results." http://star.cde.ca.gov/ star2000F.

———. 2002a. "The California English Language Development Test (CELDT)." *Assessment Notes ... From the Standards and Assessment Division.* California Department of Education. January 31.

———. 2002b. "SBE Meeting Highlights: A Summary of Key Actions by the California State Board of Education, January 2002." http://www.cde.ca.gov/board/highlights/ pdf/highlights0102.pdf. (Accessed February 2002.)

———. 2002c. "SBE Meeting Highlights: A Summary of Key Actions by the California State Board of Education, February 2002." http://www.cde.ca.gov/board/highlights/ highlights0202.pdf. (Accessed February 2002.)

———. 2003. *Fact Book 2003: Handbook of Education Information.* Sacramento: California Department of Education. http://www.cde.ca.gov/resrc/factbook/factbook03.pdf. (Accessed November 1, 2003.)

———. "English Language Acquisition." http:/www.cde.ca.gov/sp/el/ii/index.asp. (Accessed June 25, 2004.)

———. "Guidelines for Reclassification." http://www.cde.ca.gov/statetests/celdt/ reclass1.htm. (Accessed January 25, 2002.)

———. "Immigrant Student Demographics: Title III." http://www.cde.ca.gov/el/title3/ immdemographics.html. (Accessed November 15, 2003.)

———. "Number of English-Learner Students in California Public Schools, by Language, 2001 through 2002." http://www.cde.ca.gov/demographics/reports/statewide/ leplcst2.htm. (Accessed November 15, 2003.)

———. "Number of Limited-English-Proficient Students in California Public Schools, by Language, 1993 through 2000." http://www.cde.ca.gov/demographics/reports/statewide/leplcst.htm. (Accessed November 15, 2003.)

———. "Standardized Testing and Reporting." http://star.cde.ca.gov/.

Cheng, Jennifer. 2001. "Educational Outcomes." In *A Portrait of Race and Ethnicity in California: An Assessment of Social and Economic Well-Being,* edited by Belinda I. Reyes (47–70). San Francisco: Public Policy Institute of California.

Conchas, Gilberto Q. 2001. "Structuring Failure and Success: Understanding the Variability in Latino School Engagement." *Harvard Educational Review, Special Issue: Immigration and Education* (fall): 475–504.

Conchas, Gilberto Q., and Patricia A. Clark. 2002. "Career Academies and Urban Minority Schooling: Forging Optimism Despite Limited Opportunity." *Journal of Education for Students Placed At Risk* 7 (3): 287–311.

Cornelius, Wayne A., and Enrico A. Marcelli. 2000. "The Changing Profile of Mexican Migrants to the United States: New Evidence from California and Mexico." Institute for the Study of Labor Discussion Paper No. 220. Bonn, Germany: Institute for the Study of Labor.

Crawford, James. 1997. "Best Evidence: Research Foundations of the Bilingual Education Act." Washington, DC: National Clearinghouse for Bilingual Education, George Washington University.

CTB/McGraw-Hill. "About the SABE/2 STAR Program." http://www.ctb.com/SABE2STAR/e_aboutsabe.html. (Accessed August 30, 2001.)

Cummins, Jim. 1981. "Empirical and Theoretical Underpinnings of Bilingual Education." *Journal of Education* 163 (1): 16–29.

———. 1986. "Empowering Minority Students: A Framework for Intervention." *Harvard Educational Review* 56 (1): 18–36.

———. 1994. "Primary Language Instructions and the Education of Minority Language Students." In *Schooling and Language Minority Students: A Theoretical Framework,* edited by Charles F. Leyba (3–46). Los Angeles: Evaluation, Dissemination and Assessment Center, California State University.

de Cos, Patricia L. 1999. "Educating California's Immigrant Children: An Overview of Bilingual Education." Sacramento: California Research Bureau of the California State Library.

Dey, Ian. 1993. *Qualitative Data Analysis: A User-Friendly Guide for Social Scientists.* New York: Routledge.

Downes, Thomas A., and Thomas F. Pogue. 1994. "Adjusting School Aid Formulas for the Higher Cost of Educating Disadvantaged Students." *National Tax Journal* 47 (1): 89–110.

Drucker, Peter. 2001. "Survey: The Near Future." Economist.com, February 10.

Duncombe, William, and John Yinger. 1997. "Why Is It So Hard to Help Central City Schools?" *Journal of Policy Analysis and Management* 16 (1): 85–113.

Emerson, Robert M., Rachel I. Fretz, and Linda L. Shaw. 1995. *Writing Ethnographic Fieldnotes.* Chicago: University of Chicago Press.

Epstein, Joyce L. 1991. "Effects of Teacher Practices of Parent Involvement on Student Achievement in Reading and Math." In *Advances in Reading/Language Research, Vol. 5: Literacy through Family, Community, and School Interaction,* edited by Steven B. Silvern (261–76). Greenwich, CT: JAI Press.

Fix, Michael E., Wendy Zimmerman, and Jeffrey S. Passel. 2001. "The Integration of Immigrant Families in the United States." Washington, DC: The Urban Institute.

Fresno (California) Unified School District. 2000. "FUSD Master Plan for English Learners." http://multilingual.fresno.k12.ca.us/mastplan/mastplan.htm. (Accessed February 2002.)

Fuentes, Emma, Daniel Liou, Patricia Sánchez, and Andrea Dyrness. 2000. "Interim Report from the English Language Learner Committee." Berkeley: University of California Diversity Project.

Galper, Alice, Allan Wigfield, and Carol Seefeldt. 1997. "Head Start Parents' Beliefs about Their Children's Abilities, Task Values, and Performances on Different Activities." Ann Arbor, MI: Society for Research in Child Development, Inc.

Gándara, Patricia, Julie Maxwell-Jolly, Eugene García, Jolynn Asato, Kris Gutiérrez, Tom Stritikus, and Julia E. Curry-Rodríguez. 2000. "The Initial Impact of Proposition 227 on the Instruction of English Learners." Santa Barbara, CA: Linguistic Minority Research Institute. http://lmri.ucsb.edu/resdiss/2/pdf_files/prop227effects.pdf. (Accessed August 29, 2003.)

García, Eugene E., ed. 2000. *Bilingual Research Journal* 24 (1/2). http://brj.asu.edu/ v2412/. (Accessed February 22, 2002.)

García, Eugene E., and Julia E. Curry-Rodríguez. 2000. "The Education of Limited English Proficient Students in California Schools: An Assessment of the Influence of Proposition 227 in Selected Districts and Schools." *Bilingual Research Journal* 24 (1/2). http://brj.asu.edu/v2412/. (Accessed February 22, 2002.)

Gershberg, Alec Ian. 2000. "Empowering Parents and Building Communities: The Role of School-Based Councils in Educational Governance and Accountability." New York: New School University, Community Development Research Center.

———. 2002. "New Immigrants and the New School Governance in New York: Defining the Issues." Working Paper No. 2002-002. New York: The New School University, Community Development Research Center. http://www.newschool.edu/ milano/cdrc/pubs/wp/wp.2002.02.pdf.

Greene, Jay P. 1998. "A Meta-Analysis of the Effectiveness of Bilingual Education." Austin, TX: Tomas Rivera Policy Institute.

Grimes, Barbara F., and Joseph E. Grimes, eds. 2001. *Ethnologue: Languages of the World*, 14th ed. Dallas, TX: SIL International. http://www.ethnologue.com/ web.asp.

Gutiérrez, Kris D., Patricia Baquedano-López, and Jolynn Asato. 2000. " 'English for the Children': The New Literacy of the Old World Order, Language Policy and Educational Reform." *Bilingual Research Journal* 24 (1/2). http://brj.asu.edu/v2412/. (Accessed February 22, 2002.)

Hakuta, Kenji, Yuko Goto Butler, and Daria Witt. 2000. "How Long Does It Take English Learners to Attain Proficiency?" Policy Report 2000-1. Santa Barbara: The University of California Language Minority Research Institute.

Hanushek, Eric A. 1986. "The Economics of Schooling: Production and Efficiency in Public Schools." *Journal of Economic Literature* 24 (3): 1141–77.

———. 1996. "School Resources and Student Performance." In *Does Money Matter? The Effect of School Resources on Student Achievement and Adult Success*, edited by Gary Burtless (43–73). Washington, DC: Brookings Institution Press.

Heath, Shirley Brice. 1983. *Ways with Words.* Cambridge, England: Cambridge University Press.

Henderson, Anne T. 1987. "The Evidence Continues to Grow: Parent Involvement Improves Student Achievement. An Annotated Bibliography." Columbia, MD: National Committee for Citizens in Education.

Heubert, Jay P., and Robert M. Hauser, eds. 1999. *High Stakes: Testing for Tracking, Promotion, and Graduation.* Washington, DC: National Academy Press.

Hudson, John C., and Edward B. Espenshade, eds. 2000. *Goode's World Atlas.* 20th ed. Skokie, IL: Rand McNally.

Iatarola, Patrice, and Leanna Stiefel. 2000. "Intradistrict Equity in New York City." Unpublished manuscript, New York University.

Jaramillo, Ann, and Laurie Olsen. 1999. "Turning the Tides of Exclusion: A Guide for Educators and Advocates for Immigrant Students." Oakland: California Tomorrow.

Jasso, Guillermina, Mark R. Rosenzweig, and James P. Smith. 1998. "The Changing Skill of New Immigrants to the United States: Recent Trends and Their Determinants." NBER Working Paper 6764. Cambridge, MA: National Bureau of Economic Research.

Jepsen, Christopher, and Steven Rivkin. 2002. *Class Reduction, Quality, and Academic Achievement in California Public Elementary Schools.* San Francisco: Public Policy Institute of California.

Johnson, Kevin R., and George A. Martinez. 2000. "Discrimination by Proxy: The Case of Proposition 227 and the Ban on Bilingual Education." *UC Davis Law Review* 33 (4): 1227–76.

Kaestner, Robert, and Neeraj Kaushal. 2001. "Immigrant and Native Responses to Welfare Reform." NBER Working Paper 8541. Cambridge, MA: National Bureau of Economic Research.

Kao, Grace, and Marta Tienda. 1995. "Optimism and Achievement: The Educational Performance of Immigrant Youth." *Social Science Quarterly* 76 (1): 1–19.

Kaushal, Neeraj. 2002. "New Immigrants' Location Choices: Magnets without Welfare." Unpublished manuscript, Department of Economics, The Graduate Center of the City University of New York, New York.

Keith, Patricia B., and Marilyn V. Lichtman. 1994. "Does Parental Involvement Influence the Academic Achievement of Mexican-American Eighth Graders? Results from the National Education Longitudinal Study." *School Psychology Quarterly* 9 (4): 256–72.

Kennedy, Erin. 2000. "Language Unlocked: Valley Cambodians Learn the Khmer Tongue and Their Heritage." *The Fresno Bee*, June 5. http://psrtec.clmer.csulb.edu/Khmer_site/keep.htm.

Kindler, Anneka. 2002. "Survey of the States' Limited English Proficient Students and Available Educational Programs and Services: 1999–2000 Summary Report." Washington, DC: National Clearinghouse for English Language Acquisition and Language Instruction Educational Programs. http://www.ncela.gwu.edu/pubs/seareports/99-00/sea9900.pdf.

Kirst, Michael W., Gerald Hayward, Juila Koppich, Neal Finkelstein, Linda Petersen Birky, and James Guthrie. 1995. "Conditions of Education in California 1994–95." Berkeley: Policy Analysis for California Education.

Krashen, Stephen D. 1994. "Bilingual Education and Second Language Acquisition Theory." In *Schooling and Language Minority Students: A Theoretical Framework,* edited by

Charles F. Leyba (47–75). Los Angeles: Evaluation, Dissemination and Assessment Center, California State University.

Lareau, Annette. 1989. *Home Advantage: Social Class and Parental Intervention in Elementary Education.* New York: Falmer Press.

Leyba, Charles F., ed. 1994. *Schooling and Language Minority Students: A Theoretical Framework,* 2nd ed. Los Angeles: Evaluation, Dissemination, and Assessment Center, California State University.

Linn, Robert L. 2000. "Assessment and Accountability." *Educational Researcher* 29 (2): 4–16.

Lofland, John, and Lyn H. Lofland. 1995. *Analyzing Social Settings: A Guide to Qualitative Observation and Analysis,* 3rd ed. Belmont, CA: Wadsworth Publishing Co.

Lopez, Mark Hugo. 2000. "Evaluating California's Proposition 227." Unpublished paper, School of Public Affairs, University of Maryland.

Massey, Douglas S., and Nancy A. Denton. 1993. *American Apartheid: Segregation and the Making of the Underclass.* Cambridge, MA: Harvard University Press.

McDonnell, Lorraine M., and Paul T. Hill. 1993. *Newcomers in American Schools: Meeting the Educational Needs of Immigrant Youths.* Santa Monica, CA: RAND.

Mehan, Hugh, Irene Villanueva, Lea Hubbard, Angela Lintz, and Dina Okamoto. 1996. *Constructing School Success: The Consequences of Untracking Low-Achieving Students.* Cambridge, England: Cambridge University Press.

Mendel, Edward. 2002. "Bilingual Education Foe Faults State Board." *San Diego Union Tribune,* February 12.

Moll, Luis C., Cathy Amanti, Deborah Neff, and Norma González. 1992. "Funds of Knowledge for Teaching: Using a Qualitative Approach to Connect Homes and Classrooms." *Theory into Practice* 31 (2): 132–41.

National Clearinghouse for Bilingual Education (NCBE). 1999. "Biennial Report to Congress on the Emergency Immigrant Education Program (1994–96)." Washington, DC: NCBE, George Washington University. http://www.ncela.gwu.edu/ncbepubs/reports/eiep99/index.htm.

National Clearinghouse for English Language Acquisition and Language Instruction Educational Programs (NCELA). 2002. "Biennial Report to Congress on the Emergency Immigrant Education Program: 1998–2000." Washington, DC: NCELA. http://www.ncela.gwu.edu/pubs/reports/eiep02/eiepfull.pdf.

New York City Board of Education. 2000. "ELL Subcommittee Research Studies Progress Report: Longitudinal Study of Bilingual and ESL Education in New York City Schools." New York: New York City Board of Education.

Nieto, Sonia. 2002. *Language, Culture, and Teaching: Critical Perspectives for a New Century.* Mahwah, NJ: Lawrence Erlbaum Associates.

Noguera, Pedro A. 2001. "Racial Politics and the Elusive Quest for Excellence and Equity in Education." *Education and Urban Society* 34 (1): 18–41.

Oakland Tribune. 2001. "Critics Give State's English Fluency Test an 'F,'" December 10.

Ogbu, John U. 1982. "Cultural Discontinuities and Schooling." *Anthropology & Education Quarterly* 13 (4): 290–307.

———. 1991. "Immigrant and Involuntary Minorities in Comparative Perspective." In *Minority Status and Schooling: A Comparative Study of Immigrant and Involuntary Minorities,* edited by Margaret Gibson and John Ogbu (3–36). New York: Garland Publishing, Inc.

Ogbu, John U., and Herbert Simons. 1998. "Voluntary and Involuntary Minorities: A Cultural-Ecological Theory of School Performance with Some Implications for Education." *Anthropology & Education Quarterly* 29 (2): 155–88.

Olsen, Laurie. 1997. *Made in America: Immigrant Students in Our Public Schools.* New York: The New Press.

Olsen, Laurie, and Marcia Chen. 1988. "Crossing the Schoolhouse Border: Immigrant Students and the California Public Schools." Oakland: California Tomorrow.

Olsen, Laurie, and Carol Dowell. 1989. "Bridges: Promising Programs for the Education of Immigrant Children." Oakland: California Tomorrow Immigrant Students Project.

Olsen, Laurie, and Ann Jaramillo. 1999. "Turning the Tides of Exclusion: A Guide for Educators and Advocates for Immigrant Students." *California Tomorrow Equity-Centered School Reform Series.* Oakland: California Tomorrow.

Olsen, Laurie, Ann Jaramillo, Zaida McCall-Pérez, Judy White, and Catherine Minicucci. 1999. "Igniting Change for Immigrant Students: Portraits of Three High Schools." *California Tomorrow Equity-Centered School Reform Series.* Oakland: California Tomorrow.

Olsen, Laurie, Hedy Nai-Lin Chang, Denise De La Rosa Salazar, Carol Dowell, Cecilia Leong, Zaida McCall-Pérez, Greg McClain, and Lisa Raffel. 1994. "The Unfinished Journey: Restructuring Schools in a Diverse Society." California Tomorrow Research and Policy Report from the Education for a Diverse Society Project. Oakland: California Tomorrow.

Ovando, Carlos J. 2003. "Bilingual Education in the United States: Historical Development and Current Issues." *Bilingual Research Journal* 27 (1): 1–24.

Padilla, Amado M., and David Durán. 1995. "The Psychological Dimension in Understanding Immigrant Students." In *California's Immigrant Children: Theory, Research, and Implications for Educational Policy,* edited by Rubén G. Rumbaut and Wayne A. Cornelius (131–60). San Diego: Center for U.S.-Mexican Studies, University of California, San Diego.

Parrish, Thomas B. 1994. "A Cost Analysis of Alternative Instructional Models for Limited English Proficient Students in California." *Journal of Education Finance* 19 (Winter): 256–78.

———. 2001. "Effects of the Implementation of Proposition 227 on the Education of English Learners, K–12. Year 1 Report." Sacramento: California Department of Education, Language Policy and Leadership Office.

Portes, Alejandro, and Rubén G. Rumbaut. 2001. *Legacies: The Story of the Immigrant Second Generation.* New York: Russell Sage Foundation.

Portes, Alejandro, and Richard Schauffler. 1994. "Language and the Second Generation: Bilingualism Yesterday and Today." *International Migration Review* 28 (4): 640–61.

Putnam, Robert D. 2002. "Bowling Together." *The American Prospect* 13 (3), February 11. http://www.prospect.org/print/V13/3/putnam r.html.

Rivera-Batiz, Francisco. 1995. "The Education of Immigrant Children: The Case of New York City." Paper presented at organizational meeting, New York Community Trust Project, International Center for Migration, Ethnicity and Citizenship, The New School for Social Research, New York, November 28.

———. 1996. "The Education of Immigrant Children in New York City." *ERIC Clearinghouse on Urban Education Digest* 117.

Roebuck, Karen. 2002. "Growing Hispanic Student Population Facing Educational Crisis." Associated Press, August 16.

Rossell, Christine H. 2000a. "The Federal Bilingual Education Program." In *Brookings Papers on Education Policy: 2000,* edited by Diane Ravitch (215–64). Washington, DC: Brookings Institution Press.

———. 2000b. "Teaching Language Minorities: Theory and Reality." Boston, MA: Boston University Press.

Rossell, Christine, and Keith Baker. 1996. "The Educational Effectiveness of Bilingual Education." *Research in the Teaching of English* 30 (1): 7–74.

Rothenberg, Daniel. 2000. *With These Hands: The Hidden World of Migrant Farmworkers Today.* Berkeley: University of California Press.

Rubin, Herbert J., and Irene S. Rubin. 1995. *Qualitative Interviewing: The Art of Hearing Data.* Thousand Oaks, CA: Sage Publications.

Ruiz-de-Velasco, Jorge, and Michael Fix. 2000. "Overlooked and Underserved: Immigrant Students in U.S. Secondary Schools." Washington, DC: The Urban Institute.

Rumbaut, Rubén G. 1995. "The New Californians: Comparative Research Findings on the Educational Progress of Immigrant Children." In *California's Immigrant Children: Theory, Research, and Implications for Educational Policy,* edited by Rubén G. Rumbaut and Wayne A. Cornelius (17–69). San Diego: Center for U.S.-Mexican Studies, University of California, San Diego.

Santosuosso, Joseph A. 1999. "When in California . . . In Defense of the Abolishment of Bilingual Education." *New England Law Review* 33 (3): 837–78.

Sassen, Saskia. 1998. *Globalization and Its Discontents: Essays on the New Mobility of People and Money.* New York: The New Press.

Schirling, Elsa, Frances Contreras, and Carlos Ayala. 2000. "Proposition 227: Tales from the Schoolhouse." *Bilingual Research Journal* 24 (1/2). http://brj.asu.edu/v2412/. (Accessed February 22, 2002.)

Schmid, Carol L. 2001. "Educational Achievement, Language-Minority Students, and the New Second Generation." *Sociology of Education* Extra Issue: 71–87.

Schnur, Bruce. 1999. "A Newcomer's High School." *Educational Leadership* 56 (7): 50–52.

Schwartz, Amy Ellen. 1999. "School Districts and Spending in the Schools." In *Selected Papers on School Finance 1997–1999,* edited by William J. Fowler Jr. NCES 1999-334. Washington, DC: U.S. Department of Education, National Center for Education Statistics.

Schwartz, Amy Ellen, and Alec Ian Gershberg. 2000. "The Experience of Recent Immigrants in New York City Public Schools: Enrollment Resources and Outcomes." New York: The New School University, The International Center of Migration, Ethnicity and Citizenship.

———. 2001. "Immigrants and Education: Evidence from New York City." *National Tax Association Proceedings—2000* (125–34).

Shaeffer, Sheldon. 1994. *Participation for Educational Change: A Synthesis of Experience.* Paris: UNESCO, International Institute for Educational Planning.

Sonstelie, Jon, Eric Brunner, and Kenneth Ardon. 2000. *For Better or Worse? School Finance Reform in California.* San Francisco: Public Policy Institute of California.

Spears, Phil. 2001. "Apportionment Information Reports for the 2001 California English Language Development Test (CELDT)." Memo, August 23. Sacramento: California

Department of Education, Standards and Assessments Division. http://www.cde.ca
.gov/statetests/celdt/admin/adminform.pdf. (Accessed January 2002.)

Stanton-Salazar, Ricardo D. 2001. *Manufacturing Hope and Despair: The School and Kin Support Networks of U.S.-Mexican Youth.* New York: Teachers College Press.

Stanton-Salazar, Ricardo D., and Sanford M. Dornbusch. 1995. "Social Capital and the Reproduction of Inequality: Information Networks among Mexican-Origin High School Students." *Sociology of Education* 68 (2): 116–35.

Stritikus, Tom T., and Eugene García. 2003. "The Role of Theory and Policy in the Educational Treatment of Language Minority Students: Competitive Structures in California." *Education Policy Analysis Archives* 11 (26). http://epaa.asu.edu/epaa/v11n26/. (Accessed August 29, 2003.)

Suárez-Orozco, Carola, and Marcelo Suárez-Orozco. 2001. *Children of Immigration.* Cambridge, MA: Harvard University Press.

Suárez-Orozco, Marcelo M. 1991. "Immigrant Adaptation to Schooling: A Hispanic Case." In *Minority Status and Schooling: A Comparative Study of Immigrant and Involuntary Minorities,* edited by Margaret A. Gibson and John U. Ogbu (37–61). New York: Garland Publishing, Inc.

Thompson, Marilyn S., Kristen E. DiCerbo, Kate Mahoney, and Jeff MacSwan. 2002. "¿Exito en California? A Validity Critique of Language Program Evaluations and Analysis of English Learner Test Scores." *Education Policy Analysis Archives* 10 (7). http://epaa.asu.edu/epaa/v10n7/. (Accessed February 6, 2002.)

Trueba, Enrique (Henry) T., and Lilia I. Bartolomé. 2000. *Immigrant Voices: In Search of Educational Equity.* Lanham, MD: Rowman & Littlefield.

Valdés, Guadalupe. 2001. *Learning and Not Learning English: Latino Students in American Schools.* New York: Teachers College Press.

Valenzuela, Angela. 1999. *Subtractive Schooling: U.S.-Mexican Youth and the Politics of Caring.* Albany: State University of New York Press.

Vernez, Georges, and Allan Abrahamse. 1996. *How Immigrants Fare in U.S. Education.* Santa Monica: RAND.

White, Michael J. 1986. "Segregation and Diversity Measures in Population Distribution." *Population Index* 52 (2): 198–221.

World Bank Group, The. "Countries and Regions." http://web.worldbank.org/WBSITE/EXTERNAL/COUNTRIES/0,,pagepk:180619~theSitePK:136917,00.html. (Accessed June 25, 2004.)

Wyckoff, James H., and Michelle Naples. 2000. "Educational Finance to Support High Learning Standards: A Synthesis." *Economics of Education Review* 19 (4): 305–18.

Yi, Daniel. 2001. "Program Testing English Fluency Faulted." *Los Angeles Times,* December 9.

Zehr, Mary Ann. 2001. "Study: Dearth of Programs for Older Immigrant Students." *Education Week,* January 24.

Additional Readings

Alamillo, Laura, and Celia Viramontes. 2000. "Reflections from the Classroom: Teacher Perspectives on the Implementation of Proposition 227." *Bilingual Research Journal* 24 (1/2). http://brj.asu.edu/v2412/. (Accessed February 22, 2002.)

Anstrom, Kris. 1997. "Academic Achievement for Secondary Language Minority Students: Standards, Measures, and Promising Practices." Washington, DC: National Clearinghouse for Bilingual Education, George Washington University.

Bali, Valentina A. 2001. "Sink or Swim: What Happened to California's Bilingual Students after Proposition 227?" *State Politics and Policy Quarterly* 1 (3): 295–317.

Barron, Rachel. 2000. "The Education Outlaws." *El Andar Magazine,* Winter.

Bedard, Kelly, William O. Brown Jr., and Eric Helland. 1999. "School Size and the Distribution of Test Scores." Claremont Colleges Working Papers in Economics 1999-11. Claremont, CA: Claremont McKenna College.

Bohrnstedt, George W., and Brian M. Stecher, eds. 1999. "Class Size Reduction in California: Early Evaluation Findings, 1996–1998." Sacramento: California Department of Education.

Butler, Yuko G., Jennifer Evelyn Orr, Michele Bousquet Gutiérrez, and Kenji Hakuta. 2000. "Inadequate Conclusions from an Inadequate Assessment: What Can SAT-9 Scores Tell Us about the Impact of Proposition 227 in California?" *Bilingual Research Journal* 24 (1/2). http://brj.asu.edu/v2412/. (Accessed February 22, 2002.)

California Code of Regulations. Title 5, Division 1, Chapter 11, California English Language Development Test.

California Commission on Teacher Credentialing. http://www.ctc.ca.gov/codcor.doc/989805/989805.html. (Accessed September 20, 2001.)

California Department of Education. "EIEP Demographics." http://www.cde.ca.gov/eiep/newcomer.html. (Accessed November 18, 2003.)

California Education Code. Sections 44253.3 (b); 51120, Article 2; 51130, Article 3.

Casserly, Michael, Executive Director, Council of Great City Schools. Letter dated September 17, 2001. http://www.cgcs.org/. (Accessed April 5, 2003.)

Dixon, Carol, Judith Green, Beth Yeager, Doug Baker, and María Fránquiz. 2000. " 'I Used to Know That': What Happens When Reform Gets Through the Classroom Door." *Bilingual Research Journal* 24 (1/2). http://brj.asu.edu/v2412/. (Accessed February 22, 2002.)

Dolson, David. 1999. "Designing a Standards-Based Accountability System for Language Minority and Immigrant Student Populations. A Guide for School District Personnel and Program Evaluators, Second Edition." Sacramento: California Department of Education, Language Policy and Leadership Office.

Fix, Michael E., and Jeffrey S. Passel. 1994. "Immigration and Immigrants: Setting the Record Straight." Washington, DC: The Urban Institute.

Fix, Michael E., and Wendy Zimmerman. 1993. "Educating Immigrant Children. Chapter 1 in the Changing City." Urban Institute Report 93-3. A Report of the Immigration Policy Program. Washington, DC: The Urban Institute.

Gándara, Patricia. 2000. "In the Aftermath of the Storm: English Learners in the Post-227 Era." *Bilingual Research Journal* 24 (1/2). http://brj.asu.edu/v2412/. (Accessed February 22, 2002.)

García, Augustine. 2000. "Informed Parent Consent and Proposition 227." *Bilingual Research Journal* 24 (1/2). http://brj.asu.edu/v2412/. (Accessed February 22, 2002.)

García, Eugene E. 1999. *Student Cultural Diversity: Understanding and Meeting the Challenge*, 2nd ed. New York: Houghton Mifflin Company.

Griffith, James. 1996. "Relation of Parental Involvement, Empowerment, and School Traits to Student Academic Performance." *Journal of Educational Research* 90 (1): 33–41.

Hakuta, Kenji. 2000. "Points on SAT-9 Performance and Proposition 227." Stanford, CA: Stanford University. http://www.stanford.edu/~hakuta/SAT9/SAT9_2000/bullets.htm.

Helfand, Duke. 2001. "District Loses Fight Over Belmont Bills." *Los Angeles Times*, June 9, page B-1.

———. 2001. "District to Scrap Student Clinic." *Los Angeles Times*, June 15, page B-3.

Howe, Christopher K. 1994. "Improving the Achievement of Hispanic Students." *Educational Leadership* 51 (8): 42–44.

Hunter, James, and Craig B. Howley. 1990. "Undocumented Children in the Schools: Successful Strategies and Policies." *ERIC Digest.* http://www.ed.gov/databases/ERIC_Digests/ed321962.html. (Accessed February 10, 2002.)

Huss-Keeler, Rebecca L. 1997. "Teacher Perception of Ethnic and Linguistic Minority Parental Involvement and Its Relationship to Children's Language and Literacy Learning: A Case Study." *Teaching and Teacher Education* 13 (2): 171–82.

International Monetary Fund. 2001. "Real Gross Domestic Product: Advanced Economies." *World Economic Outlook Database* (May). Washington, DC: International Monetary Fund. http://www.imf.org/external/pubs/ft/weo/2001/01/data/index.htm. (Accessed July 2001.)

———. 2001. "Real Gross Domestic Product: Developing and Transition Countries." *World Economic Outlook Database* (May). Washington, DC: International Monetary Fund. http://www.imf.org/external/pubs/ft/weo/2001/01/data/index.htm. (Accessed July 2001.)

Jamieson, Amie, Andrea Curry, and Gladys Martinez. 2001. "School Enrollment in the United States—Social and Economic Characteristics of Students." *Current Population Reports.* Population Characteristics (P20). Washington, DC: U.S. Census Bureau.

Kane, Thomas J., and Douglas O. Staiger. 2002. "Volatility in School Test Scores: Implications for Test-Based Accountability Systems." In *Brookings Papers on Education Policy—2002,* edited by Diane Ravitch (235–83). Washington, DC: Brookings Institution Press.

Los Angeles Unified School District. "Emergency Immigrant Education Program." http://www.lausd.k12.ca.us/lausd/offices/bilingual/eiep.html. (Accessed July 2001.)
————. "Master Plan for the Education of English Learners." http://www.lausd.k12.ca.us/lausd/offices/bilingual/mp/welcome.html. (Accessed July 2001.)

Maxwell-Jolly, Julie. 2000. "Factors Influencing Implementation of Mandated Policy Change: Proposition 227 in Seven Northern California School Districts." *Bilingual Research Journal* 24 (1/2). http://brj.asu.edu/v2412/. (Accessed February 22, 2002.)

McWhirter, Ellen Hawley, Gail Hackett, and Deborah L. Bandalos. 1998. "A Causal Model of the Educational Plans and Career Expectations of Mexican American High School Girls." *Journal of Counseling Psychology* 45 (2): 166–81.

Orr, Jennifer E., Yuko G. Butler, Michele Bousquet, and Kenji Hakuta. 2000. "What Can We Learn About the Impact of Proposition 227 from SAT-9 Scores? An Analysis of Results from 2000." Stanford, CA: Stanford University.

Palmer, Deborah K., and Eugene E. García. 2000. "Voices from the Field: Bilingual Educators Speak Candidly about Proposition 227." *Bilingual Research Journal* 24 (1/2). http://brj.asu.edu/v2412/. (Accessed February 22, 2002.)

Paredes, Sara M. 2000. "How Proposition 227 Influences the Language Dynamics of a First- and Second-Grade Mathematics Lesson." *Bilingual Research Journal* 24 (1/2). http://brj.asu.edu/v2412/. (Accessed February 22, 2002.)

Portes, Alejandro. 1995. "Segmented Assimilation among New Immigrant Youth: A Conceptual Framework." In *California's Immigrant Children: Theory, Research, and Implications for Educational Policy,* edited by Rubén G. Rumbaut and Wayne A. Cornelius (71–76). San Diego: Center for U.S.-Mexican Studies, University of California, San Diego.

Portes, Alejandro, and Rubén G. Rumbaut. 1996. *Immigrant America: A Portrait,* 2nd ed. Berkeley: University of California Press.

Ramos, Lucila, and Arthur R. Sanchez. 1995. "Mexican-American High School Students: Educational Aspirations." *Journal of Multicultural Counseling and Development* 23 (October): 212–21.

Rivkin, Steven G. 1994. "Residential Segregation and School Integration." *Sociology of Education* 67 (4): 279–92.

Rumbaut, Rubén G., and Wayne A. Cornelius, eds. 1995. *California's Immigrant Children: Theory, Research, and Implications for Educational Policy.* San Diego: Center for U.S.-Mexican Studies, University of California, San Diego.

Shaeffer, Sheldon. 1992. *Collaborating for Educational Change: The Role of Teachers, Parents, and the Community in School Improvement.* Paris: UNESCO, International Institute for Educational Planning.

Sonstelie, Jon. 2001. "Toward Cost and Quality Models for California's Public Schools." In *School Finance and California's Master Plan for Education,* edited by

Jon Sonstelie and Peter Richardson (103–23). San Francisco: Public Policy Institute of California.

Stecher, Brian M., and George W. Bohrnstedt, eds. 2000. *Class Size Reduction in California: The 1998–1999 Evaluation Findings.* Sacramento: California Department of Education.

Stewart, David. 1994. "Immigrant Laws Are Education Laws Too." *Phi Delta Kappan* 75 (7): 556–58.

Stiefel, Leanna, Patrice Iatarola, Norm Fruchter, and Robert Berne. 1998. "The Effects of Size of Student Body on School Costs and Performance in New York City High Schools." New York: New York University, Institute for Education and Social Policy.

Stritikus, Tom T., and Eugene E. García. 2000. "Education of Limited English Proficient Students in California Schools: An Assessment of the Influence of Proposition 227 on Selected Teachers and Classrooms." *Bilingual Research Journal* 24 (1/2). http://brj.asu.edu/v2412/. (Accessed February 22, 2002.)

Suárez-Orozco, Marcelo M., and Carola E. Suárez-Orozco. 1995. "The Cultural Patterning of Achievement Motivation: A Comparison of Mexican, Mexican Immigrant, Mexican American, and Non-Latino White American Students." In *California's Immigrant Children: Theory, Research, and Implications for Educational Policy,* edited by Rubén G. Rumbaut and Wayne A. Cornelius (161–89). San Diego: Center for U.S.-Mexican Studies, University of California, San Diego.

Sui-Chu, Esther Ho, and J. Douglas Willms. 1996. "Effects of Parental Involvement on Eighth-Grade Achievement." *Sociology of Education* 69 (2): 126–41.

Tanners, Lisa. 1997. "Immigrant Students in New York City Schools." *Urban Education* 32 (2): 233–55.

U.S. Congress. House. Committee on Education and the Workforce. 2001. "House Education and the Workforce Committee Fact Sheet: Bilingual Education Reform." http://edworkforce.house.gov/issues/107th/education/nclb/bilingualfactsheet.htm.

U.S. Department of Education. Overview of Executive Summary, No Child Left Behind Act of 2001. http://www.ed.gov/nclb/overview/intro/execsumm.html?exp=0.

U.S. Department of Justice. Immigration and Naturalization Service. 1999. "Asylees, Fiscal Year 1997." Annual Report No. 3 of the Office of Policy and Planning, Statistics Branch, July. http://uscis.gov/graphics/shared/aboutus/statistics/asylee97.pdf.

———. 1999. "Refugees, Fiscal Year 1997." Annual Report No. 4 of the Office of Policy and Planning, Statistics Branch, July. http://uscis.gov/graphics/shared/aboutus/statistics/refugeerep97.pdf.

———. "Asylees." *1986 Statistical Yearbook of the Immigration and Naturalization Service.* P. 25. Washington, DC: U.S. Government Printing Office.

———. "Asylees." *1989 Statistical Yearbook of the Immigration and Naturalization Service.* Pp. 29–30. Washington, DC: U.S. Government Printing Office.

———. "Asylees." *1991 Statistical Yearbook of the Immigration and Naturalization Service.* Pp. 77–89. Washington, DC: U.S. Government Printing Office.

———. "Refugees." *1986 Statistical Yearbook of the Immigration and Naturalization Service.* Pp. 22–24. Washington, DC: U.S. Government Printing Office.

———. "Refugees." *1989 Statistical Yearbook of the Immigration and Naturalization Service.* Pp. 25–28. Washington, DC: U.S. Government Printing Office.

————. "Refugees." *1991 Statistical Yearbook of the Immigration and Naturalization Service.* Pp. 74–76. Washington, DC: U.S. Government Printing Office.

————. *1982 Statistical Yearbook of the Immigration and Naturalization Service.* (Ref 2.2) p. 98. Washington, DC: U.S. Government Printing Office.

Vernez, Georges. 1998. "Education's Hispanic Challenge." Working Paper No. 228. Annandale-on-Hudson, NY: The Levy Economics Institute of Bard College.

Waldinger, Roger, and Mehdi Bozorgmehr, eds. 1996. *Ethnic Los Angeles.* New York: Russell Sage Foundation.

White House, The. 2002. "Fact Sheet: No Child Left Behind Act." http://www.whitehouse. gov/news/releases/2002/01/20020108.html.

Zehr, Mary Ann. 2001. "Immigrant Students Find U.S. Schools Less Demanding." *Education Week,* January 17.

————. 2001. "New York City Modifies Bilingual Education." *Education Week,* January 17.

About the Authors

Alec Ian Gershberg is associate professor at the New School's Robert J. Milano Graduate School of Management and Urban Policy in New York City, where he teaches courses on education policy, public and private finance, and international development. Currently, he is a senior education economist at the World Bank, on leave from the New School for the 2004–2005 academic year. Dr. Gershberg is a research associate at the National Bureau of Economic Research and has previously served as a visiting fellow at the Public Policy Institute of California and a visiting professor at Stanford University's School of Education. He has conducted extensive research and policy analysis on education reform in developing countries in Latin America and Africa. Dr. Gershberg's work on the United States has concentrated on immigrant education in New York and California. His articles have appeared in such publications as *Comparative Education, Economics of Education Review, World Development,* and the *National Tax Journal.*

Anne Danenberg is a research associate at the Public Policy Institute of California (PPIC) whose work focuses on educational issues in California. Before joining PPIC in 1998, her research included projects on educational outcomes for immigrants, residential segregation in the Bay Area, and school population projections. While studying at Brown University, Ms. Danenberg held a teaching assistantship, was a recipient of the National Institute of Child Health and Human Development (NICHD) Demography Traineeship, and was associated with the Population Studies Training Center (PSTC).

Patricia Sánchez is an assistant professor of culture, literacy, and language in the Division of Bicultural-Bilingual Studies at the University of Texas at San Antonio. She has also served as a research assistant at the Public Policy Institute of California and at SRI International (formerly the Stanford Research Institute), conducting research on immigrants and public schools. While studying at the University of California, Berkeley, she helped found the Center for Popular Education and Participatory Research and also worked as an adjunct professor at the University of San Francisco. Dr. Sánchez's current research focuses on globalization, transnationalism, and second-generation immigrant youth. Her most recent work, "At Home in Two Places: The Lives of Transnational *Mexicana* Youth," will appear as a chapter in the forthcoming book, *Transformations of La Familia on the U.S.-Mexico Border Landscape* (University of Notre Dame Press). She has also published in the Australian journal, *Discourse: Studies in the Cultural Politics of Education.*

Index